Great
Italian Desserts

❧ ❧

Also by Nick Malgieri

NICK MALGIERI'S PERFECT PASTRY

Great Italian Desserts

BY

NICK MALGIERI

ILLUSTRATED BY CHRISTINE BUHR

LITTLE, BROWN AND COMPANY
BOSTON   TORONTO   LONDON

First Edition

Library of Congress Cataloging-in-Publication Data
Malgieri, Nick.
    Great Italian desserts / by Nick Malgieri; illustrated by
Christine Buhr.
        p.   cm.
    Includes bibliographical references and index.
    ISBN 0-316-54519-8
    1. Desserts.   2. Cookery, Italian.   I. Title.
TX773.M237   1990
641.8′6—dc20   90-6263

10 9 8 7 6 5 4 3 2 1

RRD IN

Book Design by Robert G. Lowe

*Published simultaneously in Canada
by Little, Brown & Company (Canada) Limited*

PRINTED IN THE UNITED STATES OF AMERICA

⁓⁓ ⁓⁓

For my mother and father, Ann and Nufre Malgieri,
who taught me to appreciate all that is Italian;
and the memory of my grandmother Clotilde Lo Conte,
whose example made me dedicate my life to baking.

ৡড় ড়ৡ

Contents

Acknowledgments

Many friends and colleagues have contributed immeasurably to the making of this book. Anna Teresa Callen encouraged my interest in Italian desserts more than ten years ago, spurring me to research, experiment with, and teach others how to create them first at her school. Paula Wolfert provided valuable advice about unusual recipes she had encountered and generously put me in contact with her friends in Sicily, who gave me a cordial welcome, wonderful recipes, and further introductions.

My editor, Jennifer Josephy, gave me free rein to create the book that I had always dreamed of doing. Her advice and astute editing have turned it into what I had always hoped it would be.

Deborah Jacobs, the copyeditor, made the process of readying the final manuscript a pleasure.

Christine Buhr, who did the illustrations, is a pastry chef as well as a gifted illustrator. Her innate understanding of the techniques and presentations have added clarity to the recipes and beauty to the pages that I could have never achieved with mere words.

Jim Scherer, who took the jacket photograph, has a great eye for detail and is also extremely easy to work with. David Edgcumbe, the most talented pastry chef I know, prepared most of the desserts on the jacket and organized everything for the trip to Boston for the photograph.

My dear friend Sandy Leonard traveled to Italy with me and drove, made reservations, offered valuable suggestions and advice, and generally kept our trips organized while I was lost in contemplation of one recipe or another. His patience, generosity, and unflagging capacity to taste yet one more dessert are enormous. *Grazie*, Sandro.

Anna Amendolara Nurse gave me information regarding specialties from Apulia, as well as her good advice, patient ear, and continual support. Julia della Croce shared her knowledge of Sardinian pastries with me. Peter Fresulone gave me some of his treasured family recipes. Dali Cahill pointed me toward the best cannoli in Palermo. Emory Thompson of White Lily Foods again provided me with technical information about flour, taking time from his busy schedule to run tests on samples of Italian flour and provide a comparison with American flours.

Josh Eisen helped me test recipes during the beginning of the process; then Leonard Remo continued testing, in addition to ordering supplies, assisting with classes, and being generally indispensable.

Fellow members of the International Association of Culinary Professionals in Italy led me to interesting specialties and shared recipes, and gave me invaluable information about regional traditions. They are Michi Ambrosi, Jo Bettoja, Ada Parasiliti, Paola Pettini, and Fulvia Sesani.

More than to anyone else in Italy I am indebted to Professore Salvatore Schifano of the hotel school of Favara, near Agrigento, who put me in touch with chefs throughout Italy and gave me information about traditional Sicilian pastries. Chef Schifano accompanied me on several occasions to the Santo Spirito Monastery, in Agrigento. Special thanks are due him and Madre Maria Ildegarde Pirrone, Madre Mafalda Pascucci, and Suora Benedetta of the monastery.

Dottoressa Emilia Chiriotti, publisher of *La pasticceria internazionale*, and Olga de Fonzo, publisher of *Il lavoro turistico*, both provided valuable contacts at pastry shops and restaurants in northern Italy.

The following pastry shop owners invited me into their establishments, offering generous samples and often recipes for their creations: Sergio Benedetto of the Pasticceria Maggio, in Saint Vincent; Augusto Boch of the Pasticceria Boch, in Aosta; Corrado

Costanza of the Pasticceria Rubino, in Noto; Maria Grammatico of the Pasticceria del Convento, in Erice; Salvatore Maggio of the Pasticceria Maggio, in Trapani; Rolando Morandin of the Pasticceria Morandin, in Saint Vincent; Giulio and Nina Nostro of the Pasticceria Margherita, in Reggio Calabria; Pietro Robiglio of the Pasticceria Robiglio, in Florence; Ermenegildo Rosa Salva of the Pasticceria Rosa Salva, in Venice; and Lucio Vogrig of Gubana Vogrig, in Cividale del Friuli.

Many restaurant chefs offered their advice, opinions, and hints on the best pastry shops in their areas. Among them are Paolo Gallo of Ristorante P & G, in Trapani; Pasqualino Giudice of Ristorante Jonico, in Siracusa; Giorgio Nardelli of the Parkhotel Laurin, in Bolzano; and Tonino and Claudia Verro of La Contea, in Neive, near Alba.

Dottore Roberto Seppi gave me an interesting historical and political perspective on the Trentino–Alto Adige region. Dottore Aurelio Ceresoli of Lazzaroni in Saronno generously guided me through the factory there and provided me with information about natural yeast used in the industrial production of *panettone*. My thanks to Cindy Ayers of Campbell's for arranging the visit. Margherita Simili of Bologna pointed me toward that city's best pastry shops.

My many cousins in Italy shared original recipes and family traditions. They are Michele and Pupetta Basile; Maria and Immacolata Spera; Nannina Scoppetuolo; Aida Donnarumma; Ina, Angelo, and Enzo Marcellino; and Carmelina, Augustino, and Michele Branciforte.

Ceri Hadda lent her unerring editorial hand at the eleventh hour with the Bibliography. Last and heartfelt thanks go to Peter Kump, who has continually encouraged me and who has always provided most generous support for my work.

Great
Italian Desserts

ல்ல ல்ல

Introduction

I was raised on Italian food. My maternal grandmother, Clotilde Lo Conte, lived with us when I was a child, and her greatest pleasure was in cooking and baking. Since she spoke little English, I had the good fortune as a baby to learn Italian simultaneously with English, and I cut my teeth on the delicious *biscotti* that Mammanonna prepared.

The stories my grandmother told me were of day-to-day life in her beloved village of Grottaminarda, and I grew up with a knowledge and appreciation of her favorite people, places, and events there.

All of our family meals were simple, rustic southern Italian cooking — scores of pasta dishes, based on freshly made or dry pasta, sometimes with a meat *sugo* (sauce) containing pork rind, beef, and veal, sometimes with one of the many vegetable- and tomato-based sauces. There were *minestre* (soups) of vegetables, occasionally including dried beans or lentils, often colored and flavored with the sweet, fresh-tasting tomatoes that my grandmother packed in jars herself each fall. Variety meats occupied a large place in our menus, and dishes of brains, lungs, sweetbreads, and lamb's head appeared regularly. These were often accompanied by homemade preserved peppers, eggplant, or other pickled vegetables.

But my grandmother's greatest glory was her desserts. Having had the good fortune to learn baking from a pastry chef from Naples who had retired to Grottaminarda, she possessed a knowledge of fine pastries and cakes that was greater than that of the average Grottaminarda housewife. She fearlessly sculpted hearts and baskets from *Croccante* (page 249) and thought nothing of preparing thirty or forty *pizze* and *torte* for our own use and the delight of friends and relatives on important holidays such as Christmas and Easter.

How often in my preschool years she would say in her mountain dialect: *"Mo' fagimma 'na rroge"* (*"Now let's make something sweet"*). I would watch rapturously while she prepared the many cookies, fritters, cakes, and creams in her vast repertoire. Invariably friends and neighbors would be the recipients of this bounty, the quantities she would produce being excessive for a family of four.

By the time I was old enough to begin experimenting with baking on my own, Mammanonna had ceased all activity in the kitchen. She died only months before I began my course at the Culinary Institute (then in New Haven, Connecticut), but I have often felt that her benevolent spirit has guided me in the course of my career.

I first visited Italy in 1973, during a weekend break from my kitchen apprenticeship in Zurich. I was going to a job interview in Monte Carlo and stopped over in Milan. Of course, the pastries that greeted me there were nothing like the southern Italian specialties at home or in the pastry shops of Newark's old Fourteenth Avenue Italian community, where I grew up. The slick-looking cakes and frozen desserts in the large, elegant pastry shops filled me with curiosity, and I soon began to explore another aspect of the type of baking I so dearly loved. I went from one pastry shop to another, making notes, asking questions of the salespersons, and often having the opportunity to meet and question the pastry cooks themselves. Throughout the course of the following seventeen years, that exploration continued, and I have had the good fortune to visit every region of Italy — exploring, tasting, questioning, and learning from the best professional and domestic cooks and bakers.

The journey has been a glorious one, and I have had the pleasure to meet some extraordinarily generous and enthusiastic people, eager to share their techniques, recipes, and opinions. It has led me, often in the company of friends like Sandy Leonard and Miriam and Lester Brickman, from the tops of precariously high mountains to the cool sanctity of cloistered convents, to find an obscure recipe or taste a little-known dessert.

I have taught many professional and amateur cooks to prepare Italian pastries, and the result has unanimously been one of happy revelation. Content with what Italian-American pastry shops have to offer, many believe Italian pastries to be rather limited in scope. But most students, after seeing and tasting the great variety of traditional, modern, and regional specialties that make up the vast range of Italian desserts, undergo a full-scale conversion to the Italian style of baking: simplicity, deep flavor, and richness only where necessary to complement flavor and texture.

Italian pastries have a long and varied history. Many, like *mostaccioli,* are holdovers from classical times, originating with the Romans. Medieval specialties like *panforte* and *cassata* abound and vie for popularity with foreign dishes that have been incorporated into the Italian dessert repertoire, like *gubana,* strudel, and couscous. Modern preparations like *tiramisú* and *tegole d'Aosta* are entering into the tradition, though an internationalizing trend and a reliance on convenience products in many commercial establishments often blur the boundary between Italian and foreign specialties in present-day Italy.

Home cooking is being abandoned by some Italians in favor of fast food and other types of commercially prepared foods, and this change is beginning to erode the custom of traditional cooking and baking in many large urban areas. Concerned regionalists and food writers have recorded the cooking and baking lore of Italy's many locales during the past ten years in an attempt to preserve traditions.

This book is my humble effort to contribute to that preservation effort, as well as an attempt to introduce a food-conscious American public to many Italian desserts not readily available in the United States. My greatest wish is to see the wonderful Italian baking tradition take its rightful place beside the French and Viennese schools as one of Europe's and the world's most refined.

~∂∽ ∽∂~

A Note About Authenticity

The cooks and bakers of Italy are, for the most part, fiercely independent in their approach to their work. Although many swear by particular versions of certain dishes, most feel free to add and subtract ingredients according to personal taste, seasonal availability, and whim.

During my visits to Italy over the course of more than seventeen years, the many Italian cooks and bakers I have met, observed, and interviewed have been almost unanimous in their nondogmatic approach and most willing to share information about how they have changed, modified, or improved traditional specialties or created specialties of their own. In addition, Italian cooking and baking have undergone waves of foreign influence over the course of centuries, so that elements of cuisines from France, England, North Africa, Yugoslavia, Austria, and, most recently, the United States have all left their mark.

To define an "authentic" Italian recipe presents a few problems. Must it have originated in Italy, free of foreign influence? This would, of course, eliminate last week's adaptation of a cake from a French magazine, but it would also eliminate the Sicilian version of Moroccan couscous, Neapolitan *Krapfen* derived from German and Austrian carnival fritters, and Milanese fruit tarts in the French style.

However, if we use foreign-influenced foods that have withstood the test of time and popularity as a yardstick for what is authentically Italian, we would be eliminating the many contemporary specialties that use up-to-date ingredients like white choc-olate and tropical fruits.

Naturally, we should also consider the personal creativity of individuals, chefs and pastry chefs who daily strive to perfect their craft and their recipes and presentations in the interest of both artistic achievement and commercial success. And to eliminate industrially made products would leave Milan bereft of *panettone* and Siena without *panforte*.

If we accept the foods that have traveled to Italy with foreign invaders and emigrants, as well as modern foods made in domes-tic, artisanal, and industrial circumstances, whose version do we accept as authentic? Does home cooking that embodies family traditions have a greater claim to authenticity than a pastry shop or restaurant that serves the specialties of a particular region? (Families in different regions, even small villages, prepare mark-edly different interpretations of the same foods, varying ingredi-ents or shape to suit convenience or personal taste.) Or do industrial manufacturers who have an interest in maintaining tra-ditions to increase trade in their products present more authentic versions of recipes?

It is a cliché that Italian-American examples of some classic Italian pastries bear no resemblance to the originals in Italy. But modern Italian pastries in Italy often bear no resemblance to past-ries and desserts of the same name recorded in classic Italian cooking and baking literature.

In light of the nebulous authenticity of many Italian foods, I have chosen and documented the recipes in this book in the fol-lowing ways:

1. When I have received a recipe for a particular dish from an individual, I have named him or her and stated his or her connection to the dish and its tradition.
2. When I have tasted a pastry or dessert in a particular place and developed a recipe that duplicates the appearance, taste, and texture of the original, I have stated the place where it was tasted and any other pertinent facts about its history.

3. When I have used secondary sources to identify ingredients and techniques, after tasting a particular food, I have named both the secondary source and the place. All recipes adapted from secondary sources cite the source.

4. When a dish stems from a particular foreign influence or tradition, I have attempted to trace how and when it developed into an Italian food and to describe its difference from the original foreign food.

5. When the ingredients used to prepare a recipe in Italy are unavailable in the United States, I have suggested alternate ingredients that will not change its nature. When an essential ingredient is unavailable, I have signaled this fact and stated how different ingredients will affect the preparation and how the finished product will differ from the recipe prepared with its original ingredients.

6. In the case of standard Italian ingredients that differ markedly from American ones in form (vanilla powder; scented, premeasured baking powder; candied fruit) or performance (flour, natural yeast, purchased bread dough), I have freely substituted the American ingredient that provides similar, and often identical, results.

7. When a recipe stems from an Italian-American source or tradition, I have cited it, and, where possible, I have described its difference from the Italian original.

8. Finally, in several instances I have created desserts that I find to be in the Italian style, though I have not discovered them anywhere in my travels. One such example is the *Torta Stregata* (page 162), a cake perfumed with Strega liqueur, filled with pastry cream, and covered with meringue — all typically Italian components and flavors but not encountered in that combination. I have cited these inventions as my own and have no wish to indulge in any deception about their origin.

During a recent trip to Italy I had the honor and pleasure of teaching an impromptu class at Paola Pettini and Rosalia Cippone's beautiful cooking school in Bari. After I had prepared chocolate chip cookies and apple pie for some forty members of Paola and Rosalia's Club di Cucina, one of the club members named the cookies *biscottini con le goccie di cioccolato* (cookies with chocolate drops). All the ingredients were indisputably and authentically Italian, I had written the recipe in metric weights, and the finished product was given an officially Italian name.

Perhaps this recipe, distributed to more than forty of Bari's most avid cooking enthusiasts, will enter the tradition of Barese baking and proudly stand alongside *carteddate* and other specialties of Apulia.

Perhaps it will even become "authentic."

❧ 1 ❧

Basic Ingredients and Recipes

Ingredients for Italian Desserts

Most of the ingredients needed for preparing Italian desserts and pastries are only as far away as your supermarket. The following guidelines specify the nature of standard ingredients, like flour and eggs, and define any unusual ingredients — kept to a minimum — that you may need to purchase. See Sources of Equipment and Ingredients for ordering.

STAPLES

Flour — The typical Italian flour for baking is called Farina Doppio Zero (Double Zero). It is slightly weaker (lower in gluten-forming proteins) than our all-purpose bleached flour but not so different as to warrant major adjustment. All-purpose bleached flour is used in all recipes.

Sugar — Regular granulated sugar is used in all recipes.

Honey — Use a dark, robust variety in the recipes that call for honey.

Cornmeal — Stone-ground cornmeal is preferable, but the recipes will work with plain yellow cornmeal. In the cake recipes a finer cornmeal is used; reduce standard cornmeal to a powder in a blender or coffee grinder, or see Sources of Equipment and Ingredients.

DAIRY PRODUCTS

Milk — Whole milk.

Cream — Heavy whipping cream.

Butter — Unsalted butter.

Eggs — Large eggs.

Ricotta — Whole-milk ricotta (see page 17).

Mascarpone — This rich Italian cream cheese is easy to prepare (see page 20).

LEAVENERS

Yeast — All recipes state quantities for both active dry yeast and compressed yeast. If you live in an area where 2-ounce yeast cakes are available, use one-third of the cake when 2/3 ounce compressed yeast is called for. If the small triangular yeast cakes are available where you live, use one for 2/3 ounce yeast.

Bicarbonate of ammonia — This leavener, used in some *biscotti*, has the added side effect of promoting dryness, ensuring crispness. It is usually available in pharmacies and in areas with an Italian, German, or Scandinavian population. All the recipes that call for it also specify quantities of baking powder and baking soda to substitute. See Sources of Equipment and Ingredients for mail order houses.

Baking powder — Double-acting baking powder.

DRIED AND CANDIED FRUIT

Dried figs — Calimyrna figs (dried white or green), not the black mission figs.

Candied fruit — Use the best quality you can find or prepare your own. See *Zuccata*, page 15, and Homemade Candied Orange Peel, page 17.

NUTS AND NUT PRODUCTS

Almonds — Whole, unblanched almonds still have the brown skin on the kernel. To blanch, bring to a boil in a pan of cold water, drain, rub in a towel to loosen the skins, and then pop off skins.

Hazelnuts — For ground hazelnuts, leave the skin on. For

other uses, bake for 10 minutes at 350 degrees, rub in a towel, and go over one at a time to remove most of the skin.

Pistachios — Purchase the greenest ones you can find, shelled, whole, and unsalted. Follow the same procedure for blanching as given for almonds.

Ground nuts — Use a rotary nut grinder or pulse carefully in a food processor, making sure the nuts do not become pasty but remain powdery.

Pine nuts — Sold in small jars at high prices. If they are purchased in bulk, taste them to make sure they are not bitter and rancid. Store in the freezer to retain freshness.

Almond paste — Use the canned variety; Solo is the most widely available brand. Avoid the type in the cellophane tube.

WINES, LIQUORS, LIQUEURS

Marsala — Use the imported variety from Sicily. Pellegrino and Florio are widely available brands.

White wine, red wine — Jug wine will do, or use white or red vermouth.

Dark rum, white rum — Use a good brand like Meyers or Bacardi.

Brandy — Stock brand or another Italian brandy gives the most authentic flavor.

Grappa — If unavailable, substitute brandy.

Strega — Yellow herb liqueur from southern Italy; if you can't find it, substitute Chartreuse.

Alchermes — Spicy red liqueur that derives its color from cochineal, a natural dye made from cochineal insects, like lady-bugs. The recipe for *Zuppa Inglese*, page 179, gives a substitution.

FATS AND OILS

Lard — Use good-quality leaf lard.

Olive oil — Use a light-colored, mild-flavored, pure olive oil, rather than extra virgin, for desserts.

Frying oil — Use a light or pure olive oil rather than extra virgin, or a mild vegetable oil. Canola and safflower are also good for deep-frying.

CHOCOLATE AND COCOA

Chocolate — Use semisweet chocolate available in the supermarket in 1-ounce squares. This is the closest equivalent to the Italian *cioccolata fondente*, the chocolate used in most Italian desserts.

Cocoa — Use unsweetened alkalized (Dutch-process) cocoa powder, like Hershey's European-style, or an imported Dutch brand.

Some Basic Recipes

Though I prefer not to cross-reference subrecipes endlessly, I have grouped in this section some basic recipes that will be referred to later in the book, because they are too long to include in the recipes for the desserts that use them. Where possible, I have attempted to work out a simplified version of some of these preparations that sacrifices none of the flavor of the original, more time-consuming process.

These recipes are some of the most important foundations of authentic Italian desserts and make all the difference between a pedestrian result and one that is particularly fine.

ᔭ ᒣ

Conserva di Amarene

Sour Cherry Preserves

Sour cherry preserves are frequently used in Italian desserts, especially those from Rome southward. Though you may substitute good-quality commercial preserves (British and German brands sometimes use the term "Morello cherries"), this recipe produces a quick, easy batch of the preserves that keeps well in the refrigerator. Use the preserves as they are, or use only the cherries for desserts like *Zeppole di San Giuseppe* (page 47) and *Crostata di Visciole alla Romana* (page 77).

3 *pounds sour cherries,*
  fresh or individually
  quick-frozen
3 *cups sugar*
2-*inch piece of cinnamon*
  stick

Rinse, stem, and pit the cherries, if using fresh, and place in a nonreactive pan. Add the sugar and stir it in. Add the cinnamon stick and bring to a boil over low heat, stirring frequently. Skim off the froth that rises to the surface.

At the boil, remove the cherries to a bowl with a slotted spoon or skimmer. Insert a candy thermometer in the syrup and cook until the syrup reaches 220 degrees, continuing to skim froth as necessary.

Add the cherries and the juice that has accumulated with them to the pan and continue cooking until the syrup again reaches 220 degrees.

Pack the boiling *conserva* into 6 hot, sterilized half-pint mason jars, filling them to within ½ inch of the top. Wipe the rims of the jars with a clean, damp cloth and immerse the caps in boiling water. Place the caps on the jars with tongs, place the rings over the caps, and screw the rings down immediately. Cool the jars at room temperature, with plenty of space between them.

If you do not wish to keep the *conserva* a long time, cool it and store in plastic containers with tight-fitting lids. Store the *conserva* in the refrigerator up to several months.

Makes about 3 pints

◈◈ ◈◈

CANDIED FRUIT

Many of the recipes for Italian desserts contain dried and candied fruit. Although American raisins and currants rank with any in Italy, the quality of Italian candied fruit is superior to that available in the United States. If you can locate a source of candied peel — orange, lemon, or citron sold by the piece (it will resemble halves or quarters of the peel left intact) — by all means use this and dice it yourself, rather than use the diced, packaged variety. Or consult the mail order houses listed in Sources of Equipment and Ingredients. If, as a last resort, you must use the standard supermarket variety of diced candied fruit or peel, be sure to rinse it well, chop it more finely, and soak it in rum or orange liqueur for a few hours before using it in a dessert.

◈◈ ◈◈

Zuccata

Homemade Candied Fruit

The difficulty in finding good-quality candied fruit led me to investigate the possibility of preparing it in small quantities at home. Though the process is a long one, it is not particularly difficult.

The procedures here are based on a description of the preparation of the classic Sicilian *zuccata 'ncilipata,* or syrup-candied zucchini. I admit that the idea of candied zucchini seems bizarre; in Sicily, a type of long, tender, light-colored squash that has only the slightest resemblance to our zucchini is used for this. I am indebted to Madre Maria Ildegarde Pirrone, abbess of the Santo Spirito Monastery, in Agrigento, for describing this preparation.

Since the type of zucchini used for this preparation is unavailable in the United States, I have also given instructions for using watermelon rind or underripe cantaloupe.

3 pounds long-necked
    zucchini, watermelon
    rind, or very underripe
    cantaloupe
2 cups coarse salt
3 cups sugar
1 cup light corn syrup
1 cup water

If using the zucchini or watermelon rind, cut it into 2-inch chunks. For cantaloupe, halve, seed, and peel the melon before weighing it and cutting it into chunks.

Place the chunks in a nonreactive pan and pour on the salt. Toss the chunks in the salt and allow to stand, loosely covered with plastic wrap, at room temperature for 24 hours.

Rinse off the chunks and return to the pan. Cover with water. Place the pan in the sun and change the water 6 times daily for 3 days, until the water no longer tastes salty. (You can prepare this indoors, since the sun is not essential, but make sure the water is changed frequently.)

Drain the chunks. Place them in a nonreactive pan and cover with water. Bring to a boil and lower to a simmer; simmer very gently for 1 to 1½ hours, until tender. Drain and cool to room temperature.

Coarsely grate the cooked chunks either by hand or in a food processor, or pass through a meat grinder fitted with the coarse blade. Take handfuls of the grated zucchini or melon and squeeze out as much water as possible.

Bring the sugar, corn syrup, and water to a boil in a large pan and add the grated zucchini or melon. Return to a boil and lower to a very gentle simmer. Cook for 3 hours. As the mixture cooks, the water will evaporate and the syrup will thicken. If the syrup seems very thick, add ½ cup water, return to a full boil, and lower to a gentle simmer again. Repeat the addition of the water as necessary while the mixture is cooking.

After the 3 hours of cooking, the *zuccata* will be translucent and the syrup will be very dense. Add ½ cup water to the pan, return to a boil, and drain the *zuccata* in a colander in the sink. Cool the *zuccata*, pack it in plastic containers with tight-fitting lids, and store in the refrigerator.

Makes about 3 pounds

ডে৩ ৫৩৫

Scorzette di Arance
Candite

———

Homemade Candied Orange Peel

Though the process of making candied peel is similar to that of making *Zuccata* (preceding recipe), there are different procedures for preparing candied orange peel. This recipe works well, and the peel keeps almost indefinitely in the refrigerator.

Score the oranges in 5 or 6 places from stem to blossom ends and remove the peel (both the colored part and the white part beneath it). Weigh the pieces of peel. There should be about 1 pound.

Place the peel in a large saucepan or casserole and cover with water. Bring to a boil and drain. Repeat the process 7 more times to remove the bitterness from the peel and to soften it.

Combine the sugar, corn syrup, and water in a large saucepan or casserole. Bring the syrup to a boil and add the blanched orange peel. Bring to a boil, lower to a simmer, and cook until the syrup is very thick. Add ¼ cup water, return to a boil, and cool. Pack the candied peel, with its thick syrup, in plastic containers, cover tightly, and store in the refrigerator. Before using the candied peel, rinse under warm running water.

Makes about 1½ pounds, drained

6 large oranges
Sugar equal to the weight of the peel (2 cups per 1 pound peel)
Light corn syrup equal to half the weight of the sugar (1 cup per 1 pound peel)
Water equal to one-fourth the weight of the sugar (½ cup per 1 pound peel)

ডে৩ ৫৩৫

RICOTTA

Whether it is made from cow's, ewe's, or goat's milk, Italian ricotta is smoother and firmer than its commercial American counterpart. Sometimes the difference in the ricotta's texture can change the nature of the dessert prepared from it.

If you live in a city that has an Italian neighborhood, it should be fairly easy to find freshly made ricotta, either loose or, more commonly, in perforated containers, which maximizes the drainage of water from the cheese and ensures its firmness. Pastry shops often use a kind of ricotta known as *impastata*, a mixture of ricotta and a very dry whey cheese (like that used for the filling of a cheese Danish, for example) that is pureed smooth to make the curd less apparent. This *impastata* is very firm and is used for cannoli filling and other ricotta fillings where firmness is important and standard commercial American ricotta would be too liquid.

∾ ∽ "Improved" Commercial Ricotta

Here is a simple method for improving the smoothness and firmness of the commercial ricotta available in the supermarket.

2 containers whole-milk ricotta, 15 ounces each
1 cup milk
2 teaspoons red wine vinegar
Cheesecloth, a linen napkin or tea towel, or coffee filters

Puree the ricotta, one container at a time, in a blender or food processor. Combine all the ricotta with the milk in a large nonreactive pan. Heat, stirring over low heat, to about 170 degrees. Add the vinegar and continue stirring until the curds begin to separate and the whey begins to drain away.

Line a large stainless steel strainer or colander with the cheesecloth, napkin or towel, or coffee filters.

Place the strainer or colander over a bowl and pour the pureed ricotta into it. Cover the top of the strainer or colander tightly with plastic wrap and refrigerate overnight to allow the ricotta to drain. Before using the ricotta, force the drained cheese through a strainer or colander to lighten it.

Makes about 2 pounds

ౚౚ ౚౚ

Homemade Ricotta

Robert Alleva, Sr., proprietor of the Alleva Dairy on Grand Street in New York's Little Italy, recently shared some of his knowledge about making fresh ricotta — the indispensable milk product for many Italian pastries. The Allevas, originally from Benevento, in southern Italy, have been in the *latticini* (Italian cheeses and milk products) business since 1892.

I was surprised to find that the process of making ricotta is a simple one. Alleva stated that the pH of the milk is altered from its normal 7.0 to 5.9 by the addition of lemon juice, vinegar, citric acid, or sour milk, then heated to 175 degrees. Next, the coagulated ricotta is skimmed from the surface and placed in perforated containers to drain. The longer the ricotta is "cooked" — held at the coagulating temperature — the finer and drier the curd becomes.

Rushing home with several gallons of milk, I tried the process numerous times with excellent results. You need the following equipment to make a pound of ricotta: a 5-quart stainless steel or enamel casserole, a slotted spoon or skimmer, an instant-read thermometer, a strainer or colander, and cheesecloth or a napkin. You can use the homemade ricotta on its own or in combination with commercial ricotta.

Combine the milk and vinegar in a 5-quart enamel or stainless casserole and place over low heat. Place the thermometer in the liquid, without allowing it to touch the bottom of the pan, and continue to heat until the liquid reaches 175 degrees. Be careful to regulate the heat, lowering it substantially at about 160 degrees so that the liquid just reaches 175 degrees but does not exceed it.

While the liquid is heating, rinse the cheesecloth or napkin

3 quarts whole milk (replace 1 cup of the milk with cream to make a richer ricotta)

3 tablespoons red wine vinegar

and use it to line a strainer or small colander placed in a bowl. When the ricotta forms on the surface of the liquid, remove it with a slotted spoon or skimmer and place it in the lined strainer. To make the ricotta more dry and firm, continue to heat the curds 5 minutes longer before placing them in the strainer.

To make the ricotta smooth before using it in a recipe, pulse it in a food processor fitted with the metal blade until creamy.

Makes approximately 1 pound ricotta

ல் ௦

Ricotta Pecorina

Ewe's Milk Ricotta

Much of the ricotta made in Italy, especially in the south and in Sicily, is made from ewe's milk, resulting in a sweet, though slightly gamy-tasting ricotta that retains its identity even after sweetening for cannoli or *cassata* filling. Though ewe's milk ricotta is not widely available in the United States, Paula Lambert's Mozzarella Company in Dallas (see Sources of Equipment and Ingredients) makes it every year during the spring.

As a substitute, I sometimes add some mild goat cheese to whole-milk ricotta to approximate the taste of the ewe's milk (see *Cannoli alla Siciliana* variations, page 51).

ல் ௦

Mascarpone

Italian Cream Cheese

Mascarpone, one of the richest cheeses imaginable (close to 80 percent milk fat), is essential to several Italian desserts, among them *tiramisù*. Excellent *mascarpone*, imported from Italy, is available under several different labels. Unfortunately, it is not very widely distributed and, outside major cities with large Italian populations, may be difficult to find.

To develop a recipe for *mascarpone*, I spoke with Paula Lambert, president of the Mozzarella Company. Ms. Lambert's company prepares many types of European-style cheeses difficult to find in the United States, including *mascarpone*. She explained that the procedure is a simple one: heavy cream is heated, curdled slightly by the addition of a combination of tartaric and citric acids, and drained so that the watery whey drains away from the fat-rich curd. The yield from the cream is approximately 50 percent, making the yield from 1 quart of cream about 1 pound of *mascarpone*.

You will need the same equipment to make *mascarpone* as was used in Homemade Ricotta, page 19.

Choose a stainless steel bowl that fits inside a large saucepan without touching the bottom of the pan. Add water to the pan and place the bowl in the pan so that the bowl touches the surface of the water but still sits firmly on the rim of the pan. Remove the bowl, place the pan on medium heat, and bring the water to a boil.

Place the cream in the bowl and place over the boiling water. Adjust the heat under the pan to medium and heat the cream, checking the temperature often with an instant-read thermometer, to 190 degrees; stir occasionally. Stir in the vinegar, continuing to stir gently until the cream begins to curdle. Remove the pan from the heat, cover, and allow the curds to firm up for 10 minutes.

Line a strainer or colander with dampened cheesecloth, napkin, or coffee filters. Set the strainer or colander over a bowl and carefully spoon the curds into the strainer. Allow the *mascarpone* to cool to room temperature, cover the strainer tightly with plastic wrap, and refrigerate for 24 hours to allow the cheese to finish draining and become firm.

1 quart heavy whipping cream (NOT ultrapasteurized)
1 tablespoon white wine vinegar or lemon juice

Store in the refrigerator in a tightly covered container. Use the *mascarpone* within 3 or 4 days.

Makes about 1 pound

∽ ∾

Vino Cotto

Cooked Wine

An important ingredient in many southern Italian pastries and desserts, *vino cotto* is a type of preserve made from wine, grape juice, or even figs or prunes. Sometimes referred to as *mosto cotto*, the preserve may also be made from must, the freshly pressed juice of grapes drained off before the fermentation that would turn it into wine begins. The terms are used interchangeably, though, and whether made from wine or must, the preserve is commonly known as *vino cotto.*

Vino cotto is usually made during the *vendemmia*, or grape harvest season, when the must is plentiful, and it is a simple matter for Italians to acquire a few gallons of the freshly pressed grape juice. If you know someone who makes wine, by all means use the actual must. If not, this recipe suggests appropriate substitutes. Or try the next recipe, which uses bottled wine as a substitute for the must.

In Calabria and Sicily, it is customary to flavor the *vino cotto* with orange zest, cinnamon, and clove. If you wish to flavor it, add the finely grated zest of 2 oranges, 2 cinnamon sticks, each about 3 inches long, and 2 whole cloves after 30 minutes of cooking. Strain through a fine-meshed strainer before bottling.

4 quarts must of red muscat grapes, or 6 to 7 pounds red muscat grapes, or 4 quarts unsweetened muscat grape juice, available in health food stores

If using the must, place in an 8-quart enameled iron or stainless steel casserole.

If using the grapes, strip them from the stems, rinse them quickly, and drain. Place the grapes, in batches, in a stainless steel colander set over a large bowl and crush them coarsely, squeezing with your hands and allowing the juice to drain into the bowl. Reserve the squeezed grape skins. After crushing all the grapes, run the reserved skins through a food mill fitted with the finest blade, letting their juice drain into the bowl with the other juice. Pour all the juice into an 8-quart enameled iron or stainless steel casserole.

Bring the must or grape juice to a boil over medium heat and lower to a simmer. The must will foam a great deal while it is simmering. Be careful that it does not boil over. Cook the must for about 1 hour, stirring often, until it is thick and syrupy and reduced to about 1 quart. Cool the *vino cotto*, pour it into a clean glass jar or bottle, cover, and store in the refrigerator. The *vino cotto* will keep indefinitely.

Makes about 1 quart

ଡ଼ଡ ୧ଡ଼

Vino Cotto with Bottled Wine

If you manage to find a fairly sweet wine for this, leave out the sugar; the flavor will be deeper and less sugary.

Combine the wine and sugar in an 8-quart enameled or stainless steel casserole and cook as in the previous recipe.

1 gallon red jug wine
2½ cups sugar

❧ 2 ❧

Yeast-Risen Pastries

I have limited the pastries in this chapter to the large yeast-risen cakes so popular for holidays and special occasions in Italy. Many of these, like *panettone* and *colomba*, are almost exclusively prepared in factories nowadays, by large producers like Motta, Alemagna, and Lazzaroni. The versions here are home-style ones, not to be confused with their commercially made counterparts.

Many of these pastries contain dried and candied fruit. Read the sections on these in Basic Ingredients and Recipes for information on quality in these products, and see Sources of Equipment and Ingredients for mail order houses.

Working with Yeast

All the recipes that call for yeast state the amount in terms of both active dry yeast and compressed yeast. Although there is not an enormous difference between the way each performs, compressed yeast dissolves on contact with warm liquid, while active dry yeast needs a few minutes to soften. I treat both the same way, whisking the yeast into warm liquid and then adding the liquid to the flour to form a sponge. Since the sponge is fairly loose, fermentation begins immediately and the yeast begins to multiply. When the sponge is added to the dough, the yeast already has a head start and the dough's fermentation begins more quickly, thus reducing the time spent waiting for fermentation.

LIEVITO NATURALE

Among professional bakers in Italy, actual yeast is often not used; a kind of sourdough known as *lievito naturale* or *lievito madre* (natural yeast or mother yeast) is used in its place. These natural yeasts are products of a natural fermentation of flour and water (sometimes naturally yeast-ridden foods, such as grape skins or hops, are used to begin a natural yeast) and contain certain acids and enzymes that also promote long-standing freshness in the pastries they leaven. As the natural yeast is used, a little is saved and more flour and water are added to renew it and make a sufficient quantity for the next use. Such is the cult of natural yeast in Italy that when Italian bakers travel, they take some of their precious natural yeast with them. When the great commercial establishments finish the last of their natural yeast before closing for annual cleaning, a competitor will contribute a bit from which to start a new batch upon reopening.

HINTS FOR SUCCESS IN WORKING WITH YEAST

• Always use warm liquid, about 105 degrees, to dissolve yeast. A cold liquid may dissolve the cell walls of dry yeast, and a hot one may cook both dry and compressed yeast and kill them.
• After preparing the sponge, proceed immediately to the remaining part of the recipe. It is better for the dough to wait for the sponge to be sufficiently fermented than to have the sponge wait and overferment.
• Always wait until the dough has fermented enough before proceeding to the next step in the recipe. Fermentation not only produces the gas that leavens the dough; it is also largely responsible for the flavor of the finished product and needs to develop fully if the baked pastry is to be both light and flavorful.
• Proofing, the final fermentation before baking, is the most important part of the process. Forming the pastry expels most of the accumulated gas, so that the formed pastry needs to fer-

ment again to restore its lightness before baking. Rushing the process by baking an underproofed pastry will result in a heavy texture and an excessively yeasty taste.

• Cooling is important. Cool all yeast-risen pastries on a rack to make sure that their steamy yeastiness dissipates before serving them. Also, wrapping a yeast-risen pastry while it is still warm will result in a soggy texture and increase the likelihood of mold.

ॐ ॐ

Ciambella Lucchese

Sweet Raisin and Anise Bread from Lucca

The narrow, winding streets of Lucca strongly evoke an era when it was possible to visit European cities without fear of being hit by a tour bus. Relatively calm and not at all crowded, Lucca preserves many traditions of antique Tuscan cooking, among them the circular *ciambella*, sometimes called *buccellato*, from the Latin for "bracelet."

I like the *ciambella lucchese* because it is sweet and cakelike yet, since it contains no fat of any kind, is relatively low in calories. Really a bread dough with sugar and seasonings added, the *ciambella* makes a good breakfast or tea bread.

SPONGE
1 cup all-purpose flour
½ cup water
1½ envelopes active dry yeast or ½ ounce compressed yeast

For the sponge, place the flour in a small bowl. Measure warm tap water (about 105 degrees) and whisk the yeast into the water. Stir the yeast mixture into the flour. Cover tightly with plastic wrap and allow to ferment at room temperature until double, about 30 minutes.

For the dough, place the flour, sugar, water, and salt in the bowl of a heavy-duty mixer or a mixing bowl. Add the sponge and beat on the lowest speed with the paddle until smooth and elastic; this should take about 5 minutes by machine. If you are mixing by hand, use your hand to squeeze the dough together, then turn the dough out onto a lightly floured surface and knead it by folding it over on itself repeatedly until smooth and elastic, about 10 minutes.

Add the raisins and anise seeds to the dough and mix in gently, by machine or by hand. Cover the bowl and allow to ferment until double, about 3 to 4 hours.

Scrape the dough out onto a floured surface and fold it over on itself several times to deflate. Form the dough into a cylinder about 24 inches long and place it on a paper-lined cookie sheet. Connect the ends of the cylinder to form a circle and cover with a towel. Allow to proof until double, about 2 to 3 hours.

Bake the *ciambella* at 375 degrees for about 45 minutes until well risen and a deep golden color, and until a thin knife blade inserted into the thickest part emerges clean. Cool on a rack and then cover well with plastic wrap.

Makes 1 large ring-shaped loaf

VARIATION

Form the dough into 2 long, narrow loaves, each about 12 inches long. Place each on a paper-lined pan; proof and bake as before. Although this version of *ciambella* does not take the bracelet shape of its nickname, *buccellato*, it is often sold in this form in the bakeries of Lucca. Making this variation will give you a loaf to freeze for later use.

DOUGH
2½ cups all-purpose flour
⅔ cup sugar
⅔ cup warm water
½ teaspoon salt
⅓ cup raisins
1 tablespoon anise seeds

രു ലെ

Colomba Pasquale

———

Easter Dove

The Easter dove, a symbol of the Resurrection, is a traditional pastry throughout Italy. Made from a yeast dough, the *colomba* is easy to prepare and simple to shape. It is usually encrusted with coarse sugar granules, but this version leaves the surface plain, to be lightly dusted with confectioners' sugar after baking. For an alternate presentation, divide the dough in half and shape into 2 round loaves, baking each on a separate parchment-lined sheet.

This recipe is based on one made by my friend Anna Teresa Callen, a great teacher of Italian cooking and baking.

SPONGE
¾ *cup milk*
1 *envelope active dry yeast*
    or ⅔ ounce compressed
    yeast
1 *cup all-purpose flour*

DOUGH
3 *large eggs*
1 *large egg yolk*
½ *cup sugar*
8 *tablespoons (1 stick)*
    unsalted butter
½ *teaspoon salt*
1 *teaspoon vanilla extract*
1 *teaspoon grated orange*
    zest
1 *teaspoon grated lemon zest*
2¾ *cups all-purpose flour*
½ *cup dark or golden raisins*
½ *cup mixed candied fruit*

Confectioners' sugar for
    finishing

For the sponge, heat the milk to lukewarm, about 100 to 105 degrees, in a small saucepan over low heat. Remove from the heat and whisk in the yeast. Stir in the flour and cover with plastic wrap. Allow to ferment 30 minutes or until double.

For the dough, whisk the eggs and yolk together and whisk in the sugar. Melt and cool the butter and whisk in. Stir in the salt, vanilla, and zests, then the flour. Use your hand to beat in the sponge, or transfer the dough to the bowl of a heavy-duty mixer fitted with the paddle and beat on the lowest speed until smooth, no more than 2 or 3 minutes. Beat in the raisins and candied fruit.

Place the dough in a buttered bowl and cover with plastic wrap. Allow to ferment until double, about 1 hour. Remove the dough from the bowl and deflate by folding it over on itself several times on a lightly floured surface. Divide in half and shape each piece of dough into a dove, forming each one on a separate parchment-lined cookie sheet, according to the illustration; use raisins for the eyes. Cover loosely and allow to proof at room temperature until double, about 1 hour.

Bake the *colombe* at 375 degrees for about 20 minutes, until golden and firm to the touch. Cool the *colombe* on racks. Keep them tightly wrapped in plastic at room temperature, or freeze for later use.

Dust with the confectioners' sugar before serving.

Makes about 16 servings

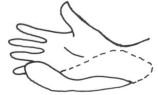

Gubana

Fruit- and Nut-Filled Yeast-Risen Cake

A specialty of the Natisone valleys, near the Yugoslavian border, the *gubana* was traditionally offered by brides to their wedding guests, as well as being an Easter pastry. *Gubana* means "rolled up" in the local Slavic dialect and refers to the dough's being covered with a rich fruit-and-nut filling, rolled up, and baked in a pan in the form of a spiral. When the *gubana* is sliced, the interior spiral of filling is revealed. There are several versions of the pastry, some made with puff pastry, others with a sweetened yeast dough, as this one is.

This version is based on the *gubana Vogrig*, one of the best commercial *gubane*, from Cividale del Friuli, a small town near Udine, well known for the excellence of its *gubana*. The Vogrig family was one of the first to commercialize the *gubana* and offer it throughout the year. They began in their native village of Grimacco and in the mid-1960s established a large plant at Cividale. Lucio Vogrig, son of the founder, Attilio, was kind enough to share information on both the lore and preparation of the *gubana* when I visited his immaculate factory in Cividale.

SPONGE
½ cup milk
1 envelope active dry yeast
* or ⅔ ounce compressed*
* yeast*
¾ cup all-purpose flour

For the sponge, heat the milk to lukewarm and whisk in the yeast. Pour into the flour and stir until smooth. Cover with plastic wrap and allow to ferment about 30 minutes.

For the dough, place the flour, eggs, and yolk in a heavy-duty mixer fitted with the paddle and beat on low speed until well mixed. Or combine the ingredients in a bowl and mix well with a wooden spoon or rubber spatula. Add the sponge and mix until smooth, about 3 to 4 minutes by machine. By hand, stir in the sponge as well as possible, turn the dough out onto

DOUGH

2 cups all-purpose flour

2 large eggs

1 large egg yolk

½ teaspoon salt

½ cup sugar

8 tablespoons (1 stick)
   unsalted butter, melted

FILLING

1 cup whole almonds,
   blanched or unblanched

1 cup walnut pieces

⅓ cup pine nuts

1 cup golden raisins

⅓ cup grappa, brandy, or
   dark rum

Grated zest of 1 lemon

⅓ cup candied orange peel,
   diced

8 tablespoons (1 stick)
   unsalted butter

½ cup dry bread crumbs

1 large egg

1 large egg and granulated
   sugar for finishing

a lightly floured surface, and knead by folding the dough over on itself repeatedly until smooth, about 5 to 6 minutes. Beat or knead in the salt, sugar, then the butter, and continue beating the dough until it is smooth and elastic. Scrape the dough into a buttered bowl, cover it, and allow it to ferment until double, about 1 hour.

For the filling, chop the almonds and walnuts coarsely and place in a bowl with the pine nuts. In a small saucepan, cover the raisins with water, bring to a boil, drain, and add the *grappa*. Allow to soak while preparing the rest of the filling. Add the lemon zest and diced orange peel to the nuts. Melt the butter and cook the bread crumbs in it until they are golden, then add to the bowl. Stir in the egg, then the raisins and *grappa*. Set aside, covered, and keep at room temperature until the dough is ready.

Scrape the dough from the bowl onto a floured surface. Press the dough well with the palms of the hands to deflate it but *do not* fold it over, which would render it too elastic to shape. Press the dough into a rectangle about 20 × 10 inches and spread it evenly with the filling. Roll up the filling in the dough, starting from the wide end. Butter a 10-inch spring-form pan and arrange the dough loosely in the pan in a spiral. Beat the egg and paint the top of the *gubana* with it, then sprinkle with the sugar. Cover loosely with a towel and allow to proof until the spiral grows together, about 1 hour. Bake the *gubana* at 350 degrees for about 50 minutes. Cool in the pan on a rack. Release the sides of the springform pan and slide the *gubana* off the pan bottom onto a platter. Cover loosely with

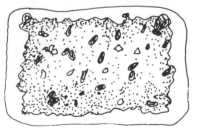 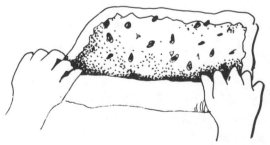 

plastic wrap. Serve the *gubana* cut into slices. It is common to serve a slice of *gubana* sprinkled with *grappa.*

The *gubana* keeps well: double-wrap in plastic and store in the refrigerator up to 2 weeks. Unwrap, cover loosely with a towel, and allow to come to room temperature before serving.

Makes 12 servings

☙ ❧

Nadalin

Christmas Bread from Verona

In his wonderful book about the cooking of Verona, Giovanni Capnist cites the *nadalin* (literally, little Christmas) as the first assignment given to young girls learning to cook at home. An ancestor of Verona's most famous Christmas bread, the *pandoro,* it is more commonly made at home, while the *pandoro* is left to professionals.

Sprinkle the yeast over the water in a small bowl. Wait 5 minutes until the yeast has dissolved. Beat the eggs in a large mixing bowl and beat in the sugar, salt, and vanilla. Melt the butter and beat it in; then beat in the yeast mixture and finally stir in the flour. Beat the dough until it is smooth and elastic, either by hand in the bowl or in a heavy-duty mixer fitted with the dough hook on low speed, about 10 minutes.

Place the dough in a buttered bowl and turn it over so that the entire surface is buttered. Cover the bowl loosely with plastic wrap and allow the dough to ferment until it has doubled in bulk, about 2 hours. Turn the dough out onto a lightly floured work surface and fold it over on itself several times to deflate.

Butter a star-shaped *pandoro* mold and half fill the mold with the dough. Cover the mold loosely with plastic wrap and

1 envelope active dry yeast or ⅔ ounce compressed yeast

⅓ cup warm water

4 large eggs

⅔ cup sugar

½ teaspoon salt

1 tablespoon vanilla extract

12 tablespoons (1½ sticks) unsalted butter

4 cups all-purpose flour

Confectioners' sugar and 3 tablespoons melted butter for finishing

allow the *nadalin* to proof until the mold is filled. Bake the *nadalin* in the lower third of a preheated 375-degree oven for about 40 minutes, until a long, thin knife plunged into the center comes out clean. Check the *nadalin* for doneness after about 25 minutes, to make sure that it does not overbake and become dry.

Immediately invert the *nadalin* onto a rack and remove the mold. Paint the *nadalin* all over with the melted butter and allow it to cool completely. Keep it tightly wrapped in plastic at room temperature until serving time. Before serving, dust lightly with the confectioners' sugar.

Makes 8 to 10 servings

ಬಲ ಅಲ

Pandolce Genovese

Fennel, Raisin, and Pine Nut Bread from Genoa

Rare among enriched bread doughs, the *pandolce* does not contain eggs or milk. The fennel-scented dark brown loaves are seen in all the pastry shops on the Ligurian coast, along with the locally popular lemon tart.

This version is a synthesis of different *pandolci* I tasted in Santa Margherita Ligure, Recco, and Genoa.

SPONGE
½ cup all-purpose flour
¼ cup water
1 envelope active dry yeast or ⅔ ounce compressed yeast

For the sponge, place the flour in a small bowl. Measure warm tap water and whisk the yeast into the water. Stir the yeast mixture into the flour. Cover tightly with plastic wrap and allow to ferment at room temperature until double, about 30 minutes.

For the dough, place the ingredients in the order given in the bowl of a heavy-duty mixer fitted with the paddle or in a mixing bowl. Add the sponge and beat on the lowest speed.

This should take about 5 minutes by machine. If you are mixing by hand, use your hand to squeeze the dough together, then turn the dough out onto a lightly floured surface and knead it by folding it over on itself repeatedly until smooth and elastic, about 10 minutes.

Add the raisins, candied peel, pine nuts, and fennel seeds to the dough and mix in gently, by machine or by hand. Cover the bowl and allow to ferment until double, about 3 to 4 hours.

Scrape the dough out onto a floured surface and fold it over on itself several times to deflate. Form the dough into a round loaf, place it on a parchment-lined cookie sheet, and cover with a towel. Allow to proof until double, about 2 to 3 hours.

Immediately before baking, slash the top of the *pandolce*: make 2 parallel cuts 2 inches apart on the top of the loaf, then 2 more cuts perpendicular to the first ones, to form a #.

Bake the *pandolce* at 375 degrees for about 1 hour until well risen and a deep golden color, and until a thin knife blade inserted into the thickest part emerges clean.

Cool the *pandolce* on a rack. Store well wrapped in plastic at room temperature.

Makes 8 servings

DOUGH

3 cups all-purpose flour

¾ cup sugar

⅔ cup warm water

1½ teaspoons salt

4 tablespoons unsalted
    butter, melted and cooled

⅓ cup raisins

⅓ cup candied citron or
    orange peel, rinsed and
    chopped

⅓ cup pine nuts, lightly
    toasted

1 tablespoon fennel seeds

Panettone Milanese

Yeast-Risen Christmas Cake

This is the typical Italian Christmas pastry. Made from a rich yeast dough with raisins and candied fruit, the *panettone* originated in Milan but is now made all over Italy.

Though a popular cake, *panettone* is seldom made in the home. Large-scale manufacturers like Motta and Alemagna make the bulk of the *panettone* produced in Italy, and even pastry shops sell these packaged versions, made with natural yeast for superior freshness.

XMAS CAKE

This recipe, which I have used for close to ten years, makes an excellent home-style *panettone*. While it does not have the shelf life of a commercially made *panettone*, it keeps perfectly well for several days. To ensure maximum lightness, allow the dough to ferment, then proof slowly and for as long as necessary. Rushing the process will produce a leaden texture.

SPONGE

⅔ cup milk

1½ envelopes active dry yeast or 1 ounce compressed yeast

1 cup all-purpose flour

DOUGH

12 tablespoons (1½ sticks) unsalted butter

1 teaspoon salt

½ cup sugar

1 teaspoon grated lemon zest

2 teaspoons vanilla extract

2 tablespoons dark rum

6 large eggs

4 cups all-purpose flour

¾ cup candied orange peel, rinsed and diced

¾ cup dark raisins

¾ cup golden raisins

4 tablespoons unsalted butter, melted, for finishing

For the sponge, heat the milk to lukewarm, whisk in the yeast, and stir the yeast mixture into the flour. Cover and allow to ferment at room temperature for about 45 minutes, until almost tripled in volume.

For the dough, beat the butter with the salt and sugar until light. Add the flavorings and beat until smooth. Add 2 eggs, then continue beating until the mixture is emulsified and smooth and looks like buttercream. If the mixture remains curdled, warm the bottom of the mixing bowl in a pan of warm water for a second or two and continue beating; rewarm the bowl as necessary until the mixture is smooth. Add one-third of the flour and mix in, then another 2 eggs. Repeat with another third of the flour, the last 2 eggs, and the last third of the flour. Beat in the sponge and beat the dough smooth.

Mix in the candied peel and raisins just until incorporated. Place the dough in a buttered bowl and allow to ferment until double, up to 2 hours.

Turn the dough out onto a floured surface and deflate by folding it over on itself several times. Divide the dough into 2 pieces and shape each into a ball. Place each piece of dough in a well-buttered 2- to 2½-quart charlotte mold or other straight-sided mold. Cover loosely and allow to proof until they both rise to the top of the mold, about 2 hours.

Slash an X in the top of each *panettone* with buttered scissors and bake at 375 degrees for about 50 minutes. Unmold immediately and paint all over with the melted butter. Cool on a rack.

Double-wrap each *panettone* in plastic and store in the refrigerator. Bring to room temperature before serving.

Makes 16 servings

⁓ ⁓

Panettone Valdostano

Panettone from Aosta

Although this is similar to *Panettone Milanese* (preceding recipe), it is an interesting variation. Augusto Boch of the Pasticceria Boch in Aosta, in northwestern Italy, near the French border, makes this for the French tourists who visit Aosta to take home with them. To satisfy French tastes, he substitutes raisins for the candied fruit and covers the *panettone* before baking with an almond-and-sugar glaze, more almonds, and confectioners' sugar, which gives the baked pastry a crunchy top. This *panettone* has a more practical shape, also, since it is baked in a deep layer pan and so is easier to cut into slices or wedges.

For the sponge, heat the milk to lukewarm, whisk in the yeast, and stir the yeast mixture into the flour. Cover and allow to ferment at room temperature for about 45 minutes, until almost tripled in volume.

For the dough, beat the butter with the salt and sugar until light, either by hand, with a hand mixer set at medium speed, or in a heavy-duty mixer fitted with the paddle. Add the vanilla and beat smooth. Add the eggs, one at a time, alternately with the flour, ending with the flour. Beat in the sponge and then beat the dough until smooth.

Mix in the raisins until just incorporated. Place the dough in a buttered bowl and allow to ferment until double, about 2 hours.

Deflate the dough by folding it over on itself several times and then form into a ball. Place in a buttered 9-inch springform pan, pressing lightly so that the dough reaches the sides of the pan. Cover with a towel and allow to proof until risen to the top of the pan, about 2 hours.

SPONGE
⅓ cup milk
1 envelope active dry yeast
    or ⅔ ounce compressed
    yeast
½ cup all-purpose flour

DOUGH
6 tablespoons unsalted
    butter, softened
½ teaspoon salt
¼ cup sugar
2 teaspoons vanilla extract
3 large eggs
2 cups all-purpose flour
⅓ cup dark raisins
⅓ cup golden raisins

ICING

¼ cup whole, blanched
    almonds

¼ cup sugar

1 teaspoon cornstarch

1 large egg white

¼ cup blanched, sliced
    almonds or whole,
    blanched almonds,
    coarsely chopped

Confectioners' sugar for
    finishing

While the dough is proofing, prepare the icing. Pulse the almonds and sugar in a food processor fitted with the metal blade until finely ground. Place in a bowl and stir in the cornstarch and egg white.

When the *panettone* is risen, carefully spread the icing on top, strew with the sliced almonds, and dust generously with the confectioners' sugar.

Bake at 375 degrees for about 50 minutes. Release the sides of the springform pan and slide the *panettone* off the pan bottom to a rack to cool. Do not invert to unmold or the topping will fall off.

Wrap the cooled *panettone* in plastic and store at room temperature up to 3 days. If you refrigerate the *panettone*, the icing will become sticky.

Makes 10 servings

ಬಒ ಲಇ

Zelten alla Bolzanese
———
Tyrolean Fruit and Nut Cake from Bolzano

Although the *Zelten* contain yeast, they are not breads, for they do not have the open crumb characteristic of a yeast-risen dough. The texture of the *Zelten* is that of a rich fruitcake, and the bread dough serves only to bind all the diverse elements together.

A cross between *Panforte di Siena* (page 143) and an English fruitcake, *Zelten* are the traditional Christmas dessert in the Alto Adige, Italy's only official German-speaking region, where Bolzano is located.

Be sure to make the *Zelten* several weeks in advance to give them an opportunity to mellow before serving.

FRUIT, NUTS, AND
    FLAVORINGS

1 cup raisins

For the fruits, nuts, and flavorings, combine all ingredients in a nonreactive bowl, cover with plastic wrap, and leave to macerate at least 24 hours or up to 5 days.

On the day you wish to assemble and bake the *Zelten*, prepare the dough: combine the flour and salt in a bowl and stir to mix well. Measure warm tap water (105 degrees) and whisk the yeast into it. Add to the flour mixture, stirring to mix well. Cover with plastic wrap and allow to ferment about 1 hour, until double. Turn the dough out onto a well-floured surface and fold over on itself several times to deflate (the dough will be soft — use a spatula or bench scraper if necessary). Return the dough to the bowl, cover, and allow to ferment again until double, about 40 minutes.

Add the dough to the fruit mixture, squeezing the fruit in with both hands. Continue squeezing and tossing the mixture to mix the fruit in evenly — this will take at least 10 minutes of active mixing. Cover the bowl and allow to rest 30 minutes before shaping.

For the syrup, combine all the ingredients in a saucepan and bring to a boil over low heat, stirring occasionally to dissolve the sugar. Pour the syrup into a bowl and cool.

To form the *Zelten*, divide the dough into 4 pieces and, on a lightly floured surface, shape each into a 6-inch disk about ½ inch thick. Use a spatula to shape the dough but avoid adding flour, which will toughen the *Zelten*. Arrange the *Zelten* on 2 jelly roll pans lined with buttered aluminum foil and paint lightly with the syrup, using a brush.

Bake the *Zelten* at 325 degrees for about 30 minutes, basting with the syrup every 10 minutes. The *Zelten* are done if they feel firm when pressed with a fingertip.

Remove the *Zelten* from the oven and paint again with the remaining syrup. Allow to cool completely on a rack; cover loosely with a towel and leave at room temperature until the next day. Decorate each with 5 or 6 almonds, forming a border around the edge. Wrap the *Zelten* tightly in plastic wrap, then aluminum foil, and store in a cool, dry place to age for 2 weeks to 1 month.

Makes four 6-inch cakes, about 48 small servings

1 cup dried figs, stemmed and diced

1 cup dried apples or pears, diced

½ cup pitted dates, diced

½ cup candied orange peel, rinsed and diced

½ cup candied lemon peel, rinsed and diced

⅔ cup walnut pieces

⅔ cup whole, blanched almonds, coarsely chopped

½ cup pine nuts, lightly toasted

1 teaspoon ground cinnamon

½ teaspoon ground cloves

½ cup dark rum

DOUGH

1 cup all-purpose flour

½ teaspoon salt

½ cup water

1½ teaspoons active dry yeast or ⅓ ounce compressed yeast

SYRUP

2 tablespoons water

¼ cup honey

¼ cup sugar

Whole, blanched almonds, lightly toasted, for finishing

❧ 3 ❧

Fried Pastries

Although the mention of fried pastries conjures up visions of doughnuts to most Americans, Italy's pastry tradition is replete with recipes for crisp, delicate deep-fried treats. Never heavy or greasy, these fried pastries form a large part of the Italian pastry repertoire.

Fried pastries like *Cannoli alla Siciliana* (page 48), tubes of a delicately seasoned dough that are fried hollow and filled with ricotta cream after cooling, are usually made in pastry shops, though many fried pastries are within the province of home cooks. The reason that fried desserts have been so popular is simple: as recently as forty years ago, many homes, especially rural ones in southern Italy and Sicily, did not have a stove equipped with an oven, making the preparation of baked goods and pastries in the home impossible. In fact, a great deal of cooking was done on a wood or charcoal fire, either on a stove that had a fire compartment beneath large openings into which a pan could be set, or on a grill in the fireplace. Baking was limited to holidays, and even then the pastries to be baked were sent to a communal oven, where for a small fee the oven keepers baked the pans of *biscotti* or the *torte* and *pizze*. On my first visit to my cousins in Grottaminarda, the village in southern Italy where my mother was born, I was taken to see a communal oven, run by a family as their sole means of support, on the outskirts of town. The oven's fire was built directly on the hearth and then swept aside when the baking began. Unfortunately, both the oven and the large shed in which it was housed were destroyed in the last earthquake, in 1980.

Family celebrations like a birthday or feast day are often accompanied by fried pastries, made and fried at home, eliminating the need to take pans to the communal oven to be baked. And even though the most remote areas now have gas stoves with ovens (usually powered by a large tank of gas standing prominently close by), the tradition of fried pastries persists.

The frying medium varies depending on the region, though until recently much frying throughout Italy was done in lard, the cheapest and most commonly available fat. This widespread use of lard for frying accounts for the fact that *carnevale* (literally, farewell to meat), or carnival, the day before Ash Wednesday, was much feted with fried pastries. Since Lent began the following day, there would be forty days of fasting and abstinence from meat and meat products, during which pastries fried in lard would be forbidden.

I usually use a mild-flavored olive oil for deep-frying, though I have recently tried various vegetable oils with success. Both canola and safflower oils have a high smoking point, so that it is possible to continue frying with them for a relatively long period of time before the oil begins to degenerate and foam.

Successfully cooked fried pastries are not greasy or soaked with fat but are light, delicate, and not so high in calories that they may not be an occasional treat.

HINTS FOR SUCCESS WITH FRIED PASTRIES

- Make sure the dough to be fried is not laden with flour; when the dough is placed in the hot oil, the excess flour will burn, accumulate in the pan, and cause the frying medium to degenerate quickly.
- Prepare a slotted spoon or a skimmer and a pan covered with paper towels at the same time you begin heating the oil, so that everything needed to drain the pastries is ready before you begin frying. Fried pastries cook quickly and may burn if left unattended while you search for a pan on which to drain them.

- Use a large, deep pan, like a Dutch oven, for frying. Fill the pan only halfway at most; this way if the fat begins to foam, it will not overflow.
- Use a low-to-medium heat for heating frying fat. Never use a high heat, which might cause the flame to jump up the side of the pan and ignite the fat.
- Use a thermometer to gauge the heat of the fat, and adjust the heat under the pan accordingly as the temperature fluctuates during frying.
- Severe burns may result if the pan of hot fat is jostled or if the fat splashes during frying. Make sure children, pets, and the idly curious are well away from the kitchen when you are deep-frying.
- After you finish frying, remove the pan of hot fat from the hot burner to a cool one. Cover the pan and allow the fat to cool. If you have used oil, cool and filter it through a coffee filter or paper towel and use a funnel to pour it back into a bottle; cork it tightly and refrigerate. If the oil has burned or darkened excessively, discard it by pouring it down the drain accompanied by running hot water.
- Use fried pastries for informal and family occasions, so that you may enjoy them freshly fried and warm. Some fried pastries, like cannoli, may be prepared well in advance, but *Sfingi* (page 46), *Frittelle di Riso Corrado Costanza* (page 55), and some others are best served immediately.

∾ ∾

Galani

Venetian Carnival Fritters

A typical Venetian carnival pastry, *galani* are made in one form or another all over Italy and known by many different names. They are easy to prepare and have a delicacy and richness that only a fried pastry possesses.

The typical fat for frying these in most parts of Italy is lard, though I use olive oil with equal success. Make sure that little or no flour clings to the *galani* when they go into the oil or the oil will probably break down and foam before you are finished frying.

Place the flour on a work surface or in a bowl. Make a well in the center and place the sugar, salt, butter, and eggs in the well. Gradually draw in the flour to make a soft dough.

Knead the dough briefly on a well-floured surface by folding it over on itself several times, using a spatula if the dough is sticky. Flour the dough lightly and wrap in plastic. Allow the dough to rest at room temperature for about 1 hour.

Divide the dough into 4 pieces. Flour the surface and the dough lightly and roll it out as thin as possible, dusting with flour and moving the dough often so that it does not stick to the surface or the rolling pin.

Cut the dough into 1½ × 3-inch rectangles with a pastry wheel. Slash the center of each rectangle parallel to the long ends and pass one of the short ends through it to form a knot, as in the illustration.

Heat the oil to 350 degrees and fry the *galani* a few at a time until they are a deep gold. Remove the *galani* from the oil with a slotted spoon and drain them on a cookie sheet lined with paper towels.

Cool the *galani*, dust with the confectioners' sugar, and arrange on a platter.

If there are any *galani* left over, they will keep well unless the weather is very humid. Store them at room temperature, loosely covered with plastic wrap, and give them another coat of confectioners' sugar before serving.

Makes 7 to 8 dozen

2 cups all-purpose flour
¼ cup sugar
½ teaspoon salt
4 tablespoons unsalted butter, softened
3 large eggs

1 quart light or pure olive oil, vegetable oil, or lard, for frying

Confectioners' sugar for finishing

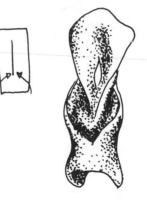

꧁ ꧂

Scaledde

Calabrian Fritters

These small pastries take their name from their amusing twisted shape, known in Calabrian dialect as "little ladders."

1 large egg
1 large egg yolk
1 tablespoon sugar
Pinch salt
1 tablespoon anisette
1 tablespoon unsalted butter, melted
1 cup all-purpose flour

Oil for frying

1 cup honey for finishing

Whisk the egg and yolk together and whisk in the sugar, salt, anisette, and butter. With a rubber spatula, stir in the flour to make a soft dough and continue stirring until the dough becomes slightly elastic, about 1 minute. Scrape the dough out of the bowl onto a floured surface and fold the dough over on itself 5 or 6 times, to make it more elastic. Flour the dough, wrap it in plastic, and let it rest at room temperature for about 1 hour.

Divide the dough into 12 pieces and roll each piece into a thin cylinder about 12 inches long. Cut the cylinders into 3-inch lengths and twist each length around the oiled handle of a wooden spoon, about ⅜ inch in diameter, according to the illustration. Push the spirals of dough off the handle onto a pan to dry for 30 minutes.

Heat the oil to 350 degrees and fry the *scaledde*. Drain and cool them on paper towels. Heat the honey and drizzle it over the *scaledde*.

Makes about 4 dozen small pastries

Note: For advance preparation, fry the *scaledde* but only add the honey before serving.

ꙮ ꙮ

Struffoli

Caramelized Wreath of Crisp Fritters

A popular Italian Christmas pastry, *struffoli* are tiny, crisp fritters bound together with caramel. In some regions it is traditional to prepare the caramel with honey, but I find that the sugar caramel holds up better and is less sweet. The addition of the pine nuts is optional, but they do dress up both the appearance and taste of the *struffoli*.

For the dough, rub the flour and butter together in a bowl. Beat the eggs and vanilla together and stir into the flour. Mix and allow to stand 1 minute so that the flour absorbs the liquid. Knead lightly by folding the dough over on itself 6 or 8 times, on a generously floured surface, and wrap in plastic. Allow the dough to rest 1 hour at room temperature.

Divide the dough into 6 or 8 pieces and roll each into a rope about ½ inch in diameter. Cut each rope into ½-inch lengths. Arrange the pieces of dough on 2 generously oiled sheets of wax paper and leave them to dry for a few minutes.

Heat the oil to 350 degrees in a large pan. Fry the pieces of dough in 2 batches, tipping the wax paper to allow the pieces of dough to slide into the oil. Stir the fritters while they are frying so that they color evenly; cook until they are a deep golden color, about 3 minutes. Drain the fritters on a pan lined with paper towels. Repeat with the second batch. Place the still-warm fritters in a large buttered bowl.

While the fritters are still warm, prepare the caramel: combine the sugar and lemon juice in a saucepan and stir to mix. Place on medium heat, stirring occasionally until the sugar

DOUGH
1½ cups all-purpose flour
1½ tablespoons unsalted butter, softened
3 large eggs
1 teaspoon vanilla extract

1½ quarts light or pure olive oil or vegetable oil, for frying

CARAMEL
1½ cups sugar
1 teaspoon lemon juice

½ cup toasted pine nuts (optional)

Candied fruit for finishing (optional)

melts and caramelizes. Do not allow the caramel to become too dark.

Pour the caramel over the fritters in the bowl and quickly add the pine nuts. Stir rapidly to coat the fritters and the pine nuts evenly with the caramel, and turn the mixture out onto a buttered platter.

Quickly and carefully, shape the mass of fritters into a wreath. Wear buttered rubber gloves if you fear burns. Decorate with the candied fruit. Loosen the wreath from the platter before the caramel hardens completely.

To serve the *struffoli*, break the wreath into rough pieces at the table with the point of a knife. Let guests help themselves, breaking the fritters apart a few at a time. This is finger food for an informal occasion.

Makes 8 servings

ᘐᘗ ᘖᘘ

Carteddate al Miele

Fried Honey Wheels from Bari

These spirals of fried pastry are mostly a vehicle to hold honey or *Vino Cotto* (page 22). Popular in Apulia as well as in Calabria, the *carteddate* are one of the pastries I remember my grandmother preparing in my early childhood.

This recipe comes from Paola Pettini, a native of Rome, who now makes her home in Bari. Signora Pettini generously shared the recipes for many Barese and Apulian specialties with me.

For the dough, mix the flour, baking powder, salt, and grated zests in a bowl. Combine the oil, wine, and liqueur and stir into the flour mixture to form a stiff, dry dough. Knead the dough on a work surface to make it as smooth as possible. Wrap the dough in plastic and let rest at room temperature for 1 hour.

Pound the dough gently with a rolling pin until it is about ¼ inch thick. Flour the dough lightly and pass it through a pasta machine, beginning with the widest setting. Pass it through the next setting, then the next, and divide the dough into 6 pieces. Pass each piece through the machine on the next settings, ending with the thinnest.

With a serrated pastry wheel, trim the long edges of one of the strips to scallop them, then divide into 4 narrow ribbons, about 1½ inches wide. Fold the ribbons lengthwise so that they are about ¾ inch wide, as in the illustration. Pinch the cut edges together every 2 inches. Then, with the fold on the bottom, roll up the ribbon of dough into a concentric spiral, not too tightly. Repeat with the other 3 ribbons, then with the other 5 strips.

Arrange the *carteddate* on generously oiled pans and let them dry at room temperature about 4 hours, so that they do not come apart while frying.

Heat the oil to 350 degrees and fry the *carteddate* 3 or 4 at a time, making sure that you remove them from the oil folded side up; this way they will not trap a large quantity of oil. Drain them on pans lined with paper towels, folded side up, allowing any excess oil to drain off.

After all the *carteddate* are fried, arrange them on a pan, folded side down. Heat the honey in a pan until it is hot and liquid. Spoon the honey over the *carteddate*, making sure it enters the folded areas. Cool and sprinkle with the grated chocolate.

Makes 24 pastries

DOUGH

3 cups all-purpose flour
1 teaspoon baking powder
½ teaspoon salt
Grated zest of 1 lemon
Grated zest of 1 orange
Grated zest of 1 tangerine, if available
⅓ cup mild olive oil or vegetable oil
⅓ cup white wine
3 tablespoons sweet liqueur, such as anisette or Strega

1½ quarts light or pure olive oil or vegetable oil, for frying

1 cup honey or Vino Cotto, *page 22*
2 ounces semisweet chocolate, finely grated

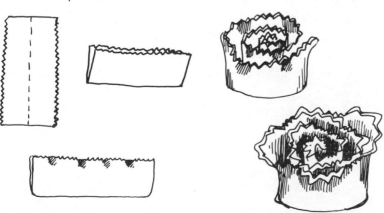
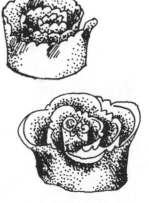

VARIATIONS

The traditional Barese recipe entails bringing a quart of honey to a boil and immersing the *carteddate* in it. If you prefer them sweeter, by all means try this method.

To flavor the *carteddate* with *vino cotto* instead of honey, bring 3 cups of *vino cotto* to a boil, then immerse the *carteddate*, a few at a time, in the hot *vino cotto*. Transfer to a pan to cool and drain; sprinkle with the colored sugar granules called *diavolilli* or *diavoletti*, known in English as nonpareils (see Sources of Equipment and Ingredients).

∂﹏ ﹏∂

Sfingi

Cream Puff Fritters

Sfingi taste wonderfully delicate and complex even though they are one of the easiest pastries to make. Nothing more than teaspoon-sized bits of cream puff paste (*pasta bignè*) dropped into hot oil and fried until golden and puffed, then rolled in flavored sugar, *sfingi* have an elusive delicacy that makes you want to taste yet another to determine its source. One important note: since the paste itself contains no sugar, you must roll *sfingi* in the sugar while still slightly warm or they will be dull and tasteless.

CREAM PUFF PASTE
1 cup water
8 tablespoons (1 stick)
   unsalted butter
½ teaspoon salt
1 cup all-purpose flour
4 large eggs

For the cream puff paste, bring the water, butter, and salt to a boil in a heavy pan. Remove from the heat and add the flour all at once. Stir until smooth and return the pan to the heat to dry out the paste, until the bottom of the pan is filmed. Remove to a mixing bowl and beat with a wooden spoon for a few seconds to cool.

Add the eggs one at a time, beating until smooth between each addition.

Heat the oil in a 3-quart saucepan and drop the batter into it, by level measuring teaspoonfuls, 10 or 12 in rapid succession. Fry the puffs, stirring often with a slotted spoon, until they are well risen and a deep golden color, about 3 minutes.

Drain the fritters on paper towels and roll half of them in the cinnamon sugar and the other half in the lemon sugar while they are still warm. Arrange the differently flavored fritters on separate platters and serve immediately.

Makes about 100 small fritters

1½ quarts light or pure olive oil or vegetable oil, for frying

CINNAMON SUGAR
1 cup sugar mixed with ½ teaspoon ground cinnamon

LEMON SUGAR
1 cup sugar mixed with grated zest of 1 lemon

ත්‍ර ද්‍ර

Zeppole di San Giuseppe

Saint Joseph's Day Fritters

These fritters are prepared for the feast of Saint Joseph, on March 19. An important holiday in Italy, it is celebrated with as much fervor as Thanksgiving is here. These light fritters are filled with an orange cream and preserved sour cherries.

For the orange pastry cream, bring the milk, orange zest, and half the sugar to a boil in a saucepan. Whisk the egg yolks in a bowl, then whisk in the remaining sugar. Sift the flour over the yolk mixture and whisk it in. When the milk mixture boils, whisk one-third of it into the yolk mixture. Return the remaining milk to a boil and whisk the yolk mixture into it. Continue whisking until the cream thickens and returns to a boil. Remove from the heat and beat in the vanilla. Pour the cream into a bowl, cover the surface directly with plastic wrap, and refrigerate until cold.

For the cream puff paste, bring the water, butter, and salt to a boil in a small saucepan. Remove from the heat and stir in the flour all at once. Return to the heat and cook the mixture until it leaves the sides of the pan. Pour the paste into a mixing

ORANGE PASTRY CREAM
1 cup milk
Grated zest of 1 orange
⅓ cup sugar
3 large egg yolks
¼ cup all-purpose flour
2 teaspoons vanilla extract

CREAM PUFF PASTE

⅔ cup water

5 tablespoons unsalted butter

¼ teaspoon salt

⅔ cup all-purpose flour

3 large eggs

2 teaspoons sugar

Grated zest of 1 orange

1½ quarts light or pure olive oil or vegetable oil, for frying

½ cup Conserva di Amarene, *page 13*

Confectioners' sugar for finishing

bowl and beat in the eggs, one at a time. Beat in the sugar and orange zest.

With a pastry bag and a ½-inch star tube (Ateco #4), pipe the paste into 3½-inch circles, piping each circle on a separate piece of parchment. Heat the oil to 375 degrees and fry the *zeppole* a few at a time, peeling away the parchment. Turn the *zeppole* once during cooking. Drain on paper towels and cool.

To assemble the fritters, place a spoonful of orange pastry cream in the center of each *zeppola* and top with some of the cherries, drained from the *conserva*. Dust the fritters with the confectioners' sugar.

Makes 24 fritters

Note: For advance preparation, make the orange pastry cream and the cream puff paste up to 1 day in advance and refrigerate. Fry the fritters up to 4 hours before serving, but only fill them about 1 hour before serving.

❧ ☙

Cannoli alla Siciliana

Sicilian Cannoli

One of the most popular of all Italian pastries in the United States, cannoli are now seen on the mainland of Italy, as well as in their native Sicily. Originally, the wealthy families of Palermo sent cannoli as gifts to friends at carnival time, always at least a dozen, and always in units of twelve. Nowadays there are many variations on this pastry, some replacing the traditional ricotta filling with vanilla or chocolate pastry cream.

My own favorite cannoli memory is of those I bought at the Monastery of Sant'Andrea in Palermo, prepared by the cloistered nuns with ricotta *pecorina*, made from ewe's milk from their farms at Piana degli Albanesi, outside the city. The cannoli shells had been fried in lard, and the hint of bacon in the shell complemented the slightly gamy flavor of the ricotta filling, with the sugar and candied orange peel providing bursts of sweetness along the way. It was the most successful combination of sweet and savory flavors that I have ever experienced.

I bought the cannoli through a *girandola*, a sort of revolving hollow column, open on one side, with shelves inside, situated in the wall that separated the cloister proper from the outer vestibule. It was used to pass merchandise in and out of the cloister without actually opening the cloister to the outside world. After I rang, a nun spoke from behind the *girandola*, and when I asked for the pastries, she disappeared for what seemed an interminable time. When she returned, she revolved the *girandola*, and three cannoli appeared on one of the shelves. I removed the cannoli and replaced them with some money, asking if she would tell me a little about the convent pastry shop. She moved to a grilled window covered with shutters from the inside, a few feet from the *girandola*, and flung open the shutters, revealing herself as a tiny, middle-aged woman dressed in the standard black Benedictine habit, plus a flour-stained blue apron. She then explained that the ricotta came from the convent's establishment at Piana, where they also run a girls' school. She also told me to go around to the back of the convent, where there was a salesroom run by a *signorina*, to find other pastries, including *cassata* and all sorts of other traditional sweets. The *signorina* turned out to be rather impatient, but I did buy some magnificent almond-paste shells filled with citron. Although there was no discussion of the recipe, tasting those cannoli was an entire education in Sicilian pastry traditions.

This is my standard version of cannoli, followed by several variations, including the Sant'Andrea ones. The cannoli tubes are fairly easy to find in department stores and kitchenware shops nowadays. If you have trouble locating them, check Sources of Equipment and Ingredients.

CANNOLI SHELLS

1½ cups all-purpose flour

2 teaspoons sugar

1 teaspoon cocoa powder

½ teaspoon salt

*½ teaspoon ground
cinnamon*

*2 tablespoons mild olive oil,
vegetable oil, or lard*

1 tablespoon vinegar

*¼ cup sweet Marsala or
other fortified wine*

*1½ quarts light or pure olive
oil or vegetable oil, for
frying*

RICOTTA FILLING

*2 pounds firm whole-milk
ricotta, commercial or
homemade*

2 cups confectioners' sugar

1 teaspoon vanilla extract

*½ teaspoon ground
cinnamon*

*1 ounce bittersweet
chocolate, chopped*

*2 tablespoons citron or
candied orange peel,
chopped*

*1 large egg white, lightly
beaten, for sealing*

*2 tablespoons chopped,
blanched pistachios; and
confectioners' sugar, for
finishing*

For the shells, mix the dry ingredients together and rub in the oil. Mix the vinegar and Marsala and stir into the flour mixture. The dough will be very firm and dry. Form the dough into a rough rectangle about ½ inch thick, wrap in plastic, and allow to rest at room temperature about 1 hour.

Flour the dough and roll it out, pressing hard, to a ¼-inch thickness. Pass the dough through a pasta machine's widest setting repeatedly, folding it over on itself after every pass through the rollers, until it is smooth, about 12 or 15 times in all. Wrap and let rest again for 1 hour at room temperature. (The dough may be refrigerated a day or two at this point.)

Divide the dough in half and rewrap one half. Flour the other half and pass it through the pasta machine, beginning with the widest setting, then through every other setting, ending with the thinnest. Place the strip of dough on a floured work surface and cover with plastic wrap to prevent it from drying and crusting. Repeat this process with the other piece of dough. Using a floured cutter or a small bowl as a pattern, cut the dough into disks. Each disk should be about 1½ inches shorter than the length of the tube it will be fried on. Roll a rolling pin over each disk once to lengthen it slightly and make it oval, as in the illustration.

To form the cannoli, place an oval of dough on the work surface and center a metal cannoli tube on it lengthwise. Wrap one edge of the dough around the tube, without stretching it, and moisten the top of the dough with a very small amount of the egg white, without letting the egg white drip onto the metal tube. Wrap the other edge of the dough around the tube to cover the first one and lift from the work surface, pressing the 2 edges of dough together well. Repeat with the other disks of

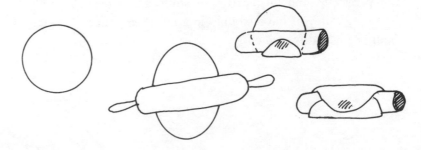

dough. (If you do not have enough tubes for all disks, keep the extra prepared ovals of dough tightly wrapped with plastic until the tubes used to fry the first batch of cannoli have cooled; then form as before.)

Fry the cannoli a few at a time in oil preheated to 350 degrees until they are a deep gold. Place on a pan lined with paper towels and remove from the tubes immediately or they will shrink as they cool and shatter when taken off the tubes. With one hand, grip the fried shell with several thicknesses of paper towel, then pull out the metal tube with tongs or a pot holder held in the other hand. Cool the shells on paper towels.

For the filling, beat the ricotta and sugar until very light, either with a hand mixer set at medium speed or in a heavy-duty mixer fitted with the whip. Beat in the vanilla and cinnamon and stir in the chocolate and citron.

No more than 1 hour before serving, fill the shells using a pastry bag fitted with a ½-inch plain tube (Ateco #6). Sprinkle the ends of the cream with the pistachios. Dust the cannoli with the confectioners' sugar.

Makes 12 to 15 cannoli

VARIATIONS

Cannoli alla Messinese
Add ¼ cup chopped *Croccante* (page 249) to the filling. Omit the pistachios and leave the ends plain.

Cannoli del Monastero di Sant'Andrea
Add ½ cup mild goat cheese, such as Montrachet, to the ricotta and sugar before beginning to beat the filling, to approximate the flavor of ricotta *pecorina*, almost unobtainable in the United States. Use candied orange peel, not citron, in the filling. Fry the shells in lard.

Cannoli alla Cioccolata
Fill the cannoli with *Crema Pasticciera alla Cioccolata*, page 220. Fold in 1 ounce chopped bittersweet chocolate and 2 tablespoons chopped citron or candied orange peel.

ळ्ऽ ल्ळॐ

Cannoli di Catania e della Sicilia Orientale

Cannoli from Catania and Eastern Sicily

The following is a less seasoned dough found more often on the east coast of Sicily, notably in Catania, and is more appropriate for cannoli with pastry cream fillings.

1½ cups all-purpose flour
1½ teaspoons sugar
½ teaspoon salt
2 tablespoons mild olive oil
    or vegetable oil
1 tablespoon vinegar
¼ cup water

Mix the dry ingredients together and rub in the oil. Mix the vinegar and water and stir into the flour mixture. Proceed as for *Cannoli alla Siciliana.*

ळ्ऽ ल्ळॐ

Ravioli Dolci di Ricotta

Fried Ravioli with Sweet Ricotta Filling

Though these are a Sicilian version of this sweet, there are many other versions in other regions of Italy, usually served at Christmastime. Make sure the filled ravioli have an opportunity to rest for a couple of hours after they are filled to minimize the chances of their opening or bursting during frying.

DOUGH
2½ cups all-purpose flour
¼ cup sugar
½ teaspoon salt
6 tablespoons unsalted butter
2 large eggs
¼ cup water

For the dough, combine the flour, sugar, and salt in a mixing bowl and stir to mix. Rub the butter in finely so that the mixture remains dry and powdery and does not become pasty. Whisk the eggs and water together and stir into the flour mixture with a folk. Continue stirring until the dough masses together in the bowl. Turn the dough out onto a lightly floured surface and fold the dough over on itself several times. Wrap in plastic and chill for 1 hour (or up to 2 days).

For the ricotta filling, press the ricotta through a sieve or fine strainer into a bowl. Whisk in the remaining filling ingredients.

To form the ravioli, flour the dough and roll it out to a ¼-inch thickness. Pass the dough through a pasta machine until the third setting. Divide the dough into 4 pieces and pass each piece of dough through the machine's settings, ending with the next-to-last setting.

Arrange the 4 strips of dough on a work surface and drop teaspoonfuls of the filling onto the dough at 4-inch intervals, about 1½ inches from the edge. Paint the dough around the filling very lightly with the beaten egg white on one strip at a time, then fold over the top half of the dough to enclose the filling, as in the illustration. Press well with your fingertips

around the filling, then cut the dough into 3-inch squares around the filling to form the ravioli, as in the illustration.

Arrange the ravioli on lightly floured pans and allow to rest at room temperature about 2 hours. Heat the oil to 350 degrees and fry the ravioli about 6 at a time until they are a deep golden color, about 5 minutes, stirring them gently with a slotted spoon while they are frying.

Drain the ravioli on paper towels and cool.

Before serving, dust lightly with the confectioners' sugar.

Makes about 2 dozen

RICOTTA FILLING

1 cup well-drained whole-milk ricotta, commercial or homemade

¼ cup sugar

½ teaspoon ground cinnamon

2 teaspoons vanilla extract

1 ounce semisweet chocolate, coarsely grated

1 egg white, lightly beaten, for sealing

1½ quarts light or pure olive oil or vegetable oil, for frying

Confectioners' sugar for finishing

⮞⮜ ⮞⮜

Tortelli di Natale

—

Little Christmas Cakes

These small cakes are a traditional pastry for Christmas from Bologna southward. Known by many different names, they have a history in almost every region, especially southern Italy and Sicily. Though there are subtle variations on name and ingredients, the idea remains the same — a thin dough pocket enclosing a chestnut or chick-pea filling flavored with chocolate and raisins or candied fruit. They may be dusted with confectioners' sugar, as in this recipe, or drizzled with warmed honey or *Vino Cotto* (page 22) before serving.

DOUGH

2 cups all-purpose flour

¼ cup sugar

½ teaspoon baking powder

3 tablespoons mild olive oil, vegetable oil, or melted butter

2 large eggs

2 tablespoons rum or brandy

FILLING

½ pound fresh chestnuts

½ cup apricot preserves

3 ounces semisweet chocolate, melted and cooled

1 teaspoon ground cinnamon

For the dough, combine the dry ingredients in a bowl and stir to mix. Whisk the oil, eggs, and rum or brandy together and stir into the dough with a fork. Continue stirring until the dough masses together, then scrape the dough out onto a lightly floured surface. Fold the dough over on itself several times, flour it well, wrap in plastic, and chill 1 hour.

For the filling, cut an X in the flat end of each chestnut and cook them in boiling salted water for about 20 minutes. Drain and peel the chestnuts. Place them in a food processor fitted with the metal blade and puree them. Add the apricot preserves and chocolate and puree again. Stir in the spices, rum, and raisins.

To form the *tortelli*, flour the dough and roll it out to a ¼-inch thickness. Pass the dough through a pasta machine until the third setting. Divide the dough into 4 pieces and pass each piece of dough through the machine's settings, ending with the next-to-last setting.

Arrange the 4 strips of dough on a work surface and place

the filling on the dough by teaspoonfuls at 4-inch intervals, about 1½ inches from the edge. Paint the dough around the filling very lightly with the beaten egg white on one strip at a time, then fold over the top half of the dough to enclose the filling, as in the illustration for *Ravioli Dolci di Ricotta* (preceding recipe). Press well with your fingertips around the filling and cut the dough into 3-inch squares around the filling to form the ravioli, as in the illustration.

Arrange the *tortelli* on lightly floured pans and allow to rest at room temperature for about 2 hours. Heat the oil to 350 degrees and fry the *tortelli* about 6 at a time until they are a deep golden color, about 5 minutes, stirring them gently with a slotted spoon while they are frying.

Drain the *tortelli* on paper towels and cool.

Before serving, dust lightly with the confectioners' sugar.

Makes about 2 dozen

¼ teaspoon ground cloves
3 tablespoons dark rum or brandy
⅓ cup raisins, coarsely chopped

1 large egg white, lightly beaten, for sealing

1½ quarts light or pure olive oil or vegetable oil, for frying

Confectioners' sugar for finishing

∽✿ ✿∽

Frittelle di Riso Corrado Costanza

Corrado Costanza's Rice Fritters

Many pastry shops in Sicily excel in one or another specialty. Others manage to prepare outstanding examples of several types of the pastry chef's art and perhaps are known for good ices and beautiful miniature pastries. Only Corrado Costanza of Noto, near Siracusa, can boast a pastry shop that excels in all branches of traditional Sicilian sweets. His expertise runs the gamut of flower-scented ices, beautifully decorated *cassate*, confections molded in the shape of religious subjects, and his favorite pursuit, re-creations of ancient pastries from the many convents and monasteries that flourished in Noto up to the time of World War I.

Noto itself has a dreamlike quality. The old city was destroyed during an earthquake at the end of the seventeenth century, and early in the eighteenth century it was rebuilt on its present site entirely in Sicilian High Baroque style. The churches, monasteries, and palaces vie with each other in splendor, and though many have seen better days, they now have a slightly dusty quality that tempers their exaggerated grandeur.

I last visited Noto and Signore Costanza with my friends Miriam and Lester Brickman, and we arrived at his pastry shop on a Sunday morning just as he was about to begin frying a batch of these *frittelle*. I was surprised to find that the rice had been cooked in chicken broth while the fritters were sprinkled with honey, sugar, and cinnamon. The combination of the meaty saltiness of the rice in the crisp fritter and the sticky sweetness of the honey transformed several ordinary flavors into an ethereally delicious whole.

One important note about serving the *frittelle:* they cannot wait and must be eaten immediately after being fried, drained, and sweetened. Prepare them for a very informal or family occasion, when you can easily spend twenty minutes in the kitchen for the frying.

¼ cup arborio or other rice and 1 cup chicken stock or salted water; or 1 cup cooked rice

BATTER
1 cup milk or water
1 envelope active dry yeast or ⅔ ounce compressed yeast
1¼ cups all-purpose flour
1 tablespoon sugar
½ teaspoon salt

1½ quarts light or pure olive oil or vegetable oil, for frying

Honey, granulated sugar, and ground cinnamon for finishing

To cook the rice, bring the stock or salted water to a boil in a small pan with a tight-fitting lid. Add the rice, stir once with a fork, cover the pan, and cook the rice over the lowest heat for about 15 minutes, checking to make sure that the liquid has not evaporated and the rice is not sticking. If necessary, add several tablespoons of boiling water to the rice if it is dry but still not cooked. When the rice is cooked it should be fairly soft. Spread the rice out on a plate to cool.

For the batter, heat the milk or water to lukewarm, about 105 degrees, pour into a bowl, and whisk in the yeast. Add the flour, sugar, and salt, stirring gently to avoid making the batter elastic. Stir in the rice and cover with plastic wrap. Allow to ferment until foamy, about 30 minutes.

Over medium heat, heat the oil to 375 degrees in a 2½- to 3-quart pan. Place one-third of the batter on a straight-edged piece of cake cardboard or cutting board and use a thin knife to shape the batter (it will be very soft and sticky) into a rectangle approximately 3 × 5 inches. Position the knife ½ inch behind the 3-inch side closest to the edge of the board. Scrape a 3 × ½-inch section of the batter into the oil, as in the illustration. Continue with the rest of the batter on the board, scraping the *frittelle* in quickly and, to avoid burns, making sure they do not splash into the oil. You will have to continually readjust the shape of the batter on the board so that it is 3 inches wide at the edge closest to the pan by pushing inward from the 2 perpendicular sides with the knife.

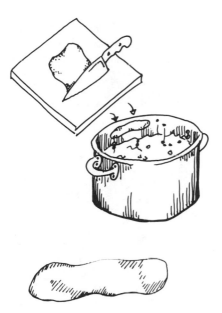

Once the *frittelle* are in the oil, stir them gently with a slotted spoon, making sure that they color evenly. Remove to a pan lined with paper towels to drain for a few minutes. Arrange the first *frittelle* on a plate and drizzle with the honey. Sprinkle with the granulated sugar and cinnamon. Serve immediately. Repeat the process with the other two-thirds of the batter, serving each batch as soon as it is fried, drained, and garnished.

Makes 24 to 30 fritters

❧☙

Krapfen

Filled Yeast-Risen Fritters

Krapfen, which means "fritters" in German, are another example of a foreign pastry very much at home in Italy. Although these probably entered Italy through the Trentino–Alto Adige region, where the Austrian influence is strong, they are seen throughout mainland Italy, even in Naples, where they are known as *i graf* in dialect.

Krapfen resemble a filled doughnut and are perfect for brunch or snacks but are not necessarily a dessert to be served at the table.

SPONGE

1 cup all-purpose flour

½ cup milk

1 envelope active dry yeast
    or ⅔ ounce compressed
    yeast

DOUGH

4 tablespoons unsalted
    butter, softened

⅓ cup sugar

½ teaspoon salt

1 teaspoon grated lemon zest

2 large eggs

1 large egg yolk

1½ cups all-purpose flour

1½ quarts light or pure olive
    oil or vegetable oil, for
    frying

1 cup jam or Crema
    Pasticciera, page 219

Confectioners' sugar for
    finishing

For the sponge, place the flour in a bowl. Heat the milk to lukewarm, about 105 degrees. Whisk the yeast into the milk and pour the mixture over the flour. Stir in to form a smooth, very soft dough. Cover the bowl with plastic wrap and allow the sponge to ferment until double, about 30 minutes.

Meanwhile, mix the dough: beat the butter, either by hand, with a hand mixer set at medium speed, or in a heavy-duty mixer fitted with the paddle. Beat in the sugar, salt, and lemon zest. Add the eggs and yolk, one at a time, beating until smooth between each addition. Beat in the flour until smooth.

When the sponge is sufficiently risen, beat it into the dough and continue mixing by hand or by machine on the lowest speed until the dough is smooth and elastic, 5 to 10 minutes. Cover the dough and allow it to ferment until double, about 1 to 1½ hours.

Generously flour a work surface and scrape the risen dough onto it. Deflate the dough by folding it over on itself several times. Be careful that the dough, which will be soft and sticky, does not stick to the surface at this point. Cover the dough with a towel and allow to rest 10 minutes. Then pat out the dough about ¼ inch thick, allow it to spring back slightly, and cut into 3-inch disks. Transfer the disks, as they are cut, to a lightly floured pan, spacing them 2 inches apart. Cover them loosely with a towel and allow to proof until double, about 1 hour.

Heat the oil to 350 degrees in a large saucepan. Fry the *Krapfen* 2 or 3 at a time, until they are a deep gold, turning them once or twice while they are frying. Remove to a pan lined with paper towels to drain. Cool.

To fill and finish the *Krapfen*, pierce each one on its side with a chopstick or thin wooden spoon handle, inserting the tool as far as the center of the fritter and revolving it slightly to make a small pocket. Place the jam or *crema pasticciera* in a pastry bag fitted with a ¼-inch plain tube (Ateco #2) and fill the *Krapfen*. Transfer them to a platter after they are filled. Dust lightly with the confectioners' sugar right before serving. Serve the *Krapfen* on the day they are made.

Makes 12 to 16 Krapfen

❧ 4 ❧

Pies and Pastries Made with
Sweet Dough

Pasta frolla, or Italian sweet pastry dough, forms the basis for many different tarts and pie-type pastries, as well as some *biscotti* in the chapter *Biscotti* and Other Cookies and some individual pastries at the end of this chapter. (Though not all are made with *pasta frolla,* they are grouped here for convenience.) As the word *frolla,* or "tender," indicates, the dough is friable or crumbly in texture rather than flaky, the norm for most French and American pastry doughs. When well made, *pasta frolla* more than compensates for its lack of flakiness with a wonderful tenderness and lightness.

The words *torte* and *pizze* roughly translate as "cakes" and "pies," yet these terms are used interchangeably to indicate pastries composed of a pan lined with dough that contains a filling, with or without a top crust. The term *crostata* usually indicates a bottom crust, filling, and lattice-top crust, and a *crostata* may be baked either on a flat pan or in a cake pan. To add to the confusion, cakes and layer cakes are also called *torte.* Since the name derives from the Latin for "round cake," it is applied equally correctly to round sweets made with pastry dough or cake layers.

BUTTER—LARD—SHORTENING

The typical fat for baking in southern Italy is leaf lard, or rendered pork fat, specifically from the hard, white fat surrounding the kidneys. It is the usual fat for making a pastry dough as well as for deep-frying. Though butter was never entirely unknown in southern Italy and Sicily, it is much more in evidence today; many, however, still cook and bake with lard.

Olive oil is also much used in southern Italian baking, and you will find recipes using oil as their principal shortening in the chapters on fried pastries and *biscotti*.

In northern Italy, the use of butter is prevalent, though some recipes still call for lard or oil.

In the recipes for pastry doughs in this chapter, I have chosen to use unsalted butter throughout. For an authentic southern Italian flavor in the *Pizza Rustica alla Grottese* (page 65) or the Sicilian *Cassata al Forno* (page 75), substitute an equal quantity of lard, as you may do in any of the southern Italian recipes.

HINTS FOR SUCCESS WITH *PASTA FROLLA*

- Leave the butter in the refrigerator while you prepare the other ingredients, so that it will not soften and cause the dough to be soft and sticky or, worse, hot and overworked.
- When you remove the butter from the refrigerator, soften it slightly by pounding with a rolling pin or squeezing it hard several times. This will allow it to work quickly into the dry ingredients and will prevent it from melting, caused by too much handling.
- Use your hands or a pastry blender to incorporate the butter. Or you may pulse the dry ingredients and butter in a food processor until the mixture resembles fine crumbs. Whatever method you use, stir the eggs, or eggs and liquid, into the dough by hand to avoid overmixing and toughening the dough.
- After the eggs have been stirred into the dough, continue stirring until the dough masses together. Then scrape the dough out of the bowl onto a floured work surface and knead lightly so that the eggs have moistened the entire quantity of dough evenly.
- Wrap the dough in plastic and refrigerate it until it is firm. If the dough is firm, it will not soften so much during the rolling and forming and will be easier to handle.

• If possible, allow the dough to chill again after forming to avoid shrinkage during baking.

ROLLING AND FORMING *PASTA FROLLA*

Most Italian recipes for *torte* and *pizze* made with *pasta frolla* call for a straight-sided cake pan rather than the sloping-sided pie pan that would normally be used in the United States for this type of pastry. The process of lining a straight-sided pan is only slightly more work than that of lining a pie pan, and the result is a professional, tailored-looking pastry.

1. Butter the pan before lining it. Aside from preventing the baked pastry from sticking to the pan, the butter makes the raw dough adhere to the pan, so that the dough holds firmly in place while being molded to the pan.

2. Fold the disk of dough in half, then in half again, to transfer it to the pan. Line up the center point of the dough with the center of the pan, then unfold the dough. This method makes it easy to align the dough perfectly in the pan.

3. Ease the edge of the dough down from the top rim of the pan so that it begins to lie flat against the side of the pan. Then press the dough well against the bottom of the pan and ease it into the inside edge, where the bottom and side of the pan meet.

4. Trim away all but ¼ inch of the excess dough at the top of the pan with a small paring knife, leaving it draped over the top edge and cutting it from the outside of the pan. This prevents the inside from collapsing before the pastry is filled.

5. Egg-wash the rim before finishing the top with lattice strips, if used, so that the strips will adhere to the side.

6. After filling, and finishing the top when necessary, trim the edge of the dough so it is even with the top inside rim of the pan. Ease it down over the filling all around to make a top edge on the pastry.

7. Use any extra dough, including trimmings, for a few simple *biscotti*. See the *biscotti* made with *pasta frolla* called *Frollini*, page 200.

⊘‍◡ ◡‍⊘

Pasta Frolla I

Although each recipe in this chapter that calls for *pasta frolla* carries quantities and instructions for preparing it, this is a more complete explanation of the technique.

This recipe is appropriate for *crostate* and some *biscotti;* the recipe that follows it is best for *pizze* and *torte* with wetter fillings.

2⅓ cups all-purpose flour
⅓ cup sugar
Pinch salt
8 tablespoons (1 stick)
   unsalted butter, cold
2 large eggs

Combine the flour, sugar, and salt in a mixing bowl. Stir well to mix. Remove the butter from the refrigerator, unwrap, and place on a work surface. Pound it gently with a rolling pin or the heel of your hand to make it pliable. After 3 or 4 strokes, the butter should have softened sufficiently. Use a scraper to remove it from the work surface and add it to the bowl with the flour mixture.

Toss the butter to coat it with flour and break it into 6 or 8 pieces, using your fingertips. Continue breaking the butter into smaller pieces and rubbing it into the flour mixture with your fingers. At the same time, work the flour mixture upward from the bottom of the bowl so that it mixes evenly with the butter. The whole process should take no more than 2 minutes. Work quickly to ensure that the mixture remains cool and powdery and does not become pasty, which would be a sign that the butter is melting and that the resulting dough will be tough.

Break the eggs into a small bowl or cup, beat lightly with a fork, and stir into the butter-flour mixture. Continue stirring with the fork until the dough begins to hold together.

Empty the contents of the bowl onto a lightly floured work surface and squeeze the dough together gently until it is smooth, very briefly, without overworking it. Shape the dough into a thick disk, about 4 inches in diameter, and wrap in plastic. Chill the dough until needed. It may be prepared up to 3 days ahead.

Makes enough dough for a 9-inch torta *with a lattice crust*

ও৫৫ ৫৫৩

Pasta Frolla II

Use this dough for *Pizza di Ricotta alla Grottese* (page 64), *Pizza di Crema alla Grottese* (page 69), or any other *torta* or *pizza* with a creamy, wet filling. The baking powder in the dough causes it to expand slightly during baking, so that the bottom crust is always in contact with the hot bottom of the pan, ensuring that it bakes through and colors well.

Use the same method as in the preceding recipe, *Pasta Frolla I*, combining the dry ingredients, working in the butter, and then beating the egg and milk or water together before adding them to the butter-flour mixture.

To prepare half a batch of the dough, halve all ingredients and use only the egg to moisten the dough.

Makes enough dough for a 9-inch torta *with a lattice crust*

2½ cups all-purpose flour
½ cup sugar
¼ teaspoon salt
½ teaspoon baking powder
10 tablespoons (1¼ sticks) unsalted butter
1 large egg
4 tablespoons milk or water

Torte, Pizze, e Crostate

Pies, Pastries, and Tarts

༚ ༙

Pizza di Ricotta alla Grottese

Ricotta Cheesecake from Grottaminarda

This is the traditional sweet ricotta pastry from Grottaminarda, the village of my mother's family, near Avellino and Benevento in southern Italy. Though it is normally an Easter dessert, *pizza di ricotta* is made on special occasions throughout the year. Feel free to vary the flavoring of the filling. Some prefer to leave out the anisette; other add toasted, slivered almonds or chopped chocolate.

PASTA FROLLA
2½ cups all-purpose flour
½ cup sugar
¼ teaspoon salt
½ teaspoon baking powder
10 tablespoons (1¼ sticks) unsalted butter
1 large egg
4 tablespoons milk or water

RICOTTA FILLING
1½ pounds whole-milk ricotta, commercial or homemade
½ cup sugar
4 large eggs
1 teaspoon vanilla extract

For the *pasta frolla*, combine the dry ingredients and mix well. Rub in the butter until it is absorbed, making sure the mixture remains cool and powdery and does not become pasty. Beat the egg with the milk or water and stir in with a fork. Continue stirring until the dough holds together, then knead briefly, just until smooth. Shape the dough into a disk, wrap in plastic, and refrigerate at least 1 hour, or until firm.

For the ricotta filling, press the ricotta through a fine sieve into a mixing bowl or puree it in a food processor fitted with the metal blade. Stir in the sugar, then the eggs, one at a time. Stir in the vanilla, anisette, citron, and ½ teaspoon of the cinnamon, being careful not to overmix.

Butter a 9-inch cake pan that is 2 inches deep. To assemble, cut off one-third of the *pasta frolla* and reserve. Roll the rest of the dough into a 14-inch disk and line the prepared pan with it. Allow the dough to hang over the edge of the pan. Pour in the ricotta filling and sprinkle it with the remaining ½ teaspoon of cinnamon.

Roll out the reserved dough into a 10-inch square. Cut it into ten 1-inch-wide strips. For the egg wash, beat the egg with the salt, and paint the strips with it. Moisten the rim of the dough on the pan with the egg wash, and attach 5 strips in each direction, pressing the edges of the strips lightly onto the rim and forming a diagonal lattice. Trim the edges of the dough so they are even with the top of the pan and push the dough off the top rim of the pan so that it rests completely within the pan.

Bake at 350 degrees for about 45 minutes, until the filling is set and the pastry is a light gold. Cool in the pan before unmolding. To unmold, invert onto a flat plate, lift off the pan, replace the pan with another plate or platter, and then reinvert so that the *pizza* is right side up. Serve the *pizza* at room temperature.

Makes 10 to 12 servings

1 tablespoon anisette
*3 tablespoons candied citron,
   rinsed and finely chopped*
1 teaspoon ground cinnamon

EGG WASH
1 large egg
Pinch salt

༄ ༄

Pizza Rustica alla Grottese

Savory Carnival Pastry with *Pecorino*, Mozzarella, and Dried Sausage

This most typical savory pie is served at *carnevale* (the day before Ash Wednesday) and then again at Easter. The name derives from the village of Grottaminarda. The dough is sweet — this is the traditional way of preparing it. If the combination is not appealing, leave out the sugar; but note that the dough may be slightly dry and may need a bit more water to moisten it.

Pizza rustica makes an excellent appetizer or a main course for a light meal, as well as a convenient picnic food.

PASTA FROLLA
2½ cups all-purpose flour
½ cup sugar
¼ teaspoon salt
½ teaspoon baking powder
10 tablespoons (1¼ sticks)
    unsalted butter
1 large egg
¼ cup milk or water

FILLING
1 pound whole-milk ricotta,
    commercial or
    homemade
3 large eggs
¼ teaspoon salt
½ teaspoon freshly ground
    pepper
½ cup grated pecorino
    romano cheese
½ pound mozzarella, thinly
    sliced
½ pound dried sausage, such
    as cacciatorino or
    soppresatta, peeled and
    sliced

EGG WASH
1 large egg
Pinch salt

For the *pasta frolla*, combine the dry ingredients and mix well. Rub in the butter until it is absorbed, making sure the mixture remains cool and powdery and does not become pasty. Beat the egg with the milk or water and stir in with a fork. Continue stirring until the dough holds together, then briefly knead it, just until smooth. Shape into a disk, wrap in plastic, and refrigerate at least 1 hour, or until firm.

For the filling, press the ricotta through a fine sieve or strainer into a bowl. Beat together the ricotta, eggs, salt, and pepper. Beat in the grated cheese.

Butter a 9-inch cake pan that is 2 inches deep. To assemble, cut off one-third of the *pasta frolla* and reserve it. Roll out the rest of the dough into a 14-inch disk and line the prepared pan with it. Allow the dough to hang over the edge of the pan.

Spread one-third of the filling on the dough in the bottom of the pan. Strew with half of the mozzarella and half the sausage. Cover with another third of the filling. Strew with the remaining mozzarella and sausage. Spread with the remaining filling.

Roll out the reserved dough into a 10-inch square. Cut it into ten 1-inch-wide strips. For the egg wash, beat the egg with the salt, and paint the strips with it. Moisten the rim of the dough on the pan with the egg wash and attach 5 strips in each direction, pressing the edges of the strips lightly onto the rim and forming a diagonal lattice. Trim the edges of the dough so they are even with the top of the pan and push the dough off the top rim of the pan so that it rests completely within the pan.

Bake at 350 degrees for about 45 minutes, until the filling is set and the pastry is a light gold. Cool in the pan before unmolding. To unmold, invert onto a flat plate, lift off the pan, replace the pan with another plate or platter, then reinvert so that the *pizza* is right side up. Serve the *pizza* at room temperature.

Makes 10 to 12 servings

ᕙᕗ ᕘᕚ

Pastiera Napoletana

Neapolitan Wheat and Ricotta Easter Pie

Along with *sfogliatelle ricce*, *pastiera* is the ultimate Neapolitan pastry. It is seen in all the pastry shops in Naples and is also very popular in Rome and throughout southern Italy.

Two versions of the filling are given here: one is very traditional, a combination of cooked wheat kernels, pastry cream, and ricotta. The second filling is less traditional and omits the pastry cream, making the preparation less time-consuming and somewhat less rich.

The wheat kernels are easily found in Italian grocery stores in the United States, especially around Easter. If you have no Italian grocer nearby, try a health food store but make sure to buy hulled wheat kernels and not whole wheat, whose red skin would be tough. See Sources of Equipment and Ingredients for mail order houses.

For the *pasta frolla*, combine the dry ingredients in a mixing bowl. Rub in the butter with your fingertips, making sure the mixture remains cool and powdery and does not become pasty. Beat the egg and milk or water together with a fork and stir into the dough. Continue stirring until the dough begins to hold together. Knead the dough lightly on a floured surface, shape into a thick disk, wrap in plastic, and chill.

Cover the wheat kernels in water and soak overnight, if possible. Drain, rinse, and place in a pan with the salt, butter, and enough water to cover by 3 to 4 inches. Simmer until tender, about 2 hours. Add water as necessary to keep the wheat from drying out and sticking. Cool the wheat and refrigerate until needed.

PASTA FROLLA
2½ *cups all-purpose flour*
½ *cup sugar*
¼ *teaspoon salt*
½ *teaspoon baking powder*
10 *tablespoons (1¼ sticks)*
    unsalted butter
1 *large egg*
4 *tablespoons milk or water*

COOKED WHEAT KERNELS
½ *cup hulled wheat kernels*
½ *teaspoon salt*
1 *tablespoon unsalted butter*

PASTRY CREAM
3 tablespoons sugar
2 tablespoons all-purpose
    flour
½ cup milk
1 large egg
1 teaspoon vanilla extract

RICOTTA FILLING
½ pound whole-milk ricotta,
    commercial or
    homemade
¼ cup sugar
2 large eggs
½ teaspoon orange flower
    water
½ cup candied orange peel,
    rinsed and chopped
¼ teaspoon ground
    cinnamon

EGG WASH
1 large egg
Pinch salt

For the pastry cream, combine the sugar and flour in a small nonreactive saucepan. Stir well to mix, and add the milk slowly, whisking it in smoothly. Whisk in the egg. Cook over low heat, stirring constantly, until the pastry cream thickens and comes to a boil. Boil, stirring vigorously, about 30 seconds. Remove from the heat, stir in the vanilla, and scrape into a clean bowl. Press plastic wrap against the surface and chill.

To assemble the filling, beat the ricotta to soften it, then add the sugar. Beat in the eggs and remaining filling ingredients. Drain and rinse the cooked wheat and add along with the pastry cream.

Butter a 9-inch cake pan that is 2 inches deep. To assemble, cut off one-third of the *pasta frolla* and reserve it. Roll the rest of the dough into a 14-inch disk and line the prepared pan with it. Allow the dough to hang over the edge of the pan. Pour in the filling and sprinkle it with the cinnamon.

Roll the reserved dough into a 10-inch square. Cut it into ten 1-inch-wide strips. For the egg wash, beat the egg with the salt, and paint the strips with it. Moisten the rim of the dough on the pan with the egg wash, and attach 5 strips in each direction, pressing the edges of the strips lightly onto the rim forming a diagonal lattice. Trim the edges of the dough so they are even with the top of the pan and push the dough off the top rim of the pan so that it rests completely within the pan.

Bake at 350 degrees for about 45 minutes, until the filling is set and the pastry is a light gold. Cool in the pan before unmolding. To unmold, invert onto a flat plate, lift off the pan, replace the pan with another plate or platter, then reinvert so that the *pastiera* is right side up. Serve the *pastiera* at room temperature.

Makes 10 to 12 servings

VARIATION
To simplify the recipe, omit the pastry cream and use 1 pound ricotta, ½ cup sugar, and 4 eggs in the ricotta filling.

જીજ જીજ

Pizza di Crema alla Grottese
Pastry Cream–Filled Pie from Grottaminarda

My favorite Easter pastry bar none, this *pizza di crema* is probably Neapolitan in origin. It is the one Easter pastry I never prepare at any other time of the year — waiting for the right season always sharpens my appetite for it.

For the *pasta frolla*, mix all the dry ingredients together in a bowl. Rub the butter in finely, making sure the mixture remains cool and powdery and does not become pasty. Beat the egg and milk or water together with a fork and stir into the flour-butter mixture. Continue stirring until the dough masses together in the bowl. Turn out onto a work surface and knead lightly until smooth. Shape into a disk, wrap in plastic, and refrigerate until firm.

For the pastry cream, bring the milk, grated orange zest, and half the sugar to a boil in a saucepan. Whisk the egg yolks in a bowl, then whisk in the remaining sugar and sift the flour on top. Whisk the flour in smoothly. When the milk mixture boils, whisk one-third of it into the yolk mixture. Return the remaining milk mixture to a boil and whisk the yolk mixture into it. Continue whisking until the cream thickens and returns to a boil. Remove from the heat and whisk in the vanilla and cinnamon. Pour the pastry cream into a bowl, cover the surface directly with plastic wrap, and refrigerate until cold.

To assemble, cut off one-third of the *pasta frolla* and reserve. Roll out the rest of the dough into a 14-inch disk and line a buttered 9-inch cake pan with it. Allow the dough to hang over the edge of the pan.

PASTA FROLLA
2½ cups all-purpose flour
½ cup sugar
¼ teaspoon salt
½ teaspoon baking powder
10 tablespoons (1¼ sticks) unsalted butter
1 large egg
¼ cup milk or water

ORANGE PASTRY CREAM
2 cups milk
Grated zest of 2 oranges
⅔ cup sugar
4 large egg yolks
⅓ cup all-purpose flour
2 teaspoons vanilla extract
½ teaspoon ground cinnamon
1 cup Conserva di Amarene, *page 13, well drained (optional)*

EGG WASH
1 large egg
Pinch salt

Pour in half the cold pastry cream and distribute the cherries evenly over it, then cover the cherries with the remaining pastry cream.

Roll out the reserved dough into a 10-inch square and cut it into ten 1-inch-wide strips. For the egg wash, beat the egg with the salt, and paint the strips with it. Moisten the rim of the dough on the pan with the egg wash and arrange the 10 strips in a diagonal lattice, with 5 strips in each direction, pressing the edges of the strips lightly onto the rim of the dough. Trim the edges of the dough so they are even with the top of the pan and push the dough off the top rim of the pan so that it rests completely within the pan.

Bake at 350 degrees for about 45 minutes, until the pastry is a light gold. Cool in the pan on a rack before unmolding. To unmold, invert onto a flat plate, lift off the pan, replace the pan with another plate or platter, and then reinvert so that the *pizza* is right side up. Serve the *pizza* at room temperature. Refrigerate, covered with plastic wrap, if not serving within 2 hours. Unwrap and bring to room temperature before serving.

Makes 10 to 12 servings

VARIATIONS
Omit the grated orange zest from the pastry cream and add 4 ounces semisweet chocolate, finely cut, to the cream as it comes off the heat. Allow to stand 2 minutes, for the chocolate to melt, and whisk until smooth. Stir in ¼ cup diced candied citron or orange peel.

Or prepare the orange or chocolate *pizza di crema* with a top crust, as in *Torta di Crema di Limone, Santa Margherita*, page 74.

 fest→←

Torta di Riso alla Romana

Roman Rice Pastry

This *torta* is a light, delicate rice pudding baked in a *pasta frolla* crust. Vary the flavoring if you wish. Sometimes I substitute grated lemon zest and a few plumped golden raisins — not authentically Roman, but very good — for the vanilla and orange peel.

For the *pasta frolla*, combine the dry ingredients and mix well. Rub in the butter until it is absorbed, making sure the mixture remains cool and powdery and does not become pasty. Beat the egg and stir it in with a fork. Continue stirring until the dough holds together, then knead it briefly, just until smooth. Shape into a disk, wrap in plastic, and refrigerate at least 1 hour, or until firm.

For the filling, bring about 4 quarts of water to a boil and add the rice, salt, and butter. Stir to make sure the rice does not stick to the bottom of the pan, and return to a boil over high heat. Lower the heat and boil about 20 minutes, until the rice grains are split open and overcooked. Drain the rice well. Combine the rice, sugar, and milk in a heavy nonreactive saucepan and bring to a boil. Lower the heat and simmer gently, stirring often, until the mixture is very thick and creamy, about 20 minutes. Remove from the heat and cool briefly. Press the ricotta through a fine sieve or strainer or puree it in a food processor fitted with the metal blade. Beat it into the rice mixture. Beat in the remaining ingredients, one at a time.

To assemble the *torta*, on a floured surface roll the dough out into a large disk, about 13 inches in diameter. Fit it into a buttered layer cake pan 9 inches in diameter and 2 inches deep.

PASTA FROLLA
1¼ cups all-purpose flour
¼ cup sugar
⅛ teaspoon salt
5 tablespoons unsalted butter
1 large egg

RICE FILLING
½ cup arborio or long-grain rice
¼ teaspoon salt
2 tablespoons unsalted butter
½ cup sugar
2 cups milk
½ pound whole-milk ricotta, commercial or homemade
4 large eggs
2 teaspoons vanilla extract
¼ teaspoon ground cinnamon
¼ cup candied orange peel, rinsed and chopped

Press the dough well against the bottom and sides of the pan and trim the edges of the dough so they are even with the top of the pan. Pour in the filling and spread it evenly. The filling will be about ½ inch lower than the top of the pan. Fold the excess dough at the rim inward, over the filling, so that it forms a border about ½ inch wide at the edge.

Bake the *torta* in the lower third of a preheated 350-degree oven for about 45 minutes, until the filling is set and the dough is a light golden color. Cool the *torta* in the pan on a rack. When the *torta* is completely cooled, place a flat plate or pan on the *torta* and invert. Lift off the baking pan and replace it with a platter. Invert again and remove the top plate or pan. Keep the *torta* loosely covered at room temperature.

Makes 10 to 12 servings

᎒Ꮕ ᏨᎧ

Crostata di Zucca

Pumpkin ''Pie'' from the Po Valley

So different in flavor from an American pumpkin pie, this *crostata* uses the pumpkin in a similar manner, as a background for other flavors. The technique of folding the leftover dough around the edges to cover the top of the pie is an ancient one. Use a 9-inch pie pan if you want to avoid having to unmold the *crostata*.

PASTA FROLLA
1¼ cups all-purpose flour
¼ cup sugar
⅛ teaspoon salt
5 tablespoons unsalted butter
1 large egg

For the *pasta frolla*, combine the dry ingredients and mix well. Rub in the butter until it is absorbed, making sure the mixture remains cool and powdery and does not become pasty. Beat the egg and stir in with a fork. Continue stirring until the dough holds together, then knead it briefly, just until smooth. Shape into a disk, wrap in plastic, and refrigerate at least 1 hour, or until firm.

For the filling, cut the pumpkin into 2-inch dice, scrape away the filaments, and peel off the skin. Steam the pumpkin over simmering water for about 40 minutes, until it is tender. Puree the pumpkin in a blender or a food processor fitted with the metal blade and cool. If the pumpkin puree is excessively watery, cook it, stirring constantly, over medium heat, preferably in a nonstick pan, to dry it out before cooling.

Measure 2 cups of the pumpkin puree (a little more or less won't matter) into a large mixing bowl. Whisk in the sugar, cinnamon, and eggs, one at a time. Combine the ground almonds and cornmeal and stir into the pumpkin mixture. Place the candied orange peel in a strainer, rinse it under running water, and chop it finely with a sharp knife. Oil the blade of the knife to prevent it from sticking to the peel. Stir the chopped peel into the filling, then fold in the melted butter.

To assemble the *crostata*, roll the dough out on a floured surface into a large disk, about 14 inches in diameter. Fold the disk of dough in half and fit it into a buttered 9-inch × 2-inch-deep layer cake pan. Press the dough well against the bottom and sides of the pan and trim the edges of the dough so they are even with the top of the pan. Pour in the filling and spread it evenly. The filling will be about ½ inch lower than the top of the pan. Fold the excess dough at the rim inward, over the filling, so that it makes a border about ½ inch wide at the edge.

Bake the *crostata* in the lower third of a preheated 350-degree oven for about 45 minutes, until the filling is set and the dough is a light golden color. Cool the *crostata* in the pan on a rack. When the *crostata* is completely cooled, place a flat plate or pan on top and invert. Lift off the baking pan and replace it with a platter. Invert again and remove the top plate or pan. Keep the *crostata* loosely covered at room temperature.

Makes 8 to 10 servings

PUMPKIN FILLING

1 fresh sugar pumpkin, about 2 pounds, or 1 can solid-pack pumpkin, 1 pound

Pinch salt

⅔ cup sugar

1 teaspoon ground cinnamon

2 large eggs

1 cup almonds, ground

½ cup yellow cornmeal

½ cup candied orange peel

4 tablespoons unsalted butter, melted

༄ ༄

Torta di Crema di Limone, Santa Margherita

Lemon Cream Pie from Santa Margherita

I often joke that the Italian and French rivieras should secede from their respective countries and form one of their own. The two regions enjoy many cultural similarities, especially in food. Thus this lemon pie from Santa Margherita Ligure, east of Genoa, is not very different from the ones found in the old town in Nice, except for the fact that it has a top crust.

The top crust may crack during baking if the filling begins to simmer after the crust has begun to set. Pay no attention to the cracks — the *torte di limone* I saw in Santa Margherita were covered with enormous fissures, adding to their homey, rustic appearance.

PASTA FROLLA
2½ cups all-purpose flour
½ cup sugar
¼ teaspoon salt
½ teaspoon baking powder
10 tablespoons (1¼ sticks)
     unsalted butter
1 large egg
4 tablespoons milk or water

LEMON FILLING
2 cups milk
1 tablespoon grated lemon
     zest
½ cup sugar
6 large egg yolks
Pinch salt
⅓ cup all-purpose flour
2 teaspoons vanilla extract
¼ cup strained lemon juice

For the *pasta frolla*, combine the dry ingredients in a bowl and mix well. Rub in the butter until it is absorbed, making sure the mixture remains cool and powdery and does not become pasty. Beat the egg and milk or water together and stir in with a fork. Continue stirring until the dough holds together, then knead it briefly, just until smooth. Shape into a disk, wrap in plastic, and refrigerate at least 1 hour, or until firm.

For the lemon filling, bring the milk to a boil with the lemon zest and half the sugar in a 2-quart nonreactive saucepan over medium heat.

Whisk the yolks in a bowl with the salt and whisk in the remaining sugar in a stream. Sift the flour over the mixture and whisk in. Whisk in the vanilla and lemon juice.

When the milk boils, remove from the heat and whisk one-third of it into the yolk mixture. Return the remaining milk to a boil and, beginning to stir the milk first, pour in the yolk mixture. Continue stirring constantly until the cream thickens and comes to a boil. Allow to boil, stirring constantly, for 30 seconds.

Remove from the heat and pour into a clean nonreactive bowl. Press plastic wrap against the surface and refrigerate until cold.

EGG WASH
1 large egg
Pinch salt

Butter a 9-inch cake pan that is 2 inches deep. To assemble, cut off one-third of the *pasta frolla* and reserve. Roll out the remaining dough into a 14-inch disk and line the prepared pan with it. Trim the edges of the dough so they are even with the top of the pan. Pour in the lemon filling and spread smoothly. Fold the top edge of the dough over the filling. For the egg wash, whisk the egg and salt together, and carefully brush the rim of the dough with it. Roll the remaining dough into a 9-inch disk. Trim the disk evenly, using a pan or plate as a guide. Slide the disk onto the *torta*. Press it into place so that it adheres to the bottom crust. Paint evenly with the egg wash. Pierce the top crust here and there with a fork dipped in the egg wash, to allow steam to escape during baking. Press the tines of the fork all around the edge, wetting the fork with egg wash again, to seal the crust.

Bake at 350 degrees for about 45 minutes, until the filling is set and the pastry is a light gold. Cool in the pan before unmolding. To unmold, invert onto a flat plate, lift off the pan, replace the pan with another plate or platter, then reinvert so that the *torta* is right side up. Serve the *torta* at room temperature.

Makes 10 to 12 servings

Cassata al Forno

Sicilian Baked *Cassata*

Though this is similar to *Pizza di Ricotta alla Grottese* (page 64), it is really a version of *Cassata alla Siciliana* (page 154) in which pastry dough substitutes for the *pan di spagna*, or sponge cake lining. In Sicily, where the ricotta is very firm, the filling is usually prepared without eggs. Here I like to add some egg whites only, for firmness but no added richness.

This version is a re-creation of one I enjoyed at the Charleston Restaurant in Mondello, Palermo's seaside resort.

PASTA FROLLA
2½ cups all-purpose flour
½ cup sugar
¼ teaspoon salt
½ teaspoon baking powder
10 tablespoons (1¼ sticks) unsalted butter
1 large egg
4 tablespoons milk or water

RICOTTA FILLING
1 pound whole-milk ricotta, commercial or homemade
½ cup sugar
4 large egg whites
1 teaspoon vanilla extract
3 tablespoons candied orange peel, rinsed and finely chopped
1 ounce semisweet chocolate, finely chopped
¼ teaspoon ground cinnamon

Confectioners' sugar for finishing

For the *pasta frolla*, combine the dry ingredients and mix well. Rub in the butter until it is absorbed, making sure the mixture remains cool and powdery and does not become pasty. Beat the egg with the milk or water and stir in with a fork. Continue stirring until the dough holds together, then knead it briefly, just until smooth. Shape into a disk, wrap in plastic, and refrigerate at least 1 hour, or until firm.

For the ricotta filling, press the ricotta through a fine sieve into a mixing bowl or puree it in a food processor fitted with the metal blade. Stir in the sugar, then the egg whites, one at a time. Stir in the remaining filling ingredients.

Butter a 9-inch cake pan that is 2 inches deep. To assemble, cut off one-third of the *pasta frolla* and reserve it. Roll out the rest of the dough into a 14-inch disk and line the prepared pan with it. Allow the dough to hang over the edge of the pan. Pour in the filling.

Roll the reserved dough into a 9-inch disk. Place the disk of dough on top of the filling and loosen the top edge of the bottom crust from the side of the pan with a thin knife. Fold the edge of the bottom crust over the top crust.

Bake at 350 degrees for about 45 minutes, until the filling is set and the pastry is a light gold. Cool in the pan before unmolding. To unmold, invert onto a platter and lift off the pan. Dust with the confectioners' sugar just before serving. Serve the *cassata* at room temperature.

Makes 10 to 12 servings

⨾⨾ ⨾⨾

Crostata di Visciole alla Romana

Lattice Tart of Roman Sour Cherries

One of the few typically Roman pastries, this sour cherry tart is found in all the pastry shops of Rome in one version or another. If you wish, substitute fruit or berry preserves for the filling here and call the dessert a *crostata di marmellata*.

Visciole are Roman cherries, small, sour, and somewhat translucent, with a short season in late May and early June. Real *visciole* are scarce even in Rome nowadays, and any sour cherries will make a creditable version of this dessert.

For the sour cherry jam, combine the sour cherries, sugar, and cinnamon stick in a pan and bring to a boil. Remove the cherries with a slotted spoon or skimmer to a bowl and slowly, over low heat, reduce the syrup until it is thick, about 10 to 15 minutes. Remove the cinnamon stick, return the cherries to the syrup, and cook until virtually no liquid remains. Pour the jam into a bowl and cool it.

For the *pasta frolla*, combine the dry ingredients and mix well. Rub in the butter until it is absorbed, making sure the mixture remains cool and powdery and does not become pasty. Beat the eggs and stir in with a fork. Continue stirring until the dough holds together, then knead it briefly, just until smooth. Shape into a disk, wrap in plastic, and refrigerate at least 1 hour, or until firm.

Preheat the oven to 350 degrees and set a rack in the middle level. Line with parchment a cookie sheet that has no rim on at least one side. To form the *crostata*, divide the *pasta frolla* in half and roll out one half into an 11-inch disk on a floured surface. Transfer the disk of dough to the lined cookie

SOUR CHERRY JAM
4 cups drained, pitted sour cherries, fresh, frozen, or jarred
1 cup sugar
1-inch piece of cinnamon stick

PASTA FROLLA
2⅓ cups all-purpose flour
⅓ cup sugar
Pinch salt
8 tablespoons (1 stick) unsalted butter, cold
2 large eggs

EGG WASH
1 large egg yolk
Pinch salt

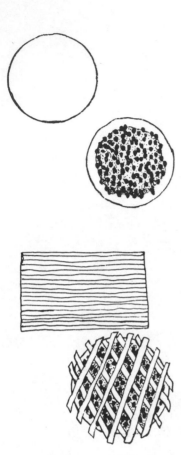

sheet and place a pattern on the dough, trimming it to a perfect 11-inch disk. Spread the jam on the dough to within 1 inch of the edge. Roll out half the remaining dough into a rectangle about 8 × 12 inches and cut it into ½-inch-wide strips. For the egg wash, whisk the egg with the salt; paint the strips with it and place them over the filling, 6 or 7 in each direction, in a diagonal lattice. Roll the remaining dough into a thin cylinder about 30 inches long. Egg-wash the rim of the pastry, then press the cylinder of dough onto it. Flatten the cylinder and score it at 1½-inch intervals with the bowl of a teaspoon and the back of a knife. Egg-wash the border. Chill the *crostata* at least 1 hour before baking it.

Bake for about 30 minutes, until deep gold. Be careful that the filling does not come to a boil during the baking. Slide the *crostata* off the cookie sheet by pulling on the parchment, and place it on a rack to cool.

Makes about 8 servings

VARIATION

Crostata di Marmellata

Substitute any good-quality jam or preserves for the sour cherry jam. This is a good winter dessert when fresh fruit is scarce.

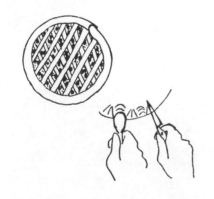

ক্থ৩ ৫৩৹

Crostata di Frutta

Mixed Fruit Tart

So different in conception from the typical French fruit tart, which has a flaky crust, pastry cream filling, and fruit, this Italian one concentrates on the fruit itself, aligning it in straight rows on a round or square crust.

The type of fruit you use depends on the season, the types available, and your own preferences. The *crostata* can be very striking with only two types of fruit or with a different fruit in every row. Use berries and other soft fruit; apples, pears, and other hard fruit will oxidize and turn brown.

The dough used here, as in the *Torta di Noci d'Aosta* (page 82), has a cakelike texture, making a tender base for the fruit topping.

For the *pasta frolla*, beat the butter until soft, then beat in the sugar in a stream, either by hand, with a hand mixer set at medium speed, or in a heavy-duty mixer fitted with the paddle. Continue beating until the mixture lightens. Add the egg yolks, one at a time, beating until the mixture is very smooth and light. Beat in the flour until it is absorbed, without overmixing.

To form the base for the *crostata*, butter a 9- or 10-inch springform pan or an 8- or 9-inch square pan and line the bottom with a piece of parchment or wax paper, cut to fit. If using wax paper, butter the paper. Press the dough into the pan with lightly floured fingertips, making an even layer. Bake the base at 350 degrees for about 25 minutes, until it is golden and feels firm when pressed with a fingertip. Do not overbake or the base will be dry and hard. Cool on a rack in the pan.

For the apricot filling/glaze, combine the preserves and rum in a saucepan and bring to a boil over low heat, stirring

PASTA FROLLA
8 tablespoons (1 stick)
unsalted butter
½ cup sugar
2 large egg yolks
1⅓ cups all-purpose flour

APRICOT FILLING/GLAZE
1½ cups apricot preserves or
jam
2 tablespoons white rum

4 cups sliced fruit and
berries, such as
strawberries, raspberries,
kiwi, orange, and sweet
cherries

3 tablespoons toasted, sliced almonds or chopped, blanched pistachios; and confectioners' sugar, for finishing

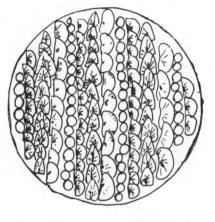

often. Strain into another pan to eliminate pulp. Just before assembling the *crostata*, return the mixture to low heat and allow to reduce until sticky, about 5 to 10 minutes.

To assemble the *crostata*, release the sides of the spring-form pan and slide the base of the pan onto a cutting board. If you have made a square base, invert onto a plate and reinvert onto a board. Paint the surface with the filling. Arrange the fruit in rows on the base, using one type of fruit per row, alternating fruits for contrast of color, as in the illustration. Paint the fruit with the glaze, using a brush. Sprinkle the almonds around the edges of the *crostata* and dust them lightly with the confectioners' sugar.

For advance preparation, arrange the fruit on the base and cover loosely with plastic wrap. Glaze the fruit no more than 2 hours before serving.

For an alternate presentation, spread the base with jarred preserves or jam and arrange the fruit on the surface. Just before serving, dust the fruit with the confectioners' sugar.

Makes about 8 servings

ॐ৲৴ ৻৴ॐ

Crostata di Fragole

Italian Strawberry Tart

In late spring, all the elegant pastry shops and prepared-food stores on the Via Montenapoleone in Milan feature magnificent tarts filled with a combination of cultivated and wild strawberries. The tarts are assembled with a row of whole or halved large strawberries around the edge and a pile of tiny wild strawberries in the center.

The wild strawberries, *fragoline* in Italian, are all but unobtainable in the United States. To try to match their intensity of flavor for this recipe, I like to macerate sliced strawberries in a little sugar and lemon juice — not the same, but an improvement on weakly flavored berries. Though they look very different from *fragoline*, these sliced berries are placed in the center of the *crostata* to approximate the appearance of the elegant Milanese tarts. The ground almonds in the *pasta frolla* add an extra dimension of flavor and texture, making the baked pastry fragile and delicate.

For a variation close to the original, use a border of whole or halved strawberries and fill in the center with whole raspberries.

Use a sharp knife to cut the *crostata* or the berries will topple, lessening the elegant symmetry of the dessert.

For the almond *pasta frolla*, combine the dry ingredients in a bowl and mix well. Rub in the butter until it is absorbed, making sure the mixture remains cool and powdery and does not become pasty. Beat the egg and stir in with a fork. Continue stirring until the dough holds together, then knead it briefly, just until smooth. Shape into a disk, wrap in plastic, and refrigerate at least 1 hour, or until firm.

Rinse and hull the strawberries. Choose the best and most symmetrical ones to form the border of the tart. (Draw a 9-inch circle on a piece of parchment or wax paper and arrange the berries inside the line to see how many you will need.) Slice the remaining berries into a bowl and add the sugar and lemon juice. Toss to combine and cover with plastic wrap. Refrigerate the sliced and whole berries until ready to assemble the *crostata*.

To form the tart base, roll out three-fourths of the dough on a floured surface into a 9-inch disk. Transfer to a cookie sheet lined with parchment or buttered wax paper. Place a 9-inch disk, like a springform bottom or plate, on the dough and trim it to a perfect 9-inch-diameter circle. Pierce the dough all over with a fork at ½-inch intervals. Combine the scraps with the remaining dough and roll into a thin cylinder, about 30 inches long. Moisten the edge of the base with water and arrange the cylinder of dough on top of it to form the sides of the tart shell. Press the cylinder with your fingertips to make it adhere and mark a series of diagonal lines on it with the back of a small knife, as in the illustration. Bake at 350 degrees for

ALMOND PASTA FROLLA
1¼ cups all-purpose flour
½ cup almonds, ground
¼ cup sugar
Pinch salt
5 tablespoons unsalted
    butter, cold
1 large egg

STRAWBERRIES
2 to 3 pints ripe strawberries
2 tablespoons sugar
1 teaspoon lemon juice

½ cup strawberry jam

Confectioners' sugar for
    finishing

about 25 minutes, until the dough is an even golden color and feels firm when pressed with a fingertip. Cool the tart shell on a rack on the cookie sheet.

To assemble the *crostata*, place the cooled shell on a platter. Spread the bottom evenly with the jam. Arrange a row of the reserved whole strawberries inside the edge. If the berries are very large, halve them. Drain the sliced berries well and pile them in the center. Dust with the confectioners' sugar before serving.

Makes about 8 servings

ᗏᔐ ᘔᗍ

Torta di Noci d'Aosta

Walnut-Filled Pastry from Aosta

This pastry could come only from a region famous for its walnuts and butter, the focal points of the recipe. Choose the freshest walnuts possible, even if you have to crack the shells by hand — it's well worth the trouble.

This version is based on one I tasted at the Pasticceria Boch, in Aosta.

WALNUT FILLING
½ cup sugar
½ teaspoon lemon juice
¾ cup honey
8 tablespoons (1 stick) unsalted butter
Pinch salt
2 cups walnuts, chopped

For the walnut filling, combine the sugar and lemon juice in a saucepan and stir well to mix. Place over medium heat and allow to caramelize, stirring occasionally. When the sugar is a pale amber color, add the honey and butter. Bring to a boil and cook about 2 minutes, until thick bubbles form. Stir in the salt and walnuts. Cool the filling.

For the *pasta frolla*, beat the butter until soft and beat in the sugar in a stream. Continue beating until the mixture lightens. Add the egg yolks, one at a time, beating until the mixture is very smooth and light. Beat in the flour until it is absorbed, without overmixing. Set the dough aside, covered.

To assemble the dessert, place half the dough in the bottom of a 9- or 10-inch springform pan that has been buttered and lined with wax paper or parchment. Press the dough with your fingertips evenly over the bottom of the pan and about 1 inch up the sides of the pan. Spread the cooled filling on the dough. Flour the remaining dough and press it into a 9- or 10-inch disk on a cardboard or tart pan bottom. Slide the dough over the filling and press it into place, making sure that the sides are straight and even. Seal the edges with the tines of a fork and pierce the top here and there with the fork.

Bake at 350 degrees for 40 to 45 minutes. Cool briefly in the pan, then unmold onto a rack to cool. Dust very lightly with the confectioners' sugar.

Makes 8 to 10 servings

PASTA FROLLA
12 tablespoons (1½ sticks) unsalted butter
¾ cup sugar
3 large egg yolks
2 cups all-purpose flour

Confectioners' sugar for finishing

ꙮ ꙮ

Torta Grassa

———

Almond Tart from Parma

Although the translation of this dessert's name (fatty or greasy tart) is less than appealing, the taste and texture of the *torta* are wonderful. The flavor has a sophisticated richness, despite the simple ingredients. This version is adapted from *L'arte della pasticceria a Parma* (The Art of Pastry-Making in Parma) by Ugo Falavigna, whose Pasticceria Torino is the best pastry shop in Parma.

For the *pasta frolla,* combine the dry ingredients in a bowl and mix well. Rub in the butter until it is absorbed, making sure the mixture remains cool and powdery and does not become pasty. Beat the egg and stir in with a fork. Continue stirring until the dough holds together, then knead it briefly, just until smooth. Shape into a disk, wrap in plastic, and refrigerate at least 1 hour, or until firm.

PASTA FROLLA
1¼ cups all-purpose flour
¼ cup sugar
Pinch salt
5 tablespoons unsalted butter, cold
1 large egg

ALMOND FILLING
5 large eggs
Pinch salt
Pinch each: ground
    cinnamon, nutmeg, and
    cloves
¾ cup sugar
2 cups blanched almonds,
    ground
¼ cup candied orange peel,
    finely diced, or 1
    tablespoon grated orange
    zest

¼ cup sliced almonds

Confectioners' sugar for
    finishing

While the dough is resting, make the filling. Whisk the eggs with the salt and spices and whisk in the sugar in a stream. Whisk in the almonds and whip the mixture, either with a hand mixer set at medium speed or in a heavy-duty mixer fitted with the whip, until it is very light in color and increased in volume, about 7 or 8 minutes. Whip in the candied orange peel or orange zest.

On a floured surface, roll out the *pasta frolla* into a 14-inch disk and line a buttered 10-inch layer cake pan with it. Trim off the excess dough at the rim of the pan. Fold about ¼ inch of the dough into the pan and press well into place against the side of the pan to make a finished top edge for the *torta*. Pour in the filling. Scatter the sliced almonds on the filling.

Bake the *torta* at 350 degrees for 30 to 40 minutes, until the filling is set and the pastry is baked through. Cool in the pan on a rack. Invert the *torta* onto a platter, remove the pan, replace with another platter, and invert. Replace any sliced almonds that fall off the surface of the *torta*. Dust lightly with the confectioners' sugar before serving.

Makes 10 to 12 servings

∾∾ ∾∾

Torta di Mandorle e Pignoli

Almond and Pine Nut Tart

Large pastries filled with almond cream and pine nuts are common in the Piedmont, and I have seen them as far south as Rome. The pine nuts contribute an elusive richness to the filling. If you have trouble finding them, or find that they are prohibitively expensive, substitute coarsely chopped slivered almonds.

Sometimes I vary this by combining the almond filling with an equal volume of pastry cream (*Crema Pasticciera*, page 219) and making enough filling for 2 *torte*. You may also spread a thin layer of raspberry preserves on the dough before adding the almond filling.

For the *pasta frolla*, combine the dry ingredients in a bowl and mix well. Rub in the butter until it is absorbed, making sure the mixture remains cool and powdery and does not become pasty. Beat the egg and stir in with a fork. Continue stirring until the dough holds together, then knead it briefly, just until smooth. Shape into a disk, wrap in plastic, and refrigerate at least 1 hour, or until firm.

For the almond filling, combine the almond paste (or ground almond mixture), sugar, and one of the eggs in the bowl of a heavy-duty mixer fitted with the paddle or in a food processor fitted with the metal blade. Mix on low speed, or pulse, until smooth. Beat or pulse in the butter, then the remaining eggs, one at a time, scraping the inside of the bowl between each addition. Beat or pulse in the vanilla and rum, then the flour.

On a floured surface, roll out the *pasta frolla* into a 14-inch disk and line a buttered 10-inch layer cake pan with it. Trim off the excess dough at the rim of the pan. Fold ¼ inch of the dough inward and press it well against the inside of the pan so that it makes a finished edge on the crust. Spread evenly with the filling and strew the pine nuts on top.

Bake the *torta* at 350 degrees for 30 to 40 minutes, until the filling is set and the pastry is baked through. Cool in the pan on a rack. Invert the *torta* onto a platter, remove the pan, replace with another platter, and invert. Dust with the confectioners' sugar before serving.

Makes 10 to 12 servings

PASTA FROLLA
1¼ cups all-purpose flour
¼ cup sugar
Pinch salt
5 tablespoons unsalted butter, cold
1 large egg

ALMOND FILLING
6 ounces canned almond paste or 1 cup whole almonds, ground finely with ½ cup sugar and ½ teaspoon almond extract
⅓ cup sugar
3 large eggs
6 tablespoons unsalted butter
1 teaspoon vanilla extract
2 tablespoons white rum
⅓ cup all-purpose flour
⅓ cup pine nuts

Confectioners' sugar for finishing

༄ ༄

Torta Ricciolina

Shredded Pasta–Filled Pastry from Bologna

I first met Margherita Simili, the extraordinary Bolognese baker, over a slice of *torta ricciolina* when she came to Peter Kump's New

York Cooking School with Marcella Hazan to demonstrate her wonderful specialties several years ago. I marveled at Margherita's talent and was thoroughly enthralled with her warmth and kindness. The breads and pastries she prepared were of outstanding quality and simplicity, like this pastry filled with shredded pasta dough. See the recipe for *Torta di Tagliatelle*, page 131, for a variation on this theme.

Ricciolina means "curly," and the curls here are provided by the raw egg-pasta filling, which is sprinkled with a mixture of almonds, sugar, and diced candied citron. The *torta* is doused with white rum as it emerges from the oven — the hot pastry makes most of the alcohol in the rum evaporate, leaving only its flavor.

This recipe was inspired by Margherita Simili's, though not based on it.

PASTA FROLLA
1¼ cups all-purpose flour
¼ cup sugar
Pinch salt
5 tablespoons unsalted
    butter, cold
1 large egg

PASTA DOUGH
1 cup all-purpose flour
1 large egg
2 large egg yolks
Pinch salt

ALMOND MIXTURE
1 cup blanched almonds
½ cup sugar
½ cup candied citron, diced

For the *pasta frolla*, combine the dry ingredients in a bowl and mix well. Rub in the butter until it is absorbed, making sure the mixture remains cool and powdery and does not become pasty. Beat the egg and stir in with a fork. Continue stirring until the dough holds together, then knead it briefly, just until smooth. Shape into a disk, wrap in plastic, and refrigerate at least 1 hour, or until firm.

For the pasta dough, place the flour on a work surface and make a well in the center. In the well, mix the egg, egg yolks, and salt. Gradually draw the flour into the egg mixture, adding a little water if the dough is too dry. Knead the dough well and set it aside to rest, covered, about 30 minutes.

While the dough is resting, combine the almonds and sugar in the bowl of a food processor fitted with the metal blade and reduce to a powder. Add the citron and continue to process until the mixture is very fine.

Divide the pasta dough into 3 pieces, flour them, and pass the pieces, one at a time, through a pasta machine, starting with the widest setting and ending with the next to last. Let the sheets of dough dry for at least 30 minutes on a floured surface.

On a floured surface, roll out the *pasta frolla* into a 14-inch disk and line a buttered 10-inch layer cake pan with it. Trim off the excess dough at the rim of the pan.

Stack the sheets of pasta dough, roll them up loosely into a cylinder, and shred them finely with a sharp chopping knife, as in the illustration.

Place alternating layers of the *tagliatelle* and almond mixture on the crust, sprinkling melted butter on the layers. Finish with a layer of the *tagliatelle* and more melted butter.

Bake the *torta* at 350 degrees for 30 to 40 minutes. Immediately after removing the *torta* from the oven, sprinkle the surface with the rum. Cool in the pan on a rack. Invert the *torta* onto a platter, remove the pan, replace with another platter, and reinvert. Dust lightly with the confectioners' sugar.

Makes 10 to 12 servings

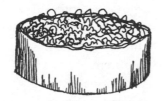

8 tablespoons (1 stick) unsalted butter, melted

Confectioners' sugar and 4 tablespoons white rum for finishing

Grigliata Umbra

Umbrian Apple Tart

When I first saw a *grigliata Umbra,* in the window of the Bottega del Pasticciere, in Assisi, I was slightly appalled that the little card proclaiming the ingredients included cocoa as part of the filling made with apples, raisins, and walnuts. One taste and I was a convert. The cocoa is used in small quantity and adds color and richness to the filling, rather than a strong chocolate flavor.

The name of the pastry derives from the strips of dough placed on the filling in the form of a grill.

The variation that follows this recipe substitutes cornmeal for the cocoa for a pastry called *brustegno* — a bit heavier than the apple *grigliata*, but an interestingly rustic dessert.

PASTA FROLLA

2½ cups all-purpose flour

½ cup sugar

¼ teaspoon salt

½ teaspoon baking powder

*10 tablespoons (1¼ sticks)
   unsalted butter*

1 large egg

4 tablespoons milk or water

APPLE FILLING

*3½ pounds tart apples, such
   as Granny Smith*

⅔ cup sugar

¼ cup water

*½ teaspoon ground
   cinnamon*

*2 tablespoons unsweetened
   cocoa powder*

1 cup walnuts, chopped

½ cup pine nuts

½ cup golden raisins

*⅔ cup or 1 small jar apple
   jelly for the glaze*

For the *pasta frolla*, combine the dry ingredients and mix well. Rub in the butter until it is absorbed, making sure the mixture remains cool and powdery and does not become pasty. Beat the egg with the milk or water and stir in with a fork. Continue stirring until the dough holds together, then knead it briefly, just until smooth. Shape into a disk, wrap in plastic, and refrigerate at least 1 hour, or until firm.

For the apple filling, peel, core, and grate the apples coarsely by hand or in a food processor fitted with the metal blade. Combine with the sugar and water in a nonreactive saucepan that has a tight-fitting lid. Place over medium heat. When the mixture begins to simmer, lower the heat, cover the pan, and cook 5 minutes, until the apples are swimming in water. Uncover, add the remaining filling ingredients, and cook over low heat, stirring often, about 15 to 20 minutes, until the filling is reduced to a thick paste. Cool the filling in a bowl at room temperature, stirring occasionally.

To assemble the pastry, butter a 10×15-inch jelly roll pan. On a floured surface, roll out two-thirds of the dough into a rectangle about 12×17 inches, roll up on the rolling pin, and unroll into the pan. Press the dough well into the pan and trim the edges of the dough so they are even with the top of the pan. Refrigerate the lined pan until the dough is firm, about 30 minutes.

Spread the filling evenly over the dough. Roll the remaining dough into a rectangle 4×15 inches. Cut into long strips, ½ inch wide. Arrange the strips on the filling, 4 in each direction, to make a "grill," or perpendicular lattice. Trim away the excess dough at the edges. Bake the *grigliata* at 350 degrees for about 35 minutes, until the pastry is baked through. Cool in the pan on a rack. When it is cool, cover with the back of another pan and invert to remove the pan in which it was baked. Place a cutting board on the pastry and reinvert, removing the other pan.

For the glaze, place the apple jelly in a small saucepan and bring to a boil over low heat, stirring occasionally. Reduce the glaze until it is sticky. Brush on the filling and cool a few minutes to allow the glaze to set. Cut the *grigliata* into 3- or 4-inch squares to serve.

Makes about 12 to 15 servings

VARIATION

Brustegno
Omit the cocoa powder from the filling. After adding all the filling ingredients to the apple mixture, sprinkle on ⅓ cup yellow cornmeal, stirring it in carefully to avoid lumps. Stir almost constantly while the filling is cooking or it will stick and scorch. Cool and prepare exactly as for the *grigliata,* omitting the lattice top.

Pasticcini

Individual Pastries

One of the great glories of the Italian style of dessert-making lies in the beauty and delicacy of its individual pastries. Many of the large desserts in this chapter may be made in smaller versions by lining twelve 3-inch brioche pans with the dough called for and dividing the filling among them. If you don't have the brioche pans, you may use standard-size muffin pans — but be sure that the pans are well buttered before you line them with the dough.

The collection of individual pastries that follows is brief but specialized. I have attempted to cull the most interesting of the ones I have seen in Italy rather than merely repeat the recipes from the first part of this chapter in smaller versions.

❧ ❧

Sfogliatelle Napoletane, or
Sfogliatelle Ricce
———
Neapolitan Flaky Pastries in the
Shape of Clams

Sfogliatelle are the Neapolitan pastry par excellence. Made from a recipe for an ancient form of puff pastry, *sfogliatelle ricce* (curly or flaky *sfogliatelle*) are shatteringly crisp and flaky on the outside, with a creamy, semolina-thickened ricotta filling within. The pastry shops in Naples that sell the *sfogliatelle* keep them in warmers, so that the fat in the dough, usually lard, does not have an opportunity to congeal and render the pastry heavy.

Another form of the pastry is *sfogliatelle frolle*, or "tender" *sfogliatelle*. Here the same filling is enclosed in *pasta frolla*, making it an easier version (see next recipe).

Although *sfogliatelle* are a bit time-consuming to prepare, the work may be divided over a period of days: make the dough one day and form the dough the next. Make the filling on the third day, then form and bake the pastries on the fourth. I have successfully frozen the formed dough for several weeks before forming and filling the pastries.

Your own *sfogliatelle*, fresh from the oven, just cooled to lukewarm, are an incomparable treat.

DOUGH
3 cups all-purpose flour
1 teaspoon salt
¾ cup warm water

For the dough, combine the flour and salt in a mixing bowl and stir in the water. The dough will be very dry. Scrape the contents of the bowl onto a work surface, and press and knead the dough together so that all the dry bits are incorporated. Press or roll out the dough about ⅓ inch thick and pass repeatedly through the widest setting of a pasta machine to work the dough smooth. Fold the dough in half after each pass through the machine and change the direction of inserting the dough occasionally. After about 12 or 15 passes, the dough should be smooth. Knead the dough into a ball, wrap in plastic wrap, and allow to rest in the refrigerator about 2 hours.

For the filling, combine the water and sugar in a saucepan. Bring to a boil and sift the semolina or cream of wheat over the boiling water gradually, stirring constantly to avoid lumps. Lower the heat and cook, stirring often, until very smooth and thick, for a minute or two.

Press the ricotta through a fine sieve, or puree it in a food processor fitted with the metal blade, and stir into the cooked semolina mixture. Cook several minutes longer, stirring often. Stir in the egg yolks, vanilla, cinnamon, and candied orange peel off the heat. Scrape the filling into a shallow bowl or glass pie pan and press plastic wrap against the surface. Refrigerate until cold and set.

Combine the lard and butter in a mixing bowl and beat until soft, fluffy, and completely mixed. Flour the dough and divide it into 4 pieces. Flour each piece of dough and pass each through the pasta machine at the widest setting. Make sure the dough emerges in a neat rectangular strip as wide as the opening of the machine. If the dough is uneven, fold it over on itself so that it is as wide as the opening and pass it through again. Pass all 4 pieces of dough, one after the other, through every other setting, ending with the last setting.

Place one of the strips of dough on a lightly floured surface and paint it generously with the lard-and-butter mixture. Begin rolling the dough into a tight cylinder from one of the short ends. Pull gently on the sides of the strip of dough as you roll

FILLING

1 cup water

½ cup sugar

⅔ cup semolina or cream of wheat

1½ cups whole-milk ricotta, commercial or homemade

2 large egg yolks

2 teaspoons vanilla extract

¼ teaspoon ground cinnamon

⅓ cup candied orange peel, rinsed and finely chopped

4 ounces lard

8 tablespoons (1 stick) unsalted butter

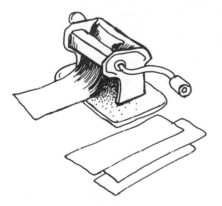
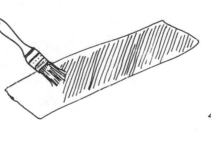

it up to make it thinner and about 8 or 9 inches wide. Paint another strip of dough with the fats and position the rolled piece on it so that the end of the first strip meets the beginning of the second; continue to pull and roll up. Proceed with the third and fourth strips in the same way. Cover the remaining lard and butter and reserve, in the refrigerator, for baking the *sfogliatelle*. The dough should form a tight cylinder about 2½ inches in diameter and 8 to 9 inches long. Wrap in plastic and chill several hours, until firm. The dough may be frozen at this point; defrost it in the refrigerator overnight before proceeding.

Preheat the oven to 400 degrees and set a rack in the middle level. Line 2 jelly roll pans with parchment. Remove the roll of dough from the refrigerator, place it on a cutting board, and trim the ends straight. Cut the roll into about 16 to 18 slices, each about ½ inch thick. Place the filling in a pastry bag that has a ¾-inch opening; a tube is not necessary.

To form the pastries, take one slice of the dough at a time and flatten it from the center outward in all directions, as in the illustration (this positions the layers of dough properly). Form it into a cone by sliding the layers away from each other with the thumbs underneath the dough and the first two fingers of each hand on top, manipulating the dough from the center outward. Holding the cone of dough on the palm of one hand and the pastry bag with the other, squeeze in the filling so that the pastry is full and plump. There is no need to seal the open end; the filling is too firm to run during baking.

Bring the lard-and-butter mixture to room temperature to soften it. Position the formed and filled *sfogliatelle* on the paper-lined pans and paint the outside of each with the lard and butter. Bake them about 20 to 25 minutes, basting once or twice with the remaining fats, until they are a deep gold. Remove from the pans to racks to cool. Serve the *sfogliatelle* warm on the day they are baked. To reheat, place on a paper-lined pan and heat at 350 degrees for about 10 minutes.

Makes 16 to 18 pastries

୨ଚ ୧ଚ

Sfogliatelle Frolle

"Tender" *Sfogliatelle*

Sfogliatelle frolle are sold in Naples right beside the flaky variety (see preceding recipe). The name constitutes a contradiction in terms, since *sfogliatelle* literally means "flaky pastries," and to prepare them with *pasta frolla*, which has a tender, cakey texture after it is baked, eliminates all possibility of flakiness. Fortunately, such contradictions are not bothersome to Neapolitans, and another excellent pastry is the result.

For the *pasta frolla,* combine the flour, sugar, and salt in a mixing bowl. Stir well to mix. Remove the butter from the refrigerator, unwrap, and place on a work surface. Pound it gently with a rolling pin or the heel of your hand to make it pliable. After 3 or 4 strokes, the butter should have softened sufficiently. Use a scraper to remove it from the work surface and add it to the bowl with the flour mixture.

Toss the piece of butter to coat it with flour and break it up into 6 or 8 pieces, using your fingertips. Continue breaking the butter into smaller pieces and rubbing it into the flour mixture with your fingertips. At the same time, work the flour mixture upward from the bottom of the bowl so that it mixes evenly with the butter. The whole process should take no more than 2 minutes. Work quickly to ensure that the mixture remains cool and powdery and does not become pasty, which would be a sign that the butter is melting and that the resulting dough will be tough.

Break the 2 eggs into a small bowl or cup, beat them lightly with a fork, and stir into the butter-flour mixture. Continue stirring with the fork until the dough begins to hold together.

Empty the contents of the bowl onto a lightly floured

PASTA FROLLA
2⅓ *cups all-purpose flour*
⅓ *cup sugar*
Pinch salt
8 tablespoons (1 stick)
    unsalted butter, cold
2 large eggs

FILLING
See Sfogliatelle Napoletane, *preceding recipe*

EGG WASH
1 large egg
1 large egg yolk
Pinch salt

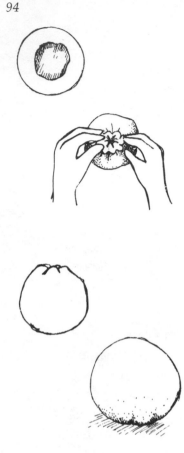

work surface and knead the dough gently until it is smooth, very briefly, without overworking it. Shape the dough into a thick disk, about 4 inches in diameter, and wrap in plastic. Chill until needed. The dough may be prepared up to 3 days ahead.

Prepare the filling and cool it. Whisk the egg, egg yolk, and salt together for the egg wash.

Divide the dough into 12 equal pieces and form the pastries: roll out each piece of dough into a 5-inch disk, then trim with a paring knife to an even 5 inches, using a plate or other pattern as a guide. Paint the dough with the egg wash and place $\frac{1}{12}$ of the filling in the center. Pull up the circumference of the dough to meet in the center, enclosing the filling, and pinch the edges together firmly. Make sure the pastries are only loosely filled or they will burst while they are baking. As the pastries are formed, invert them, so that the seam is underneath, onto a cookie sheet or jelly roll pan lined with parchment. Repeat with the remaining dough and filling.

Chill the *sfogliatelle* several hours, loosely covered with plastic wrap. Immediately before baking, carefully brush with the egg wash, using a soft brush. Bake at 375 degrees for about 20 minutes, just until the pastry is baked through. Cool the pastries on a rack.

Makes 12 pastries

❧ ☙

Baba Napoletani

———

<h1 style="text-align:center">Neapolitan Babas</h1>

Supposedly created in the eighteenth century by onetime king of Poland Stanislas Leszczynski at his court in exile in Nancy, France, the baba has become totally Neapolitan. A buttery yeast dough baked to a tender lightness is then soaked in a hot rum syrup, making the pastry moist, tender, and flavorful.

Dariole, or timbale, molds used to bake babas are available from specialty stores (see Sources of Equipment and Ingredients). This recipe uses mini-muffin pans, available at hardware and variety stores. The tiny babas are appealingly small and consequently not overly rich or substantial. The recipe may produce more babas than you need for a single occasion, but both the babas and the syrup keep well in the freezer and are wonderful to have on hand as a last-minute dessert.

For the sponge, heat the milk to lukewarm, sprinkle the yeast on the surface, and allow to stand 5 minutes. Whisk until smooth and stir into the flour. Cover the sponge and ferment 20 minutes. For the dough, beat the eggs, salt, sugar, and flour together. Beat in the sponge, then the cooled melted butter.

Pipe the dough into well-buttered miniature muffin pans, filling them half-full (this quantity of dough will make about 30 to 36 babas). Cover the pans with buttered plastic wrap and allow to proof until the dough comes to the top of the cups. Bake the babas at 400 degrees for about 10 to 15 minutes, until golden and baked through. Cool the babas on a rack.

For the syrup, combine the sugar and water in a pan and bring to a boil. Add the rum. Measure ⅓ cup and reserve for the apricot glaze.

Reheat the remaining syrup if it is not boiling hot and soak the babas in it, 3 or 4 at a time, about 1 minute, until they swell slightly. Remove the babas to a nonaluminum pan to drain. If the syrup is not boiling hot, the babas will not absorb it easily and will remain dry within.

To glaze the babas, combine the apricot preserves and ⅓ cup syrup and bring to a boil over medium heat, stirring occasionally. Strain into another pan, return to a boil, and reduce until thick. Paint the babas with the hot glaze and allow them to cool.

For the water icing, combine the confectioners' sugar and water in a small saucepan. Stir until smooth and heat gently over low heat until hot but not simmering. Quickly paint the

SPONGE
½ cup milk
1 envelope active dry yeast
    or ⅔ ounce compressed
    yeast
¾ cup all-purpose flour

DOUGH
3 large eggs
½ teaspoon salt
2 tablespoons sugar
1½ cups all-purpose flour
8 tablespoons (1 stick) butter,
    melted and cooled

SYRUP
2 cups sugar
3 cups water
½ cup dark rum

APRICOT GLAZE
1 cup apricot preserves
⅓ cup syrup (see above)

WATER ICING
1½ cups confectioners' sugar
½ cup water

babas with the icing. Cover the babas loosely with plastic wrap and keep at a cool room temperature. Serve the babas on the day they are soaked.

Makes about 30 to 36 very small babas

〜 〜

Barchette alla Mandorla

——

Pastry Boats with Almond Filling

These elegant little pastries are very much like ones I tasted at the Pasticceria Bernasconi, in Rome. It may be a little trouble to locate the barquette pans, but stores that carry imported kitchenware often stock them. They may also be ordered by mail (see Sources of Equipment and Ingredients).

PASTA FROLLA
1¼ cups all-purpose flour
3 tablespoons sugar
Pinch salt
4 tablespoons unsalted butter, cold
1 large egg

MACAROON FILLING
8 ounces canned almond paste
3 large egg yolks
1 tablespoon Maraschino liqueur

GLAZE
¼ cup light corn syrup
½ teaspoon vanilla extract

For the *pasta frolla*, combine the flour, sugar, and salt in a mixing bowl. Stir well to mix. Remove the butter from the refrigerator, unwrap, and place on a work surface. Pound it gently with a rolling pin or the heel of your hand to make it pliable. After 3 or 4 strokes, the butter should have softened sufficiently. Use a scraper to remove it from the work surface, and add it to the bowl with the flour mixture.

Toss the piece of butter to coat it with flour and break it up into 6 or 8 pieces, using your fingertips. Continue breaking the butter into smaller pieces and rubbing it into the flour mixture with your fingertips. At the same time, work the flour mixture upward from the bottom of the bowl so that it mixes evenly with the butter. The whole process should take no more than 2 minutes. Work quickly to make sure that the mixture remains cool and powdery and does not become pasty, which would be a sign that the butter is melting and that the resulting dough will be tough.

Break the egg into a small bowl or cup, beat it lightly with a fork, and stir into the butter-flour mixture. Continue stirring with the fork until the dough begins to hold together.

Empty the contents of the bowl onto a lightly floured work surface and squeeze the dough together gently until it is smooth, very briefly, without overworking it. Shape the dough into a thick disk, about 4 inches in diameter, and wrap in plastic. Chill the dough until needed. It may be prepared up to 3 days ahead.

For the almond filling, break the almond paste into 1-inch pieces and place in the bowl of a heavy-duty mixer fitted with the paddle or in a food processor fitted with the metal blade. Add one yolk and mix on the lowest speed or pulse in the processor. After the first yolk is almost absorbed, add the second and beat or process until smooth. Add the last yolk and the liqueur and work until smooth again. Cover the filling until assembling the pastries, to prevent it from forming a crust.

To assemble the pastries, first roll the dough out into a 4×12-inch rectangle and drape it over twelve 3- to 4-inch barquette pans arranged in a double row. Press the dough well into the pans, then roll over with the rolling pin to cut away any excess dough. Arrange the pans on a cookie sheet and chill them until the dough is firm, about 1 hour.

To fill the pastries, place the filling in a pastry bag fitted with a ½-inch star tube (Ateco #4). Pipe the filling in the form of a large spiral, as in the illustration. Fill all the lined pans. Bake the pastries at 375 degrees for about 20 minutes, until the filling is firm and well colored and the dough is baked through.

While the pastries are baking, prepare the glaze: combine the corn syrup and vanilla in a small saucepan and heat until bubbles form around the edges. Immediately after removing the pastries from the oven, brush them with the hot glaze. Cool in the pans before unmolding.

Makes 12 pastries

৯৩ 5 ৫৯

Puff Pastry, Strudel Dough, and Cream Puff Pastry

Though the first two of these doughs seem unrelated, they are really variations on a theme. Strudel dough, a lean, elastic dough, is capable of being pulled paper-thin, painted with butter, and rolled up with a filling inside. During baking, the layers of dough absorb the butter and the dough bakes to a flaky tenderness. Puff pastry begins with a lean dough wrapped around a block of butter and is then repeatedly rolled and folded to increase the number of layers of dough and butter. During baking, the same phenomenon of the dough's absorbing the butter occurs. Since there are more layers in puff pastry, the dough actually expands, its layers pushed apart due to the pressure of steam formed by the evaporation of water in the dough. Strudel dough and puff pastry meet head-on in *Sfogliatelle Napoletane*, page 90. In the *sfogliatelle*, the lean dough is rolled thin, painted with fat, and then rolled up jelly roll–style and sliced. The slices are fanned out into cone shapes and filled; their flakiness develops during baking.

Thinly pulled dough would seem to be a Greek and Middle Eastern invention. In the era of classical Rome it was imported to Italy, since most Roman cooks were Greek slaves. Strudel is therefore not an unlikely Italian pastry, though its present popularity throughout Italy is due to its presence in Italy's German-speaking region, the Trentino–Alto Adige.

Recent research by Charles Perry has revealed that the transition from strudel to puff pastry probably occurred in medieval Spain. Since Italian life and culture were greatly influenced by the

Spanish Bourbons, from the early eighteenth to midnineteenth century, especially in southern Italy, I think it is safe to assume that puff pastry was introduced to Italy through Naples. Most modern Italian puff pastry desserts are French in origin, though they are interpreted in a uniquely Italian style.

Pasta bignè, or cream puff pastry, is also considered here. Though it is prepared according to a different system from that used for puff pastry and strudel dough and does not contain layers, it also provides a crisp, buttery container for a filling.

Puff Pastry

Although most of us are accustomed to think of puff pastry as a French preparation, there are many Italian desserts and pastries that use this dough. In fact, the dough may have originated in Italy, rather than in France, but new research points to Spain as puff pastry's country of origin.

HINTS FOR SUCCESS WITH PUFF PASTRY

- Flour the dough and the surface often, with small amounts of flour every time, to prevent the dough from sticking and tearing.
- If the dough softens and becomes difficult to roll, slide it onto a floured cookie sheet, cover loosely with plastic wrap, and refrigerate about 15 minutes.
- If the dough is very elastic and difficult to roll, chill it 1 hour and resume the process.
- Do not be afraid to interrupt the process at any point and refrigerate the dough, as long as you resume at the same point. For example, in hot weather it may be necessary to refrigerate the dough between every rolling, instead of between every other rolling, as in the recipe.
- Make a double batch of the dough and freeze half. Then the dough is available when you need it.
- You can keep the puff pastry in the refrigerator for up to 4 days. Or freeze the dough and defrost it in the refrigerator overnight before using it.

ᖍ ᖋ

Pasta Sfogliata

Italian Puff Pastry

Sfogliata means "leaved" and refers to the alternating layers, or leaves, of dough and butter formed by repeatedly rolling and folding the package of dough and butter. Puff pastry is capable of rising to delicate, flaky heights as a result of the steam that forms between the layers in the dough during baking.

If you have never attempted this process before, choose a cool day to make the dough, turn off the telephone, and reread the instructions several times. Once you have the knack of preparing puff pastry, it is no more difficult than preparing any other dough, but it does take a little practice.

DOUGH
2 cups all-purpose flour
1 teaspoon salt
*4 tablespoons unsalted
    butter, softened*
*⅓ cup white wine or white
    vermouth*
⅓ cup cold water

BUTTER SQUARE
¼ cup all-purpose flour
*16 tablespoons (2 sticks)
    unsalted butter, cold*

For the dough, combine the flour and salt in a mixing bowl. Cut the butter into 3 or 4 pieces and rub it thoroughly into the flour with your fingertips so that no pieces of butter remain visible. Make sure that the mixture remains cool and powdery and does not become pasty.

Combine the wine or vermouth with the water. Blend the liquid into the flour-and-butter mixture with a fork, working the fork, tines up, through the mixture from the bottom of the bowl upward, being careful not to stir, which would toughen the dough. Once all of the flour-and-butter mixture is evenly moistened it will look like a mass of rough curds; do not attempt to make the dough smooth. Cover the dough loosely and refrigerate it while preparing the butter square.

For the butter square, spread the remaining flour on a work surface and unwrap the chilled butter onto it. Turn the sticks of butter to coat them with the flour and pound them with a rolling pin to soften them to the point where you can easily make an indentation by pressing with a fingertip. With floured hands, press and squeeze the butter into a rough square, about 4 inches on a side. If the kitchen is warm, refrigerate the butter square while forming the dough that will envelop it.

Scrape off any bits of butter sticking to the work surface and flour the surface. Remove the dough from the refrigerator and scrape it out of the bowl onto the surface. Press the dough well with the palms of your hands once or twice to make all the bits of dough adhere. Flour the dough very lightly and roll it gently into a 5 × 10-inch rectangle. Place the square of butter at the narrow end of the rectangle closer to you and fold the other half of the dough over it.

Turn the package of dough so that the fold is on the left and roll it into a 6 × 12-inch rectangle. Fold the top third of the dough down over the middle third, and the bottom third up over the middle, as you would fold a letter, to make 3 layers of dough. Position the dough again so that the crease is on the left and roll again to a 6 × 12-inch rectangle. This time fold each narrow end of the dough toward the middle and fold again at the middle, to make 4 layers.

Wrap the dough loosely in plastic and refrigerate about 1 hour. When you remove the dough from the refrigerator, unwrap it and position it on a floured surface so that the fold is on the left. Flour the dough and roll it again into a 6 × 12-inch rectangle, repeating the 3-layer fold. Then turn so the crease is on the left, roll the dough once more into a 6 × 12-inch rectangle, and give another 4-layer fold. The dough is now finished and needs to rest again at least 3 or 4 hours before you use it to make a dessert.

VARIATION

Pasta Sfogliata all'Uovo

Many Italians like to add an egg to puff pastry for increased tenderness. To do this, crack an egg into a measuring cup, then add water and/or white wine to make ⅔ cup liquid. Beat well with a fork before using it to moisten the dough.

❧ ☙

Farfalle

—

Puff Pastry Butterflies

These are one of the many puff pastries based on the principle of encrusting the dough with sugar so that it caramelizes while it bakes. The *farfalle* are easy and fun to make. They are an excellent example of puff pastry's power to expand.

½ batch Pasta Sfogliata,
  preceding recipe
1 cup sugar

Strew half the sugar on a work surface and place the *pasta sfogliata* on it. Strew the dough with the remaining sugar and press the sugar in with the heel of your hand. Roll out the dough, constantly sprinkling it with the sugar, on the work surface until it is a 12-inch square. Trim the edges of the dough and cut it into 4 strips, each 3 × 12 inches. Stack the 4 strips of dough together and press gently down the middle of the stack to make them adhere, as if forming the spine of an opened book, as in the illustration. Chill at least 1 hour.

Cut the stacked strips crosswise at ½-inch intervals to make 24 slices. One at a time, place the slices on the sugar-sprinkled work surface with the cut side down. Pinch each in the center, according to the illustration, and make a twist at the middle. Arrange the *farfalle* on cookie sheets lined with parchment, keeping them well apart from each other.

Bake the *farfalle* at 350 degrees for about 20 to 25 minutes, until they have expanded and caramelized well. Remove from the pan to a rack to cool.

Makes 2 dozen farfalle

⫘ ⫘

Cannoncini

Baked Cannoli

These elegant pastry tubes of caramelized, baked puff pastry are similar to *Cannoli alla Siciliana*, page 48. Since they are not fried, they are a bit less rich and are more appropriately filled with pastry cream, but use ricotta filling if you prefer it.

To bake the *cannoncini* you need 12 metal tubes, as for cannoli. See Sources of Equipment and Ingredients.

To form the *cannoncini*, roll out the *pasta sfogliata* on a floured surface into a 12-inch square. Slide the dough onto a cookie sheet and refrigerate it for at least 1 hour.

For the pastry cream filling, bring the milk to a boil with half the sugar. Whisk the egg yolks in a bowl with the salt and whisk in the remaining sugar. Sift the flour over the yolk mixture and whisk in smoothly. When the milk boils, whisk one-third of it into the yolk mixture. Return the remaining milk to a boil and whisk in the yolk mixture, continuing to whisk until the cream thickens and comes to a boil. Boil, whisking constantly to prevent scorching, for 1 minute. Off the heat, whisk in the vanilla, cinnamon, and chocolate. Scrape the pastry cream into a clean nonreactive bowl and press plastic wrap against the surface. Refrigerate until cold, about 2 hours.

Remove the dough from the refrigerator and use a pastry wheel to cut it into 12 strips, each 1×12 inches. Slide the strips onto a cookie sheet and refrigerate them.

To form the *cannoncini*, butter 12 metal cannoli tubes. Remove a strip of dough from the refrigerator, brush it lightly with water, and turn it over so that the dry side is facing upward. (Take only one strip of dough from the refrigerator at

½ batch Pasta Sfogliata, *page 100*

PASTRY CREAM FILLING
2 cups milk
½ cup sugar
6 large egg yolks
Pinch salt
⅓ cup all-purpose flour
2 teaspoons vanilla extract
½ teaspoon ground cinnamon
4 ounces semisweet chocolate, finely chopped

⅓ cup sugar

¼ cup blanched almonds, toasted and coarsely chopped

a time; they will soften and become difficult to handle if not kept cool.) Place the end of a tube at the left side of the strip and roll the tube so that the dough rolls up on it spiral fashion, as in the illustration. Be sure not to roll too tightly and not to stretch the dough or the baked pastry will be impossible to remove from the tube. Trim away any excess dough at the end of the strip, making sure that the beginning and end of the strip are on the same side of the tube; having this seam underneath during baking will prevent the strip from unraveling. Continue with the remaining strips to form 12 *cannoncini*.

Place the *cannoncini* on a jelly roll pan lined with parchment and sprinkle with the ⅓ cup sugar. Bake at 350 degrees for about 30 minutes, until the pastry is dry, baked through, and well caramelized. Remove the *cannoncini* from the metal tubes immediately by gripping the pastry in one hand, protected with a clean towel or paper towels, and pulling out the tube with tongs. Cool the *cannoncini* on a rack.

To fill the *cannoncini*, pipe the cooled filling into them using a pastry bag fitted with a ½-inch plain tube (Ateco #6). Sprinkle the ends of the filling with the chopped almonds. Fill the *cannoncini* no more than an hour before serving or the pastry will become soggy. Refrigerate leftovers and bring to room temperature before serving.

Makes 12 pastries

ର୍ଚ୍ଚ ଚ୍ଚଙ୍

Strudel Trentino

Apple Strudel from Trento

Although German is the unofficial second language of Trento, capital of the Trentino region, the city has a much more Italian feel than Bolzano, its officially German-speaking neighbor to the north.

Trento's great pastry specialty, apple strudel, has a decidedly

Italian flair, even though it is Eastern European in origin. Usually made with puff pastry rather than the more traditionally Austrian stretched dough (see *Strudel di Ricotta ed Amarene alla Bolzanese*, page 119), the Trento strudel is quick to prepare and rather light.

Roll out the *pasta sfogliata* on a floured surface into a 15- or 16-inch square. Slide the dough onto a cookie sheet and refrigerate it while preparing the filling.

For the filling, peel, core, and slice the apples into thin wedges. Place them in a bowl and add all the remaining filling ingredients except the butter, bread crumbs, and sugar.

Heat the butter in a small sauté pan and add the bread crumbs. Cook, stirring often over low heat, for about 5 minutes, until the bread crumbs turn a deep golden color. Remove to a bowl and cool.

To form the strudel, place the square of dough on a small cloth, such as an apron or large towel. Add the sugar to the filling and arrange the filling over one-third of the dough closest to you. Sprinkle the filling with the cooled buttered bread crumbs. Lift the end of the cloth closest to you and roll up the strudel, making sure that the filling remains in a compact mass and folding in the ends of the strudel several times while rolling. Continue rolling until the far edge of the dough is on the bottom of the rolled strudel. Carefully lift the strudel onto a jelly roll pan lined with a piece of buttered parchment or wax paper. For the egg wash, beat the egg and salt together, and paint the strudel with it.

Bake the strudel at 425 degrees for about 45 minutes, until it is a dark golden color and the filling is bubbling.

Lift the paper and the strudel onto a rack to cool. When cool, run a knife or spatula between the strudel and the paper to loosen it, slide both onto a platter, and, holding the strudel in place, pull away the paper.

Dust the strudel with the confectioners' sugar immediately before serving. Serve the strudel on the day it is baked.

Makes 8 generous servings

½ *batch* Pasta Sfogliata, *page 100*

APPLE FILLING
3 large Golden Delicious apples, about 1½ pounds
⅔ *cup raisins or currants*
⅔ *cup walnut pieces, coarsely chopped*
1 teaspoon grated lemon zest

3 tablespoons unsalted butter
½ *cup dry bread crumbs*

⅓ *cup sugar*

EGG WASH
1 large egg
Pinch salt

Confectioners' sugar for finishing

Note: During baking, the juices from the filling often leak out of the strudel. Since the juices contain a large proportion of sugar, they can begin to caramelize when they touch the hot pan. If you see the juices begin to exude, place another pan under the one on which the strudel is baking to absorb some bottom heat from the oven and to prevent the juices from burning and making the bottom of the strudel bitter.

ଏଠ ୦ଠ

Gubana di Pasta Sfogliata

Puff Pastry *Gubana*

Since there are different names for this dessert and the terminology can be confusing, I choose to call it merely puff pastry *gubana*. Depending on the location, the yeast-risen *Gubana* on page 29 is referred to as either *presnitz* or *potitza*. All three names — *gubana*, *presnitz*, and *potitza* — signify filled pastries that are rolled into a spiral to be baked; they may be made with a yeast dough or puff pastry. This version is supposedly a specialty of Cividale, the town where the yeast dough *gubana* was popularized, though I have seen it only in pastry shops in nearby Udine. Terminology and origin aside, it is a delicious pastry.

½ *batch* Pasta Sfogliata,
 page 100

FILLING
¾ *cup golden raisins*
¾ *cup dark raisins*
¾ *cup dried figs, stemmed
 and diced*
½ *cup dark rum*
1 *cup walnuts, finely
 chopped*

Roll out the *pasta sfogliata* on a floured surface into a 10 × 20-inch rectangle. Slide the dough onto a cookie sheet and refrigerate it while preparing the filling.

For the filling, place the raisins and figs in a saucepan, cover with water, and bring to a boil. Drain and place in a bowl and cover with the rum. Allow to stand several hours or overnight covered with plastic wrap. Stir in the remaining filling ingredients.

Remove the dough from the refrigerator and place it on a cloth. Spread the dough evenly with the filling and roll it up like a strudel. Make sure the end is on the bottom. Pull to lengthen slightly and arrange in the form of a snug spiral in a buttered 9-inch springform pan. For the egg wash, whisk the egg and salt together, and paint the top of the *gubana* with it.

Bake the *gubana* at 325 degrees for about 1 hour, until it is a deep gold and well baked through. Cool in the pan on a rack.

Release the sides of the springform pan and slide the *gubana* onto a platter. Dust with the confectioners' sugar before serving.

Makes 12 servings

⅓ cup pine nuts

2 ounces semisweet chocolate, finely chopped

¾ cup dry bread or cake crumbs

1 tablespoon grated orange zest

1 teaspoon grated lemon zest

1 large egg

EGG WASH
1 large egg
Pinch salt

Confectioners' sugar for finishing

❧ ☙

Mille Foglie all'Albicocca

Napoleon Cake with Apricot Filling

Layers of baked puff pastry stacked with a filling are usually known as *mille foglie* (thousand leaves). Infinite variations of fillings and flavorings are possible. This version, with a filling of rum-scented apricot preserves and a lemon pastry cream, is found commonly throughout Italy. Feel free to vary the kind of preserves or to use another flavor of pastry cream, such as rum or even chocolate. A layer of sliced or whole berries may be used over the preserves, or you may add a thin layer of whipped cream over the pastry cream.

Since this recipe uses only three-fourths of a batch of *pasta sfogliata*, you can use the rest for *Farfalle*, page 102, or a few *Cannoncini*, page 103.

¾ *batch* Pasta Sfogliata,
    page 100

PASTRY CREAM
1½ cups milk
1 teaspoon grated lemon zest
⅓ cup sugar
4 large egg yolks
*3 tablespoons all-purpose
    flour*
2 teaspoons vanilla extract

APRICOT FILLING
½ cup apricot preserves
*2 tablespoons white or dark
    rum*

*Confectioners' sugar for
    finishing*

For the layers, roll out the *pasta sfogliata* on a floured surface into a 10 × 15-inch rectangle. Cut the dough into 2 rectangles, each 10 × 7½ inches, then roll each into a 10 × 15-inch rectangle. Pierce the rectangles of dough all over with a fork and slide each onto a 10 × 15-inch pan, lined with a piece of parchment or buttered wax paper. Chill the layers of dough several hours or overnight.

While the layers are chilling, prepare the pastry cream: bring the milk, lemon zest, and half the sugar to a boil in a nonreactive saucepan. While the milk is coming to a boil, whisk the egg yolks in a bowl and whisk in the remaining sugar. Sift the flour over the yolk mixture and whisk it in. Whisk one-third of the boiling milk into the yolk mixture. Return the remaining milk to a boil, and, beginning to whisk the milk first, pour in the yolk mixture, whisking constantly until the cream thickens and boils. Boil, whisking, 1 minute. Whisk in the vanilla.

Pour the pastry cream into a clean bowl, press plastic wrap against the surface, and chill.

Bake the layers at 350 degrees for about 30 minutes, until they are an even, deep golden color. Change the position of the layers in the oven several times, top to bottom and back to front, to help them bake evenly. Check the layers frequently while they are baking: if they begin to puff excessively, pierce the bubbles in the dough with a fork so that the layers remain flat.

Remove the baked puff pastry layers to a cutting board and cut each layer into a 9-inch square and a 4½ × 9-inch rectangle. Return the baked layers to the pans and cool. Crumble all the scraps finely and reserve for finishing the *mille foglie*.

For the apricot filling, combine the preserves and rum in a saucepan and bring to a boil over medium heat, stirring often. Strain the mixture into another pan, return to low heat, and reduce until sticky, about 5 minutes, according to the original density of the preserves.

To assemble the *mille foglie*, place one of the puff pastry squares on a 9-inch square of stiff cardboard. Spread with half the apricot filling and allow to cool. Then spread with half the cooled pastry cream. Place the 2 rectangles on the pastry cream; spread first with the other half of the apricot filling and then, after the filling has cooled, the other half of the pastry cream. Place the second square layer on the pastry cream and use a pan to press the whole together gently.

Smooth the sides with any filling that oozes out, using a thin metal spatula, and press the reserved crumbs against the sides with the palm of your hand.

Dust the top of the *mille foglie* generously with the confectioners' sugar and keep in a cool place for no more than 3 or 4 hours before serving.

For advance preparation, make all the component parts early in the day but only assemble a few hours before serving.

Use a sharp, serrated knife to cut the *mille foglie* into rectangles or squares for serving.

Makes 8 to 12 servings

∞⌒ ⌒∞

Torta Diplomatica

Rum Cake with Sponge Cake and Puff Pastry Layers

Perhaps the epitome of rich, delicate desserts, the *torta diplomatica* is a *mille foglie* (see preceding recipe) whose middle layer of puff pastry is replaced by sponge cake soaked with rum syrup. Feel free to vary the flavoring and substitute another liquor or liqueur for the rum in the syrup and the filling. Sometimes I use Maraschino liqueur and the drained cherries from *Conserva di Amarene*, page 13. Orange liqueur and finely diced candied orange peel would also be good choices.

This is an elaborate recipe, though once all the component parts are ready, it is quick to assemble. Start several days before and make the *pasta sfogliata* one day, then the sponge cake layer and syrup the next. Make the pastry cream without finishing it with the butter, and roll out the *pasta sfogliata* on the third day. The day you plan to serve the *torta*, bake the puff pastry layers, finish the pastry cream by beating with the butter and adding the rum-soaked currants, and assemble the *torta*.

⅔ batch Pasta Sfogliata,
page 100

SPONGE CAKE
4 large eggs
2 large egg yolks
Pinch salt
¾ cup sugar
1 cup all-purpose flour

RUM SYRUP
¼ cup sugar
⅓ cup water
3 tablespoons dark rum

PASTRY CREAM FILLING
*½ cup currants or golden
     raisins*
3 tablespoons dark rum
1 cup milk
¼ cup sugar
3 large egg yolks
Pinch salt
*3 tablespoons all-purpose
     flour*
*8 tablespoons (1 stick)
     unsalted butter*

*Confectioners' sugar for
     finishing*

For the puff pastry layers, roll out the *pasta sfogliata* dough on a floured surface into a 10 × 15-inch rectangle. Cut the dough into 2 rectangles, each 10 × 7½ inches, then roll each into a 10-inch square. Pierce the squares of dough all over with a fork and slide each onto a 10 × 15-inch pan, lined with a piece of parchment or buttered wax paper. Chill the layers of dough several hours or overnight.

Bake the layers at 350 degrees for about 30 minutes, until they are an even, deep golden color. Change the position of the layers in the oven several times, top to bottom and back to front, to help them bake evenly. Check the layers frequently while they are baking: if they begin to puff excessively, pierce the bubbles in the dough with a fork so that the layers remain flat.

Remove the baked puff pastry layers to a cutting board and cut each layer into a 9-inch disk. Return the baked disks to the pans and cool. Crumble all the scraps finely and reserve for finishing the *torta*.

For the sponge cake, butter a 9-inch × 2-inch-deep round cake pan and line it with a disk of parchment or wax paper, cut to fit. Combine the eggs, egg yolks, salt, and sugar in a heatproof bowl or the bowl of an electric mixer. Whisk to mix. Place the bowl over a pan of gently simmering water and whisk until warm, about 100 to 105 degrees. Remove the bowl from the pan and whip on high speed with a hand mixer or a heavy-duty mixer fitted with the whip. Continue whipping until the egg mixture has lightened in color, cooled, and increased about 4 times over its original volume.

Sift the flour over the egg foam in 3 or 4 additions, folding it in gently but thoroughly with a rubber spatula.

Pour the batter into the prepared pan.

Bake the layer at 325 degrees for about 30 minutes, until it is well risen, firm to the touch, and a deep golden color. Remove to a work surface and insert the point of a small knife between the layer and the side of the pan. Loosen the layer from the pan and invert it onto a rack. Leave the paper in place and immediately invert the layer again, onto another rack to cool. Double-wrap in plastic and chill the layer.

For the rum syrup, bring the sugar and water to a boil in a small saucepan. Cool and stir in the rum.

For the pastry cream filling, place the currants or raisins in a saucepan and cover with water. Bring to a boil, drain, pour into a bowl, and cover with the rum. Allow to stand at room temperature while preparing the pastry cream. Bring the milk to a boil with half the sugar. Whisk the egg yolks in a bowl with the salt and whisk in the remaining sugar. Sift the flour over the yolk mixture and whisk it in smoothly. When the milk boils, whisk one-third of it into the yolk mixture. Return the remaining milk to a boil and whisk in the yolk mixture, continuing to whisk until the cream thickens and comes to a boil. Boil, whisking constantly to prevent scorching, for 1 minute. Scrape the cream into a clean nonreactive bowl and press plastic wrap against the surface. Refrigerate until cold, about 2 hours.

To finish the filling, beat the butter on medium speed until soft and light. Beat in the cooled pastry cream all at once, then continue beating until the filling is smooth and light. Stir in the rum and currants or raisins by hand.

To assemble the *torta*, place one of the puff pastry disks on a cardboard or platter. Spread with half the pastry cream filling. Moisten the top of the sponge cake layer with half the rum syrup, using a brush. Place the cake layer on the filling, top side down. Moisten the cake layer with the remaining syrup and spread with the remaining filling. Top with the other puff pastry disk. Smooth the sides of the *torta* with any filling that oozes out and press the puff pastry crumbs onto the sides. Dust the top lightly with the confectioners' sugar.

Makes about 12 servings

ꙮ ꙮ

Torta di Mele con Pasta Sfogliata

Apple Tart with Puff Pastry Crust

This tart shows off the beautiful layers in the puff pastry to great advantage. The dough lines the pan in such a way that the cut edge of the dough is uppermost when the tart bakes. The construction of the crust is a little complicated, but its striking result is well worth the trouble.

This is based on an apple tart from the celebrated Sant'Ambroeus pastry shop, Milan's most elegant.

½ batch Pasta Sfogliata,
    page 100

FILLING
5 tart apples, such as
    Granny Smith or
    Greening
1 teaspoon grated lemon zest
4 tablespoons unsalted butter
⅓ cup sugar

Roll out the dough on a floured surface into a 14-inch square. Slide the dough onto a pan and chill 1 hour.

For the filling, peel, halve, and core the apples. Reserve 3 halves, tightly wrapped in plastic, in the refrigerator for the top of the tart. Dice the remaining apples coarsely and combine with the lemon zest, butter, and all but 1 tablespoon of the sugar in a nonreactive saucepan that has a tight-fitting cover. Place the pan over medium heat. When the apple mixture begins to sizzle, cover the pan, lower the heat, and cook 5 minutes, until the apples are swimming in water. Uncover the pan and cook, stirring often, until the apples are reduced to a thick, chunky puree, about 5 to 10 minutes longer. Cool the filling.

To form the tart crust, butter a 9-inch springform pan. Remove the *pasta sfogliata* from the refrigerator and cut off 2 strips, each 14 × 2½ inches, using a sharp pastry wheel. Cut the strips on one edge in a scalloped pattern, as in the illustration. Arrange the strips against the inside of the pan, pressing them in place. Roll the remaining dough into a 12-inch square (you will be starting with a 14 × 9-inch rectangle) and cut it into a

12-inch disk. Moisten the insides of the dough lining the sides of the pan with water and ease the disk of dough into the pan so that it covers the bottom evenly and is evenly pressed against the strips of dough lining the sides. Chill 1 hour.

Pour the cooked filling into the pan and smooth it evenly over the dough. Cut the remaining apple halves into thin slices and arrange them on the filling, as in the illustration. Sprinkle with the reserved tablespoon of sugar.

Bake the *torta* at 375 degrees for about 40 minutes, until the pastry is baked through and well colored and the apples on the top are cooked. Remove from the oven and cool in the pan on a rack.

Release the sides of the springform pan and slide the *torta* onto a platter.

Makes 8 servings

Crostata di Pere con Pasta Sfogliata

Puff Pastry Pear Tart

This double-crusted pear pastry depends for its success on perfectly ripe sweet pears. I like to use Bartlett or Comice pears for their intense sweetness and melting texture. Remember to purchase the pears a few days in advance and allow them to finish ripening at room temperature.

Roll out the *pasta sfogliata* on a floured surface into a 10 × 15-inch rectangle. Cut the dough in half to make two 10 × 7½-inch

¾ batch Pasta Sfogliata, *page 100*

EGG WASH
1 large egg
Pinch salt

PEAR FILLING
5 ripe pears, about 2 pounds
2 tablespoons sugar
Pinch each: ground
   cinnamon and ginger

rectangles, then roll each into a 10-inch square. Slide each square of dough onto a cookie sheet and chill at least 1 hour.

To assemble the *crostata*, place one square of dough on a cookie sheet lined with parchment. For the egg wash, whisk the egg and salt together, and paint the dough with it. Peel, core, and slice the pears thinly and arrange them in an 8-inch disk in the center of the square of dough. Sprinkle with the sugar and spices. Top with the other square of dough and press down well all around the filling to seal the 2 layers of dough together.

Place a 10-inch-diameter bowl or pan on the pastry without pressing and cut around the bowl with a sharp pastry wheel. Remove the scraps and paint the top of the pastry with the egg wash. Use the scraps to make some decorations for the top of the pastry, like the leaves in the illustration.

Bake the *crostata* at 400 degrees for about 30 minutes, until the dough is well risen and deeply colored. Cool in the pan on a rack. Slide the *crostata* from the pan onto a platter to serve.

Makes 8 servings

Strudel Dough

To the average home cook, the phenomenon of stretching a shapeless piece of dough until it is thin and transparent and covers a large surface area would seem all but impossible. Fortunately, just the opposite is true. Over the course of the past ten years, I have seen hundreds of students who had never previously prepared strudel dough make the dough from scratch and pull it successfully with a minimum of effort.

The success of a batch of strudel dough depends on one important factor: gluten. Formed by the change in structure of certain proteins in the flour when they encounter moisture and friction, the gluten is present in the dough in the form of elastic strands. Aggressive kneading and working of the dough during the initial stage of mixing causes a strong gluten to form — essential to a good strudel dough. While the dough is resting, the springy elasticity formed during kneading relaxes, though the webbed structure of the strands remains intact; it is these strands that enable the dough to be stretched more than paper-thin without tearing.

HINTS FOR SUCCESS WITH STRUDEL DOUGH

- Always use *unbleached* all-purpose flour in the following strudel recipe. It has a higher protein content than bleached all-purpose flour, an important factor in developing the necessary degree of gluten.
- Make sure the flour is not compressed when you measure it, which could result in too much flour and a tough, overly elastic dough that is difficult to pull. Fluff up the flour with a spoon, then spoon the flour into a measuring cup before leveling it off with a straight-edged spatula.
- Measure the liquid for the dough carefully, using a glass measuring cup.
- After kneading and pounding the dough, form it into an evenly shaped ball and make sure the entire surface of the dough is oiled after turning it over in the oiled bowl — dry patches on the dough will result in tearing later on during the pulling.
- If the dough resists while you are pulling it, stop for a few minutes and allow the dough to rest briefly before continuing to pull.

∞ ∞

Pasta per Strudel
———
Hand-Pulled Strudel Dough

Strudels made with this type of dough are referred to as *Ziehteigstrudel* (pulled dough strudel) in the Alto Adige to distinguish them from those made with puff pastry, as in *Strudel Trentino*, page 104.

*3 cups unbleached
   all-purpose flour
½ teaspoon salt
2 large eggs
1 tablespoon vegetable oil
Warm water*

Combine the flour and salt in a mixing bowl. Beat the eggs and oil with a fork in a 2-cup measure. Add enough warm water to make a total of 1¼ cups (10 fluid ounces). Stir the liquid into the flour mixture with a rubber spatula, making sure that no flour sticks to the side of the bowl. The dough should be fairly soft.

Turn the dough out onto a lightly floured surface and begin to develop the gluten. Pick the dough up and slam it against the surface forcefully. Fold the dough back on itself and pick it up again from the side, detaching it from the surface with a metal scraper or spatula. Repeat this motion 100 times, until the dough, which started out rather sticky, is smooth and elastic.

Oil a small bowl, place the dough in the bowl, and turn the dough over so that the top is oiled. Press plastic wrap against the surface of the dough and rest the dough at room temperature about 1 hour, or longer if possible. Refrigerate the dough if it is to be held more than half a day. If the dough is refrigerated, let it come to room temperature before proceeding.

To stretch the dough, begin by covering a rectangular table (30 × 48 inches is ideal) with a cloth. Flour the cloth generously. Place the dough in the center of the cloth, making sure not to fold the dough at all when removing it from the bowl. Flour the dough and roll it as thin as possible with a rolling pin. Brush oil on the surface of the dough.

Pull the dough from the center outward, stretching it over the backs of your hands, fingers folded under. When the dough becomes fairly large, anchor one end over the edge of the table and pull in the other direction. When the dough is paper-thin and covers the entire table, trim away the thick edges with scissors and let the dough dry for 5 to 10 minutes. If the dough tears, patch it with dough from the edges.

Fill and bake the strudel according to the individual recipe.

Strudel di Mele alla Bolzanese

Apple Strudel from Bolzano

Chef Giorgio Nardelli from the Parkhotel Laurin in Bolzano introduced me to the mysteries of Bolzano-style strudel. According to Chef Nardelli, there should no longer be any difference between dough and filling after the real Bolzano-style apple strudel is baked.

This recipe uses a formula for strudel dough I have used successfully for a long time; the filling and method of baking are pure Bolzano.

Prepare the dough and allow it to rest, according to the preceding recipe.

While the dough is resting, prepare the filling: peel, core, and slice the apples very thin. Toss the apples in a large bowl with all the filling ingredients except the sugar. Melt the butter in a sauté pan over low heat; pour half the butter into a bowl to cool slightly for buttering the dough later. When the remaining butter sizzles, add the bread crumbs and cook, stirring often, until they are deep golden, about 5 or 6 minutes.

Pull the dough according to the instructions in the preceding recipe. Paint the surface of the dough with the reserved butter, saving a tablespoon for the outside of the strudel. Distribute the filling over all of the dough, then sprinkle with the reserved sugar and the cooled buttered bread crumbs.

1 batch Pasta per Strudel, *preceding recipe*

APPLE FILLING
2½ pounds tart apples, such as Granny Smith or Greening
1 teaspoon ground cinnamon
1 tablespoon lemon juice
¼ cup pine nuts
½ cup golden raisins
½ cup sugar

12 tablespoons (1½ sticks) unsalted butter
1 cup dry bread crumbs

Confectioners' sugar for finishing

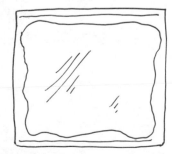

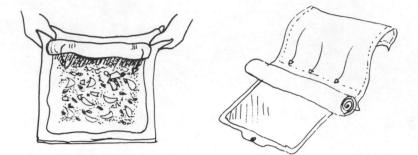

Beginning at one of the short ends, lift the cloth and roll the strudel into a tight cylinder, folding the ends in occasionally to seal them. Line a jelly roll pan with aluminum foil and butter the foil. Roll the strudel from the cloth onto the pan, bending the strudel carefully into a horseshoe shape, according to the illustration.

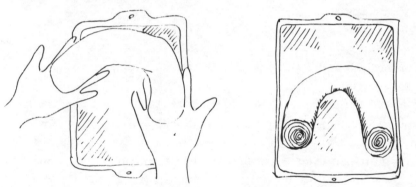

Brush the remaining butter on the outside of the strudel and bake it at 375 degrees for about 50 minutes, basting the outside of the strudel often with the juices that run out. When the strudel is baked it will be a very dark golden color and the dough will be crisp.

Cool the strudel in the pan on a rack until still slightly warm. Slide it, still on the foil, onto a large board. Loosen it from the foil by sliding a long knife or spatula between the strudel and the foil. Pull away the foil. Before serving, dust the strudel with the confectioners' sugar.

Makes 12 to 15 servings

൙ ൙

Strudel di Ricotta ed Amarene alla Bolzanese

Ricotta and Sour Cherry Strudel from Bolzano

This delicate strudel was one of the desserts I sampled at a wonderful lunch prepared by Chef Giorgio Nardelli of Bolzano. My hostess, Olga de Fonzo, publisher of *Il lavoro turistico*, a hospitality industry trade journal, kindly described the preparation so that I could attempt to reproduce it.

This recipe is the result: a rich, tender strudel delicate enough to serve even after a rich meal.

Prepare the *pasta per strudel* and allow it to rest, according to the recipe. While the dough is resting, prepare the filling.

For the filling, press the ricotta through a fine sieve or strainer into a bowl. Stir in the sugar, then the eggs, one at a time. Stir in the vanilla, lemon zest, and cinnamon.

Pull the dough according to the instructions. Paint the surface of the dough with the melted butter, saving a tablespoon for the outside of the strudel. Strew the dough with the bread crumbs. Spread the ricotta filling over about one-third of the dough, at the end that will be rolled up first, using a metal spatula. Strew the filling with the cherries from the *conserva*.

Beginning at one of the short ends, lift the cloth and roll the strudel into a tight cylinder, folding the ends in occasionally to seal them. Line a jelly roll pan with aluminum foil and butter the foil. Roll the strudel from the cloth onto the pan, bending the strudel carefully into a horseshoe shape.

Brush the remaining butter on the outside of the strudel and bake it at 375 degrees for about 50 minutes. When the strudel is baked, it will be a very dark gold and the dough will be crisp.

1 batch **Pasta per Strudel,**
  page 115

RICOTTA AND SOUR
  CHERRY FILLING
1 pound very dry whole-milk
  ricotta, commercial or
  homemade
½ cup sugar
3 large eggs
2 teaspoons vanilla extract
1 teaspoon grated lemon zest
½ teaspoon ground
  cinnamon

8 tablespoons (1 stick)
  unsalted butter, melted
½ cup dry bread crumbs

2 *cups* Conserva di
    Amarene, *page 13,*
    well drained

Confectioners' sugar for
    finishing

Cool the strudel on the pan on a rack until just slightly warm. Slide it, still on the foil, onto a large board. Loosen it from the foil by sliding a long knife or spatula between it and the foil. Pull away the foil. Before serving, dust the strudel with the confectioners' sugar.

Makes 12 to 15 servings

Cream Puff Pastry

Cream puff pastry is one of the easiest preparations to master, and it is also well suited to relatively long advance preparation. In Italy, many different types of *bignè* (puffs) are popular, and often the pastry shops offer several varieties that differ in shape, filling, and decoration. The following variations are easy, flavorful ones whose separate elements may be prepared in advance, then assembled shortly before serving.

HINTS FOR SUCCESS WITH *PASTA BIGNÈ*

- Measure ingredients accurately. Make sure the flour is not compacted when measured or the paste will be drier than necessary and consequently rather heavy after baking.
- Stand over the pan as the water, salt, and butter are coming to a boil, and be ready to proceed immediately with the addition of the flour. If the liquid reduces by continuing to boil, the ingredients will no longer be in correct proportion, and heaviness may result.
- Make sure the eggs are at room temperature — cold eggs will cool down the paste, and a cold paste does not puff as easily during baking as a warm one.
- Proceed immediately to shaping and baking the *pasta bignè* so that it is still as warm as possible when it enters the oven, for maximum expansion and lightness.
- For advance preparation, cool the baked *pasta bignè* and place in a plastic bag. Refrigerate or freeze. Before using, place on a pan and bake at 350 degrees for about 8 minutes to warm and crisp. Cool on a rack and proceed with the recipe.

∿ ∾

Pasta Bignè

Cream Puff Paste

Combine the water, butter, and salt in a small saucepan. Place over medium heat and bring to a boil, making sure the butter is melted by stirring occasionally. Remove the pan from the heat and sift in the flour, all at once, stir until smooth, and return to the heat. Cook, stirring, about 30 seconds. Pour the paste into a bowl and beat in the eggs, one at a time. Use the paste immediately as directed in the individual recipe.

⅔ cup water
5 tablespoons unsalted butter
¼ teaspoon salt
⅔ cup all-purpose flour
3 large eggs

∿ ∾

Bignè di Ricotta

Cream Puffs Filled with Ricotta

This is one of the most popular and best-loved uses for *pasta bignè*. The paste is formed into small puffs, which, after baking, are opened and filled with a smooth ricotta cream. Vary the flavoring of the cream by changing the liqueur, if you like; an herb liqueur, like Strega, would be an interesting choice.

Line 2 cookie sheets or jelly roll pans with parchment. Place half the *pasta bignè* in a pastry bag fitted with a ½-inch plain tube (Ateco #6). Pipe 8 spheres, each about 1½ inches in diameter, and space them about 3 inches apart. Pipe the *pasta bignè* by holding the bag perpendicular to the pan and about 1 inch above it, squeezing out a sphere of the paste, then releasing the pressure and pulling away from the piped puff. If there are points of the paste in the center of the puffs, moisten a

1 batch Pasta Bignè,
preceding recipe

RICOTTA FILLING

1½ pounds whole-milk
   ricotta, commercial or
   homemade

1 cup confectioners' sugar

2 teaspoons vanilla extract

2 tablespoons anisette

3 tablespoons candied orange
   peel, rinsed and finely
   chopped

2 ounces semisweet
   chocolate, finely chopped

Confectioners' sugar for
   finishing

fingertip with water and press the points smooth. Repeat with the second half of the *pasta bignè*.

Bake the *bignè* at 375 degrees for about 20 minutes, until they are well risen and a deep gold. To test one for doneness, remove it from the oven and cut it open. If there are several filaments of the unbaked paste still clinging to the inside of the puff, continue baking for another 8 to 10 minutes. Remove the puffs to a rack to cool.

For the ricotta filling, combine the ricotta and the 1 cup confectioners' sugar in the bowl of a food processor fitted with the metal blade. Process about 30 seconds, scrape down, and process another 30 seconds, until smooth. Remove to a bowl and stir in the remaining filling ingredients.

To fill the puffs, slice the top third from each one with a sharp, serrated knife. Pipe or spoon in the filling, making sure it protrudes slightly from each puff. Replace the tops and refrigerate the puffs, loosely covered with plastic wrap, for up to 4 hours before serving. If they are baked crisp enough, they should withstand the refrigerator without becoming soggy. Dust the *bignè* with the confectioners' sugar immediately before serving.

Makes about 16 puffs

৩৫ ৫৩

Bignè alla Cioccolata

Chocolate Cream Puffs

What saves these chocolate cream puffs from banality is the sprightly seasoning in the chocolate pastry cream. The cinnamon, orange zest, and rum make for an unusual flavor coupled with the dense background of the chocolate cream. Because these are rich, they are deliberately made small.

Line 2 cookie sheets or jelly roll pans with parchment. Place half the *pasta bignè* in a pastry bag fitted with a ½-inch plain tube (Ateco #6). Pipe 15 spheres onto one of the sheets or pans, each about ¾ inch in diameter, and space them about 1½ inches apart. Pipe the *pasta bignè* by holding the bag perpendicular to the pan or sheet and about 1 inch above it, squeezing out a sphere of the paste, then releasing the pressure and pulling away from the piped puff. If there are points of the paste in the center of the puffs, moisten a fingertip with water and press the points smooth. Repeat with the second half of the *pasta bignè*.

Bake the *bignè* at 375 degrees for about 20 minutes, until they are well risen and a deep golden color. Test one to see if it is sufficiently baked by removing it from the oven and cutting it open. If there are several filaments of the unbaked paste still clinging to the inside of the puff, continue baking for another 8 to 10 minutes. Remove the puffs to a rack to cool.

For the chocolate pastry cream, bring the milk and half the sugar to a boil in a 2-quart nonreactive saucepan over medium heat.

Whisk the egg yolks in a bowl with the salt and whisk in the remaining sugar in a stream. Sift the flour over the yolk mixture and whisk in.

When the milk boils, remove from the heat and whisk one-third of it into the yolk mixture. Return the remaining milk to a boil and, beginning to whisk the milk first, pour in the yolk mixture. Continue whisking constantly until the cream thickens and comes to a boil. Allow to boil, whisking constantly, for 30 seconds.

Remove from the heat and whisk in the chocolate, cinnamon, and orange zest. Let stand 2 minutes for the chocolate to melt completely, then whisk until smooth. Pour the cream into a clean nonreactive bowl. Press plastic wrap against the surface and refrigerate until cold. Immediately before filling the *bignè*, gently stir in the rum.

To fill the *bignè*, pierce each on the bottom with a small pastry tube or chopstick. Place half the filling in a pastry bag

1 batch Pasta Bignè, *page 121*

CHOCOLATE PASTRY CREAM
2 cups milk
½ cup sugar
6 large egg yolks
Pinch salt
¼ cup all-purpose flour
4 ounces semisweet chocolate, coarsely chopped
½ teaspoon ground cinnamon
1 tablespoon grated orange zest
2 tablespoons white rum

2 tablespoons unsweetened cocoa powder and 2 tablespoons confectioners' sugar for finishing

fitted with a ¼-inch plain tube and fill the *bignè* through the openings. Place them on a pan lined with clean parchment as they are filled. Repeat with the remaining filling and *bignè*. Cover loosely with plastic wrap and keep refrigerated until serving time. Immediately before serving, combine the cocoa and confectioners' sugar and place in a fine strainer. Dust the *bignè* with the mixture.

Makes about 30 puffs

⤜ 6 ⤛

Plain Cakes and Cakes with Fruit

These cakes, either plain or with fruit, are an important part of Italian baking, both domestic and commercial. Most Italians appreciate a plain cake with coffee or tea, even for breakfast. Each region has a variation on a plain cake, like the *Torta Mantovana* (page 128) or the *Ciambella Ampezzana* (page 141), distinguished by its simplicity and purity of flavor. Some, like the *Torta Caprese* (page 130), a combination of chocolate and walnuts, and the *Torta di Nocciole alla Veronese* (page 136), flavored with hazelnuts and Marsala, are richer but are still characterized by a sophisticated simplicity.

Cakes with fruit are made with both fresh and candied or dried fruit. They may be simply flavored, like the *Torta di Pesche Caramellizzate* (page 145), an upside-down cake of caramelized peaches, or rich confections, like the *Panforte di Siena* (page 143), full of nuts, candied fruit, and spices.

Most of these cakes have excellent keeping qualities, either in a tin at room temperature or in the freezer, so that making them ahead of time eliminates last-minute fuss.

HINTS FOR SUCCESS WITH PLAIN CAKES

Cakes require a greater degree of accuracy in measuring, mixing, and baking than do pastry doughs, creams, or ices. The following hints will make the process easier to understand and to execute.

- Though many recipes for desserts other than cakes allow for a variation in measuring ingredients, this can have disastrous results with cake-making. Measure ingredients accurately.
- Have all ingredients at room temperature for greater smoothness in mixing. Cold eggs added to a mixture of creamed butter and sugar will not mix in smoothly and will cause the batter to separate and the baked cake to have a rough texture.
- In case a mixture of butter and eggs separates, warm the bottom of the mixing bowl in several inches of hot water in a bowl or the sink for 2 or 3 seconds and continue mixing until the mixture becomes smooth and creamy. Repeat the process several times if necessary.
- Mix flour carefully into cake batters. Overmixing may cause a strong gluten to develop in the batter and toughen the baked cake.
- When recipes call for whipped egg whites in a batter, follow this procedure for whipping them: place the egg whites in a clean, dry bowl. Add a pinch of salt and whip on medium speed with a hand-held mixer or a heavy-duty mixer fitted with the whip. Continue whipping until the egg whites are white, opaque, and beginning to hold their shape. Increase the speed to maximum and add the sugar in a slow stream. Continue whipping until the egg whites hold a soft peak. Immediately fold the egg whites into the batter.
- Always use the pan recommended in the recipe for baking a cake or cake layer. A different pan will alter baking time, since doneness depends mostly on the depth of batter in the pan.
- Grease the pan with very soft, but not melted, butter applied with a brush. Line the bottom with a disk of parchment or wax paper, cut to fit. If the cake sticks on the side of the pan, a knife or spatula will loosen it easily. If it sticks on the bottom, it will be impossible to remove from the pan. For a pan that is not flat, butter it carefully and coat the buttered surface with flour, adding a handful of flour to the pan and tipping the pan in all directions to cover evenly with flour. Invert the pan and tap sharply against the work surface several times to remove excess flour.

- Bake cakes in the middle level of the oven for even baking. If your oven gives off a strong bottom heat, place the cake pan on a heavy jelly roll pan or insulated cookie sheet to prevent the bottom from burning. The extra pan may increase baking time slightly, so check for doneness carefully before removing the cake from the oven.

- Most cakes are done when the center feels firm when pressed with the flat palm of the hand. Or you may use a thin knife or skewer to test doneness by plunging it into the thickest part of the cake, usually the center, and seeing if the knife or skewer emerges dry.

- Cool the cake briefly in the pan, then unmold to a rack to cool. Quickly reinvert the cake so that it cools right side up, leaving the paper on the bottom of the cake. After the cake is cool, it is easy to invert the cake again and remove the paper. Leaving the paper under the hot cake holds the cake together and makes it easier to handle.

- If you prepare a cake in advance, double-wrap it in plastic after it has cooled. Refrigerate the cake. Before serving, unwrap, cover loosely with a towel, and bring to room temperature. If leftovers of a plain cake become dry, toast them under the broiler for a minute, or use them in *Zuppa Inglese*, page 179, or *Tiramisù*, page 182.

- For cakes containing dried fruit, it may be necessary to plump the fruit if it is excessively dry. Place the fruit in a saucepan and cover with water. Bring to a boil over medium heat, drain, and place the fruit on a pan lined with paper towels to absorb excess moisture. Cool and use in the recipe. Or place the fruit in a bowl and cover with boiling water. Steep for 5 minutes and drain and dry as previously.

- For cakes containing candied fruit, rinse the fruit in a strainer under warm running water. Remove to a cutting board and cut as indicated in the recipe. Oiling the knife helps to keep the fruit from sticking during cutting.

෬ఎ ఆ෬

Torta Mantovana

Mantua Cake

Light, delicate, and delicious, this pound cake is the perfect plain cake to adorn with a few berries or to serve with tea or coffee when you want something sweet but not rich. It is sometimes referred to as *torta paradiso,* undoubtedly because of its heavenly flavor and texture. This version is based on one from the Panificio Pavesi, an unpretentious but high-quality bakery in Mantua.

16 tablespoons (2 sticks)
   unsalted butter
1 cup sugar
6 large eggs, separated
2 teaspoons vanilla extract
¾ cup all-purpose flour
1 cup cornstarch
Pinch salt

Confectioners' sugar and
   unsweetened cocoa
   powder for finishing

Butter a 10-inch springform pan and line the bottom with a piece of parchment or wax paper, cut to fit.

Beat the butter until soft and light, either by hand, with a hand mixer set at medium speed, or in a heavy-duty mixer fitted with the paddle. Beat in half the sugar and continue beating until the mixture whitens, about 3 or 4 minutes. Beat in the egg yolks, one at a time, beating smooth between each addition and making sure the mixture remains smooth and does not separate. If it does, warm briefly in a bowl of hot water and continue beating until smooth. Beat in the vanilla.

Combine the flour and cornstarch in a bowl and stir well to mix. Sift once onto a piece of wax paper to aerate.

In a clean, dry bowl, whip the egg whites with the salt until they hold a very soft peak. Increase the speed of whipping and whip in the remaining sugar in a stream, continuing to whip the egg whites until they hold a soft peak.

Fold one-third of the flour-and-cornstarch mixture into the yolk mixture, then one-third of the egg whites. Fold in half of the remaining flour mixture, then half the remaining whites. Fold in the remaining flour mixture, then the remaining whites, being careful to fold gently and thoroughly and not to deflate the batter. Pour the batter into the prepared pan and smooth the top. Bake the *torta* at 325 degrees for about 1 hour, until the cake is firm in the center. Cool in the pan for 5 minutes, then release the sides of the springform pan and slide the cake off the pan bottom to a rack to cool. When the cake is cool, wrap well in plastic and store at room temperature.

Makes about 15 servings

տ֍ ֍տ

Parrozzo di Pescara

Chocolate-Covered Almond Cake from Pescara

The half-sphere shape of the *parrozzo* recalls the *pane rozzo*, or "rough bread" — a loaf eaten by those who could not afford pasta — from which this dessert takes its name. If you do not have a heat-proof 1½-quart bowl in which to bake the *parrozzo*, use a 9-inch springform pan.

    This refined version of the cake is typical of the Pasticceria Berardo at the end of the Corso near the shore of the Adriatic in Pescara, Abruzzi's seaside resort.

Butter and flour a 1½-quart Pyrex bowl or a 9-inch springform pan and tap out the excess flour.

    In a food processor fitted with the metal blade, grind the almonds with half the sugar to a fine powder. Whisk the egg yolks in a mixing bowl and whisk in the almond-and-sugar mixture, then the almond extract. Whisk or whip by machine. Fold in the flour and butter.

    In a clean, dry bowl, whip the egg whites with the salt until they hold a very soft peak. Whipping faster, add the remaining sugar in a very slow stream, whipping until the egg whites hold a soft peak. Stir one-fourth of the egg whites into the batter, then fold in the rest with a rubber spatula.

    Pour the batter into the prepared bowl or pan and bake the

1 cup whole, blanched almonds
¾ cup sugar
5 large eggs, separated
½ teaspoon almond extract
½ cup all-purpose flour
6 tablespoons unsalted butter, melted and cooled
Pinch salt
8 ounces semisweet chocolate, finely chopped
1 tablespoon vegetable oil

parrozzo for about 45 to 50 minutes, until well risen and firm to the touch. Cool in the bowl or pan on a rack for 15 minutes, then invert onto the rack, remove the bowl or pan, and finish cooling.

Place the chocolate in a clean, dry bowl over a pan of hot (but not simmering) water. Stir to melt the chocolate and stir in the oil. Cool slightly.

Slide the cooled *parrozzo* onto a platter or cardboard disk. Brush off any crumbs and spread with the chocolate. Chill briefly to set the chocolate. Keep the *parrozzo* at a cool room temperature or in the refrigerator. If refrigerated, bring to room temperature before serving.

Makes 8 to 10 servings

⳨⳨ ⳨⳨

Torta Caprese

Neapolitan Chocolate-Walnut Cake

This rich cake derives its intense flavor from walnuts and chocolate. Although it contains very little flour, it is not difficult to prepare, and it also keeps well.

The cake develops a crust on the top during baking. Allow the cake to cool in the pan for several minutes, then scrape away the crust with a sharp knife before inverting the cake onto a rack to cool.

Torta caprese is best served at room temperature. Do not refrigerate it, even if prepared the day before — slide the cake onto a platter and wrap it well in plastic, then dust with confectioners' sugar just before serving.

Butter a 10-inch round cake pan, 2 inches deep, and cut a piece of parchment or wax paper to fit the bottom.

Chop the chocolate finely and place in a small bowl over a pan of hot water to melt, stirring occasionally. Remove the bowl from the pan and allow the chocolate to cool slightly.

Beat the butter with half the sugar until soft and light, either by hand, with a hand mixer set at medium speed, or in a heavy-duty mixer fitted with the paddle. Beat in the chocolate, then the egg yolks, one at a time, scraping the bowl and beater(s) often. Continue beating until the mixture is smooth and light.

Place the walnuts in the bowl of a food processor fitted with the metal blade and grind them until fine, pulsing the machine on and off at 1-second intervals. Be careful that the walnuts do not become pasty. Stir the walnuts into the batter, then the flour.

In a clean, dry bowl, whip the egg whites until they hold a very soft peak, and whip in the remaining sugar in a slow stream. Whip the whites until they hold a soft, glossy peak. Stir one-fourth of the whites into the batter, then fold in the rest with a rubber spatula so that no streaks remain. Pour the batter into the prepared pan and smooth the top. Bake the *torta* at 350 degrees for about 40 minutes, until the center is firm when pressed with the flat palm of your hand.

Cool the cake in the pan for 10 minutes. The cake may sink slightly, but this will not affect its texture. Trim off any loose crust and invert the cake onto a rack, remove the pan, and allow to cool completely.

Dust the cake with the confectioners' sugar and slide onto a platter.

Makes about 10 servings

6 ounces semisweet chocolate

12 tablespoons (1½ sticks) unsalted butter

⅔ cup sugar

8 large eggs, separated

1⅓ cups walnut pieces

⅓ cup all-purpose flour

Confectioners' sugar for finishing

෨෴ ෴෨

Torta di Tagliatelle

Shredded-Pasta Cake from Mantua

This unusual pastry is a specialty of Mantua's, although variations are to be found as far south as Bologna (see *Torta Ricciolina*, page 85). A cake pan is filled with alternating layers of an almond-and-macaroon mixture and thinly shredded, raw egg-pasta dough.

After baking, the pasta is crisp, sweet, and delicate, almost like the shredded phyllo pastries of the Middle East.

PASTA DOUGH
2 cups all-purpose flour
¼ teaspoon salt
3 large eggs
2 tablespoons white rum or
    brandy

ALMOND MIXTURE
1 cup whole almonds
¾ cup sugar
12 amaretti (Italian
    macaroons), such as
    Amaretti di Saronno
3 tablespoons unsweetened
    cocoa powder
1 tablespoon vanilla extract

8 tablespoons (1 stick)
    unsalted butter
¼ cup sugar

For the pasta dough, place the flour on a work surface and make a well in the center. In the well, mix the salt, eggs, and rum. Gradually draw the flour into the egg mixture to make a firm dough, adding a little more rum or brandy if the dough is too dry. Knead the dough well and set it aside to rest, wrapped in plastic, for about 30 minutes.

While the dough is resting, prepare the almond mixture. Combine the almonds and sugar in the bowl of a food processor fitted with the metal blade and reduce to a powder. Add the macaroons and continue processing until they are also reduced to a powder. Sift in the cocoa powder and process a few seconds, then pulse in the vanilla. Set aside.

Divide the dough into 4 or 5 pieces, flour them, and pass the pieces, one at a time, through a pasta machine, starting with the widest setting and ending with the next to last. Let the sheets of dough dry for at least 30 minutes on a floured surface.

Loosely roll up the sheets of pasta dough, one at a time, from one of the short ends. Slice the rolls of dough crosswise with a sharp knife, making fine shreds of dough.

Butter and flour a 10-inch springform pan and arrange a layer of the shredded pasta in the bottom. Sprinkle with the almond mixture. Continue alternating layers of the pasta and the almond mixture, ending with the pasta. Dot with the butter and sprinkle with the sugar. Bake the *torta* at 350 degrees for 30 to 40 minutes. Cool in the pan, then release the sides of the springform pan and slide the *torta* off the base onto a platter.

Serve the *torta* in thin wedges, preferably with a glass of sweet wine, since the *torta* is dry and crisp. Keep any leftover *torta* loosely covered at room temperature.

Makes 12 servings

ᗝᑌ ᑌᗝ

Fregolotta Trevigiana

Crumb Cake from Treviso

In Treviso, near Venice, there is a tradition of crumb cakes like this *fregolotta* and *Torta Sbrisolona* of Mantua (see following recipe). There are many documented versions of the *fregolotta*, some actually sponge cakes containing ground nuts. This variation is a simple one, a sort of giant cookie meant to accompany a cup of coffee or tea.

Place the almonds in the bowl of a food processor fitted with the metal blade and pulse repeatedly to grind them coarsely, leaving the largest pieces about ⅛ inch across.

Combine all the remaining ingredients except the butter in a mixing bowl. Add the almonds and stir to mix with a rubber spatula. Stir in the melted butter with the spatula so that all the dry ingredients are evenly moistened with it.

Using both hands, rub the mixture between your palms to make crumbs, the largest of which should be about ¼ inch across.

Butter a 10-inch tart pan with a removable bottom or a 9-inch glass pie plate. Scatter three-fourths of the mixture in the pan or plate and press very lightly with your fingertips to compress the mixture. Scatter the remaining crumbs on top without pressing them down.

Bake the *fregolotta* in the middle level of a preheated 350-degree oven for about 25 minutes, until the *fregolotta* is a light golden color and baked through.

Cool the *fregolotta* in the pan or plate on a rack. If using the tart pan, remove the sides and slide the *fregolotta* off the pan

1 cup whole, unblanched almonds
½ cup yellow cornmeal
2 cups all-purpose flour
1 scant cup sugar
Pinch salt
16 tablespoons (2 sticks) unsalted butter, melted and cooled

base onto a platter. If using the pie plate, leave it in the plate. Store the *fregolotta* loosely covered at room temperature.

Makes about 8 servings

❦❧

Torta Sbrisolona

Crumb Cake from Mantua

A large cookie/cake like *Fregolotta Trevigiana* (preceding recipe), the *sbrisolona* is a great specialty of Mantua's. Rows and rows of them can be found in every food and souvenir store, tightly wrapped in plastic and waiting to be swept away by eager tourists. I found tasting the tourist version a sorry experience — the label proudly proclaimed that it was made with pure vegetable shortening!

This version of the *sbrisolona* is one I worked out after tasting several in Mantua. The texture is crisp and crumbly, and the almonds add extra crunch.

*8 tablespoons (1 stick)
 unsalted butter
½ cup sugar
⅛ teaspoon salt
1¼ cups all-purpose flour
½ cup whole, unblanched
 almonds*

Beat the butter with the sugar and salt, either by hand, with a hand mixer set at medium speed, or in a heavy-duty mixer fitted with the paddle. Continue beating until the mixture is soft and smooth, about 5 minutes. Stir in the flour, then the almonds, to make a very crumbly mixture.

Butter a 9- or 10-inch tart pan with a removable bottom and press the mixture gently into it, making sure the top is fairly smooth.

Bake the *sbrisolona* at 350 degrees for about 25 minutes, until it is a light gold and fairly dry. Cool in the pan on a rack. Unmold onto a platter and serve with tea, coffee, or a glass of sweet wine.

Store at room temperature, tightly wrapped in plastic.

Makes about 6 servings

৵৩ ৎ৶

Torta di Nocciole alla Piemontese

Hazelnut Cake from the Piedmont

Another variation on the combination of cake and cookie, this time from the Piedmont. The recipe is from Claudia Verro, one of Italy's most outstanding chefs, who with her husband, Tonino, runs the charming inn La Contea, near Alba. Claudia's version is a light, delicate one, more like a cake than a cookie and thus different from the typical firm versions of this sweet.

Butter a 10-inch × 2-inch-deep cake pan and line the bottom with a piece of parchment or wax paper, cut to fit.

Place the hazelnuts on a jelly roll pan and toast them at 350 degrees for about 5 to 10 minutes, until the skins darken and slip off easily. Be careful that they do not burn. Pour the hazelnuts onto a towel, fold the towel over them, and rub to loosen the skins. Go over the hazelnuts one by one to remove the skins. Cool the hazelnuts and grind them, pulsing on and off, in a food processor fitted with the metal blade, making sure they do not become pasty. Set aside.

In a mixing bowl, whisk the eggs and salt until liquid. Whisk in the sugar and continue whisking a minute or two until light. Whisk in the butter. Mix the flour and baking powder and sift over the egg mixture. Fold in gently with a rubber spatula, adding the ground hazelnuts when the flour is almost incorporated and continuing to fold until the batter is smooth. Do not overmix or the cake will be tough.

Spread the batter evenly in the prepared pan. Bake at 350 degrees for about 30 minutes, until firm and well colored. Cool in the pan 5 minutes, then invert onto a rack. Immediately reinvert and cool right side up. After the *torta* is cool, wrap it well in plastic and store at room temperature.

Makes about 10 servings

1 cup whole hazelnuts
3 large eggs
Pinch salt
1 cup sugar
12 tablespoons (1½ sticks)
    butter, melted and cooled
1¾ cups all-purpose flour
1 teaspoon baking powder

ক্ষ্ ৻৵

Torta di Nocciole alla Veronese

Hazelnut Cake from Verona

This rich and virtually flourless cake is popular in the hazelnut-growing areas outside Verona. Although the original does not demand it, the *torta* would be wonderful served with a little lightly whipped, unsweetened cream on the side.

2 cups unblanched hazelnuts
½ cup fine, dry bread
    crumbs
4 large eggs, separated
⅔ cup sugar
3 tablespoons sweet Marsala
    or dark rum
Pinch salt
8 tablespoons (1 stick)
    unsalted butter, melted

Confectioners' sugar for
    finishing

Butter and line with paper a pan that is 10 inches in diameter and 2 inches deep.

Place the hazelnuts in a food processor fitted with the metal blade and grind them finely, pulsing on and off to avoid making them oily. Pour them into a bowl and pour the bread crumbs over them without mixing.

Beat the egg yolks in a mixing bowl and beat in the Marsala or rum, then half the sugar, and continue beating until very light, either by hand, with a hand mixer set at medium speed, or in a heavy-duty mixer fitted with the whip.

In a clean, dry bowl, whip the egg whites with the salt and continue whipping until the whites hold a very soft peak, either by hand, with a hand mixer set at medium speed, or in a heavy-duty mixer fitted with the whip. Increase the speed and whip in the remaining sugar in a slow stream. Whip the egg whites until they hold a soft, shiny peak.

Fold the yolk mixture into the whites, then fold in the hazelnut-and-bread-crumb mixture. When it is half-incorporated, pour the melted butter down the side of the bowl, continuing to fold it in until the batter is smooth. Be careful not to overmix the batter or it will deflate. Cut through the center of the bowl with a rubber spatula, making sure that the end of the spatula reaches down to the bottom of the bowl on every pass through the batter so that none of the ingredients remains un-mixed at the bottom of the bowl.

Pour the batter into the prepared pan. Bake at 350 degrees for about 30 minutes, until the top is well colored and the center is firm. Cool in the pan for a minute, then loosen it from the pan with the point of a small paring knife. Invert it onto a rack, then reinvert so it cools on the paper. Dust lightly with the confectioners' sugar. Keep the *torta* tightly covered at room temperature or in the refrigerator. If it has been refrigerated, allow it to come to room temperature before serving.

Makes about 10 servings

❧❦ ❦❧

Torta di Farina Gialla

Yellow Cornmeal Butter Cake

An almond and cornmeal pound cake, this *torta* is made in one or another form throughout northern Italy. It has a pleasantly coarse texture, very different from the delicate *Polenta Dolce* (see next recipe), and is most often served as a tea or breakfast cake.

The finely ground corn flour needed for this cake is not readily available in the United States. Consult Sources of Equipment and Ingredients, or pulverize plain cornmeal in a blender or coffee grinder.

Butter a 9-inch round pan that is 2 inches deep and line the bottom with a disk of parchment or wax paper, cut to fit. Beat the butter with an electric mixer set at medium speed until soft and light. Beat in half the sugar and continue beating until light and fluffy, about 3 minutes. Beat in the egg yolks, one at a time, beating until smooth between each addition. Stir in the lemon zest and ground almonds.

12 tablespoons (1½ sticks) unsalted butter
¾ cup sugar
4 large eggs, separated
1 teaspoon grated lemon zest
1 cup blanched almonds, ground

Pinch salt

1 cup corn flour, or cornmeal finely ground in a blender or coffee grinder

Confectioners' sugar for finishing

Whip the egg whites and salt in a clean, dry bowl until they hold a very soft peak. Whip in the remaining sugar gradually, continuing to whip the egg whites until they hold a soft, glossy peak. Stir one-fourth of the egg whites into the batter. Sift one-third of the corn flour or ground cornmeal over the batter and fold it in, then add another fourth of the egg whites, folding them in. Continue alternating the corn flour or cornmeal and the egg whites, ending with the egg whites. Pour the batter into the prepared pan and bake at 350 degrees for about 30 minutes, or until a skewer inserted in the center of the cake comes out dry.

Cool the cake in the pan about 10 minutes, then invert onto a rack to complete cooling. Before serving, dust the cake with the confectioners' sugar. Store leftovers tightly covered at room temperature.

Makes 10 to 12 servings

જી જી

Polenta Dolce

Cornmeal Sponge Cake

Though this cake exists in many forms, this version is one I worked out several years ago and have used many times with great success. Use it on its own or serve it with berries. It forms an important part of *Polenta ed Osei*, from Bergamo, page 176.

5 large eggs, separated
¾ cup sugar
1 teaspoon grated lemon zest
1 cup all-purpose flour

Butter a 10-inch × 2-inch-deep cake pan and line the bottom with a piece of parchment or wax paper, cut to fit.

Place the egg yolks in a bowl and whisk to liquefy. Whisk in half the sugar and the 1 teaspoon lemon zest and continue whisking, either by hand, with a hand mixer set at medium speed, or in a heavy-duty mixer fitted with the whip.

Combine the flour and corn flour or ground cornmeal in a small bowl and stir well to mix. Set aside.

In a clean, dry bowl, whip the egg whites with the salt and continue whipping until the whites hold a very soft peak. Increase the speed of whipping and whip in the remaining sugar in a slow stream. Continue whipping until the egg whites hold a soft peak.

Fold the yolk mixture into the whites, then fold in the flour mixture, sifting it over the egg mixture in 3 or 4 additions. Be careful to fold gently to avoid deflating the batter.

Pour the batter into the prepared pan and smooth the top. Bake the cake at 350 degrees for about 35 minutes, until it is a light golden color and firm in the center. Remove from the pan immediately by inverting onto a rack. Lift off the pan and reinvert onto a rack to cool completely. Store the cake tightly wrapped in plastic at room temperature or in the refrigerator.

¾ cup corn flour, or cornmeal finely ground in a blender or coffee grinder
Pinch salt

Makes 10 servings

ର୍ଯ୍ୟ ଓ୨

Torta di Grano Saraceno

Buckwheat and Almond Cake from Bolzano

This moist cake is a traditional dessert in the Alto Adige, or Sudtirol, Italy's German-speaking region; the name in German is *Buchweizentorte*. Bolzano, the capital of the Alto Adige, is reminiscent of a medieval Austrian town, with a wonderful open-air fruit market near the center of the oldest part of the town.

Preiselbeeren, or *mirtilli rossi* (literally, red blueberries), which resemble Scandinavian lingonberries, are used to make the preserves that fill the cake. I have found that raspberry preserves, though lacking the slight bitterness of the traditional filling, make an acceptable substitute.

12 tablespoons (1½ sticks)
   unsalted butter
¾ cup sugar
4 large eggs, separated
2 teaspoons vanilla extract
1½ cups unblanched
   almonds, ground
Pinch salt
½ cup buckwheat flour
   (available in health food
   stores)

½ cup raspberry preserves

Confectioners' sugar for
   finishing

Butter a 9-inch round pan that is 2 inches deep and line the bottom with a disk of parchment or wax paper, cut to fit. Beat the butter with an electric mixer set at medium speed until soft and light. Beat in half the sugar and continue beating until light and fluffy, about 3 minutes. Beat in the egg yolks, one at a time, beating until smooth between each addition. Stir in the vanilla and ground almonds.

Whip the egg whites and salt in a clean, dry bowl until they hold a very soft peak. Whip in the remaining sugar gradually, continuing to whip the egg whites until they hold a soft, glossy peak. Stir one-fourth of the egg whites into the batter. Sift one-third of the buckwheat flour over the batter and fold it in, then add another fourth of the egg whites and fold in. Continue alternating the flour and egg whites, ending with the egg whites. Pour the batter into the prepared pan and bake at 350 degrees for about 30 minutes, or until a skewer inserted in the center of the cake comes out dry.

Cool the cake in the pan about 10 minutes, then invert onto a rack to complete cooling. The *torta* may be prepared several days in advance up to this point. Wrap well in plastic and refrigerate.

To finish, trim the *torta* evenly with a sharp, serrated knife, if necessary. Invert the cake so that the top is underneath and slice the cake through the middle to make 2 layers. Place the bottom layer on a platter and spread with the raspberry preserves. Place the other layer on the preserves and press well to make the layers adhere. Before serving, dust the cake with the confectioners' sugar. Store leftovers tightly covered at room temperature.

Makes 10 to 12 servings

Ciambella Ampezzana

Raisin Cake from Cortina d'Ampezzo

This simple cake, a light pound cake, is typical of the down-to-earth pastries and desserts from the region known as the Ampezzana. The area's capital, Cortina d'Ampezzo, is known principally as a luxury ski resort. But before the days of tourism, the area was characterized by a simple, even austere, mountain-agriculture way of life. Although part of the Veneto, the region exhibits a cooking style with a strong Austrian/Tyrolean influence. This recipe is loosely adapted from *I dolci del Veneto* (Desserts of the Veneto), by Giovanni Capnist.

Butter and flour a 2-quart fluted pan, such as a *Gugelhupf* pan.

Place the raisins in a saucepan, cover with water, bring to a boil, and drain. Spread the raisins out on a pan covered with paper towels to absorb the excess moisture.

Beat the butter with the sugar, salt, and lemon zest until it is soft and light, either by hand, with a hand mixer set at medium speed, or in a heavy-duty mixer fitted with the paddle. Beat in the egg yolks, one at a time, beating well between additions.

Sift the flour with the baking powder and toss 2 tablespoons of the mixture with the raisins in a small bowl. Stir the remaining flour into the butter mixture alternately with the milk and *grappa* or brandy, beginning and ending with the flour. Stir in the floured raisins.

Whip the egg whites in a clean, dry bowl, either by hand, with a hand mixer set at medium speed, or in a heavy-duty mixer fitted with the whip. Continue whipping the egg whites

¾ cup raisins or currants

12 tablespoons (1½ sticks) unsalted butter

¾ cup sugar

¼ teaspoon salt

1 teaspoon grated lemon zest

5 large eggs, separated

1½ cups all-purpose flour

1 teaspoon baking powder

¼ cup milk

¼ cup grappa or brandy

Confectioners' sugar for finishing

until they hold a soft peak. Stir one-fourth of the egg whites into the batter, then fold in the rest gently with a rubber spatula.

Pour the batter into the prepared pan and bake in the middle level of a preheated 350-degree oven for about 40 minutes.

Cool the *ciambella* in the pan for 5 minutes, then invert it onto a rack. Lift off the pan and finish cooling the *ciambella*. Dust the *ciambella* with confectioners' sugar before serving.

Keep the *ciambella* loosely covered at room temperature.

Makes about 12 servings

ʕ୨ ୧ʔ

Torta di Mele Ampezzana

Apple Cake from Cortina d'Ampezzo

This quickly prepared apple cake is typical of the simple and flavorful desserts of this mountain region. Use a firm, tart apple, such as Granny Smith. Pippins or Northern Spies are excellent also, if you can find them.

8 tablespoons (1 stick) unsalted butter

½ cup sugar

Pinch salt

3 large eggs

1½ cups all-purpose flour

1 teaspoon baking powder

4 large, tart apples, about 2 pounds

1 tablespoon sugar

¼ teaspoon ground cinnamon

Combine the butter, sugar, and salt in a mixing bowl and beat until soft and light, either by hand, with a hand mixer set at medium speed, or in a heavy-duty mixer fitted with the paddle. Beat in the eggs, one at a time, beating well between each addition. Combine the flour and baking powder and sift once. Stir the flour mixture into the batter. Spread the batter evenly in the bottom of a buttered and paper-lined 9-inch springform pan.

Peel, halve, and core the apples. Cut each half into 3 or 4 wedges and arrange the wedges on their sides, overlapping slightly, on the batter, about ½ inch from the sides of the pan. Fill in the center with more apple wedges, fanning them out from the center. Sprinkle with the sugar, then the cinnamon.

Bake the *torta* in the middle level of a preheated 350-degree oven for about 40 minutes, until the apples have taken on a deep golden color and the *torta* feels firm when pressed in the center with a fingertip.

Cool the *torta* in the pan for 5 minutes, then unbuckle the sides of the springform pan and slide it off the base, still attached to the paper, to cool on a rack.

After the *torta* has cooled completely, run a knife or spatula between the *torta* and the paper, slide the *torta* from the rack onto a platter, and pull off the paper.

Keep the *torta* loosely covered at room temperature.

Makes about 8 servings

ᘒᘔ ᘓᘕ

Panforte di Siena

Spiced Fruit and Nut Cake from Siena

Siena's many pastry shops prepare an array of different *panforti*, a spicy, chewy distant cousin of fruitcake. Although recipes abound, none of Siena's *panforte* manufacturers will reveal the exact formula. This version comes from my memory of eating much *panforte* in Siena and from Giovanni Righi Parenti's wonderful chapter on *panforte* in *La grande cucina toscana* (Tuscany's Great Cooking).

Old recipes for *panforte* do not contain honey as an ingredient, because formerly a special type of candied fruit, fermented in a honey syrup, was used in the dough. Nowadays honey is added to the dough to produce a similar flavor.

Usually the *panforte* is baked in a mold lined with edible wafer paper, called *ostia* in Italian and *Oblaten* in German. Stores that carry German and Eastern European foods sell *Oblaten* for making traditional Christmas cakes and cookies. See Sources of Equipment and Ingredients or use Chinese edible rice paper, available in Asian markets, which will produce equally good results.

See the recipes for *Zuccata* (page 15) and Homemade Candied Orange Peel (page 17) if you want to start from scratch.

Edible wafer paper

⅔ cup honey

⅔ cup sugar

¾ cup candied citron or
    melon, diced

¾ cup candied orange peel,
    diced

1½ cups whole, blanched
    almonds, lightly toasted

¾ cup all-purpose flour

1 teaspoon ground cinnamon

¼ teaspoon ground coriander

¼ teaspoon ground cloves

¼ teaspoon ground nutmeg

2 tablespoons all-purpose
    flour

½ teaspoon ground
    cinnamon

Confectioners' sugar for
    finishing

Butter a 10-inch tart pan with a removable bottom. Line the
bottom of the pan with edible wafer paper or parchment. If
using parchment, butter it.

Combine the honey and sugar in a saucepan and stir to
mix. Place over low heat and bring to a boil. Simmer the
mixture for 2 minutes after it comes to a boil, without stirring.

While the sugar and honey are heating, combine the candied fruit and almonds in a heat-proof mixing bowl. In another
bowl, combine the flour and spices and stir to mix. Pour the
honey-and-sugar syrup over the candied-fruit-and-almond
mixture, add the flour mixture, and stir vigorously to combine.
Immediately scrape the dough out of the bowl into the prepared
pan. Wet the palm of one hand and press the dough into place.
Do not press too hard, since the dough will still be fairly hot.
Make the top of the *panforte* as flat as possible. Combine the
flour and cinnamon and sift over the top of the *panforte* through
a small, fine strainer.

Bake at 300 degrees for about 20 minutes, checking occasionally that the dough does not come to a boil. Cool on a rack
for 10 minutes, then loosen the *panforte* from the side of the
pan with the tip of a small knife and remove the side of the pan.
Slide a knife or spatula between the *panforte* and the pan bottom and slide it onto a rack to cool completely. If parchment
was used, invert the *panforte* and peel off the paper after the
cake has completely cooled; then reinvert.

Brush the flour and cinnamon away from the top of the
panforte and dust it with the confectioners' sugar before serving.

Keep the *panforte* in a tightly covered tin at room temperature; it will stay fresh for a month.

Makes 8 to 10 servings

Torta di Pesche Caramellizzate

Caramelized Peach Cake

This wonderful cake with caramelized peaches was probably inspired by the famous French *tarte Tatin*, in which apples are cooked in caramel, covered with pastry before being baked, and then inverted so that the caramelized apples lie on top of the pastry.

Here, butter and sugar are combined and placed in the bottom of a pan, the peaches are arranged on top, and a light cake batter is then spooned over, a little like an American upside-down cake.

Peel the peaches: if they are ripe, cut an X on the blossom end of each and plunge them into boiling water, leaving them in the water for about 30 seconds. Remove from the water with a slotted spoon or skimmer and place in a bowl of cold water. Starting from the X's, pull the skin away from the peaches, using the point of a small paring knife. If the peaches resist or are underripe, peel them with a knife. Halve and pit each peach and cut each half into 4 or 5 wedges.

Melt the butter in a 9-inch nonstick sauté pan or frying pan with an oven-proof handle. Stir in the sugar and continue cooking until the mixture turns a deep golden brown, stirring constantly. (The butter may appear to have separated from the sugar — this does not matter.) If you overcook the caramel and it darkens too much, it will be bitter. Remove from the heat and immediately arrange the peach wedges in the caramel, making a row of the wedges perpendicular to the sides of the pan all around, with the wedges skinned side down. Fill in the center with more wedges, skinned side down. Then use the remaining wedges, skinned side up, to fill in between the first wedges, as in the illustration.

*4 or 5 ripe peaches, about
  2½ pounds
4 tablespoons unsalted butter
⅓ cup sugar*

CAKE BATTER
*8 tablespoons (1 stick)
  unsalted butter
½ cup sugar
¼ teaspoon salt
3 large eggs
1¼ cups all-purpose flour
1 teaspoon baking powder*

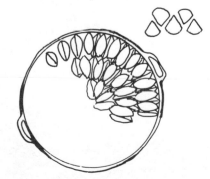

Place the pan over low heat and begin to cook the peaches. At first the caramel will melt and combine with the juices coming from the peaches. After about 5 minutes, the peaches will be swimming in caramelized juices. Continue cooking until the juices reduce to a thick syrup, about 10 minutes. If the center remains watery when the juices have thickened at the edges of the pan, remove some of the excess juice from the center with a spoon, shaking the pan gently to mix the juices without disturbing the arrangement of the peaches. Remove from the heat and cool.

Beat the butter, sugar, and salt until soft and light, either by hand, with a hand mixer set at medium speed, or in a heavy-duty mixer fitted with the paddle. Beat in the eggs one at a time, beating smooth between each addition. Sift the flour and baking powder together and stir into the butter-and-egg mixture. Spoon the batter over the peaches, making sure to cover them with an even layer of the batter.

Bake at 350 degrees for about 30 minutes, until the cake batter is baked through and the peach juices are thick and bubbling. Cool the *torta* in the pan for about 5 minutes.

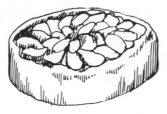

To unmold the cake, invert a platter or cardboard disk on top of the pan and, grasping both the handle of the pan and the platter, with your hands well covered with kitchen towels (mitts are perfect for this), invert the *torta* onto the platter. Leave the pan in place, give it several sharp raps, and lift it off. Watch closely as the pan comes off in case any of the peach wedges stick to the pan, so that you can remove them from the pan and replace them on the *torta.*

Serve the *torta* warm. Store it loosely covered at room temperature. Since the cake batter is moist, the juices that seep into it will not make the *torta* excessively soggy, and leftovers will keep well for a day or two.

Makes 8 servings

∽ 7 ∽

Layer Cakes

Italian cakes are rich, elaborate creations that can be surprisingly easy to prepare. Less fussy than French-style cakes, Italian ones tend to use lighter fillings, like pastry cream, whipped cream, and ricotta cream. Layers are often moistened with liqueurs or liqueur-flavored syrups before being spread with a filling, and the outsides are often finished simply with a dusting of amaretti crumbs or chocolate shavings.

I have deliberately avoided the types of cakes now popular in the pastry shops of many Italian cities, which are overly derivative of the modern French style. Filled with mousses and Bavarian creams, they are indeed lovely cakes but have little or no relation to the Italian baking tradition. Italians love to experiment with new foods, especially American ones, but I feel no need to include their experiments with foreign flavors and techniques.

Most of the layer cakes here are regional in nature. Although Sicilian *cassata* is a popular dessert throughout Italy, it will not be found in many pastry shops outside Sicily. The same is true of Parma's *Duchessa di Parma* (page 166) and of Bergamo's *Polenta ed Osei* (page 176), a lighthearted cake that imitates a mound of polenta topped with grilled quail, in the same spirit as Vienna's chocolate-almond cake masquerading as a roast loin of venison.

Related to layer cakes in that they contain the same component parts are Italy's wonderful *zuppe*, layers of cake, soaked with syrup, alternating in a bowl with soft, creamy fillings. Too delicate to be unmolded, these *zuppe* are served from the bowl in which

they are assembled, like the famous *Zuppa Inglese* (page 179) —
an Italian variation on an English trifle — and the ubiquitous *Ti-*
ramisù (page 182), a rich combination of sponge cake, espresso
syrup, and filling made with *mascarpone*, Italy's super-rich cream
cheese.

Plan ahead when making layer cakes. Remember that in most
cases all the component parts may be prepared over a span of
several days before assembling and serving the cake, allowing the
baker to be relaxed enough to enjoy the cake with the guests.

HINTS FOR SUCCESS WITH LAYER CAKES

- Have all component parts and equipment ready before beginning
  to assemble the cake.
- Make sure that the cake is completely cool before you attempt to
  slice it into thin layers. Prepare the cake a day or two in
  advance and wrap and chill it. If the cake is freshly baked, it
  will shred badly when sliced.

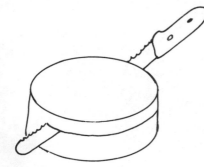

- Use a long, sharp, serrated knife for slicing a cake into thin
  layers. Even a professional pastry chef can't slice a cake into
  even layers with a short, dull knife. Holding the knife blade
  parallel to the work surface, about ⅓ or ¼ inch down from
  the top of the cake (depending on how many layers are to be
  cut) mark a line with the blade of the knife all around the side
  of the cake. Continue pressing the knife into this initial line,
  revolving the cake against the knife until you cut all the way
  through.
- Assemble the cake on a cardboard disk of the same diameter as
  the pan in which the cake was baked. You can buy boards
  from a friendly bakery or at a kitchenware or cake-decorating
  store. Paper wholesalers carry them in quantity, if you wish
  to invest and split a case with friends. Although I admit that
  the cardboard gives a slightly commercial look to a finished
  cake, the convenience and ease of handling far outweigh any
  aesthetic reservations.

- Use a thin-bladed metal spatula, preferably an offset one, for
  finishing the outside of a cake. A bulkier tool will prevent you
  from spreading the outside coating flat and straight.

༄ ༄

Pan di Spagna
Sponge Cake

This typical Italian sponge cake probably originated in Naples during the rule of the Spanish Bourbons; hence its name, which means "Spanish bread." It is a very fine-grained cake layer thanks to the addition of cornstarch. In Italy, potato starch would be more common, but the cornstarch gives identical results.

4 large eggs, separated
1 teaspoon vanilla extract
¾ cup sugar
½ cup all-purpose flour
½ cup cornstarch
Pinch salt

Butter and line with paper a 9- or 10-inch round cake pan that is 2 inches deep.

In a medium mixing bowl, whisk the egg yolks with the vanilla. Whisk in half the sugar and continue to beat until very light and frothy, about 5 minutes, either by hand, with a hand mixer set at medium speed, or in a heavy-duty mixer fitted with the whip.

Combine the flour and cornstarch and sift once to aerate.

In a clean, dry bowl, beat the egg whites with the salt until they hold a very soft peak, either by hand, with a hand mixer set at medium speed, or in a heavy-duty mixer fitted with the whip. Beating faster, add the remaining sugar in a very slow stream, beating until the egg whites hold a firm peak.

Fold the yolk mixture into the whites with a rubber spatula. Sift the flour and cornstarch over the eggs in 3 additions, folding them in gradually. Do not overmix the batter.

Pour the batter into the prepared pan and smooth the top. Bake at 350 degrees for 30 to 40 minutes, until it is well risen and feels firm when pressed gently with the palm of your hand.

Immediately loosen the layer from the side of the pan with a small knife or spatula. Invert the layer onto a rack and leave the paper stuck to it. Turn the layer right side up and cool it on a rack.

Unless you are going to use the layer within a few hours, double-wrap tightly in plastic and keep in the refrigerator up to 5 days, or freeze.

Makes one 9- or 10-inch cake layer

VARIATIONS
Flavor the batter with 1 teaspoon grated orange or lemon zest or 1 tablespoon anisette.

༄ ༀ

Torta Margherita
_____

Margherita Cake Layer

This delicate cake layer was undoubtedly named after Margherita di Savoia, Italy's second and most popular queen. As in a French *génoise*, the eggs and sugar are warmed before being whipped, so that they can absorb the air that leavens the batter while the cake is baking. These layers keep extremely well. Double-wrap them in plastic wrap and store in the refrigerator up to 5 days or in the freezer up to 1 month.

4 large eggs
2 large egg yolks
Pinch salt
¾ cup sugar
1 cup all-purpose flour

Butter a 9-inch × 2-inch-deep round cake pan and line with a disk of parchment or wax paper, cut to fit.

Combine the eggs, egg yolks, salt, and sugar in a heat-proof bowl or the bowl of an electric mixer. Whisk to mix. Place the bowl over a pan of gently simmering water and whisk until warm, about 100 to 105 degrees. Remove the bowl from the pan and whip on high speed with a hand mixer or a heavy-duty mixer fitted with the whip. Continue whipping until the egg mixture has lightened in color, cooled, and increased about 4 times over its original volume.

Sift the flour over the egg foam in 3 or 4 additions, folding it in gently but thoroughly with a rubber spatula. Pour the batter into the prepared pan.

Bake the layer at 325 degrees for about 30 minutes, until it is well risen, firm to the touch, and a deep golden color. Remove to a work surface and insert the point of a small knife between the layer and the side of the pan. Loosen the layer from the pan and invert it onto a rack. Leave the paper in place and immediately invert the layer again onto another rack, to cool. Cool to room temperature and double-wrap in plastic for storage.

Makes one 9-inch cake layer

VARIATION

For a chocolate layer, substitute ⅔ cup all-purpose flour and ¼ cup unsweetened alkalized (Dutch-process) cocoa powder for the 1 cup flour. Sift the flour and cocoa together several times to crush any lumps in the cocoa.

ళ్ళ ిళ

Meringa

———

Meringue

Though meringue is supposedly Swiss in origin, Italians are great lovers of the confection in all forms. Pastry shops abound with delicate, baroque pyramids of meringues interspersed with rosettes of whipped cream and strawberries or generous dollops of chestnut filling. Chocolate meringue, flavored with cocoa powder, is also popular, but it is not, to my knowledge, used interchangeably in desserts with plain meringue.

The type of meringue most commonly found in these desserts is an ordinary one in which the egg whites are whipped, a portion of the sugar is then whipped into the whites, and the remaining sugar is folded in by hand. The meringue is piped or shaped and baked at a low temperature until crisp and dry. For chocolate meringue, cocoa powder is added with the second part of the sugar, and it is baked at a slightly higher temperature. So-called Italian meringue, the type in which the egg whites are whipped and then doused with a hot sugar syrup, is used mainly in the preparation of *semifreddi,* or frozen desserts (see Ices and Frozen Desserts), to lighten them and is not usually baked.

4 large egg whites
Pinch salt
1 cup sugar

Place the egg whites in a clean, dry 2- to 3-quart bowl and add the salt. Whip the egg whites, either with a hand mixer set at medium speed or in a heavy-duty mixer fitted with the whip. Continue whipping until the whites become very white and opaque and begin to hold their shape. Increase the speed to the maximum and whip in half the sugar in a slow stream. Continue whipping until the mixture is very stiff but not dry and grainy. Stop whipping, scatter the remaining sugar over the mixture, and fold it in by hand, using a rubber spatula. Immediately, shape and bake the meringue according to the individual recipe.

VARIATION

Chocolate Meringue
Add 3 tablespoons cocoa powder to the second half of the sugar.

❧ ❧

Sacripantina

Sacripante Cake

The name of this dessert derives from a character in Lodovico Ariosto's poem *Orlando Furioso* called Sacripante — the name means "hoodlum" or "swashbuckler"! Supposed to have originated in Liguria, the cake is often covered with tiny dice of sponge cake. I prefer using macaroon crumbs on the outside, as in the original version of the cake, since they add a distinctive flavor as well as a subtle crunch.

For the buttercreams, place the egg yolks in the bowl of a heavy-duty mixer fitted with the whip and whisk in the sugar. Whisk in the brandy; then place the bowl over a pan of simmering water, whisking constantly, until the mixture thickens slightly. Return the bowl to the mixer and whip on medium speed until cold and increased in volume. Beat in the butter in 5 or 6 additions and continue beating until the mixture is smooth and light.

To flavor, cut the chocolate finely. Bring the water to a boil and remove from the heat. Add the chocolate and stir to melt. Cool. Then combine the instant espresso powder and water and stir to dissolve. Divide the buttercream in half and beat the cooled chocolate mixture into one half and the coffee into the other.

To assemble the cake, cut two ¼-inch slices from the layer, using a long, serrated knife. Place one slice on a cardboard cake circle and reserve the other one, covered with plastic wrap. Cut the remainder of the cake into 3 layers, then trim one to a 9-inch-round layer, the second to an 8-inch-round layer, and the third to a 7-inch-round layer. Reserve the scraps, covered with plastic wrap.

Moisten the layer on the cardboard lightly with the Marsala, then spread with one-fourth of the coffee buttercream. Place the 9-inch-round layer on the cream and moisten with the Marsala. Spread with one-fourth of the chocolate buttercream. Place the 8-inch-round layer on the cream, moisten with the Marsala, and spread with another fourth of the coffee cream. Place the 7-inch-round layer on top and moisten. Spread with another fourth of the chocolate cream. Use the scraps to form a rough 6-inch-round layer on the cream. Moisten and spread with another fourth of the coffee cream. Use more scraps to form a 5-inch-round layer, then moisten and spread with another fourth of the chocolate cream. Use the last scraps to form a 4-inch-round layer. Moisten it and spread the entire outside of the cake with the remaining coffee cream. Make a cut in the reserved layer, from the center outward to the edge,

1 Pan di Spagna, *page 149, 10 inches in diameter, baked and cooled*
1 cup sweet Marsala

COFFEE AND CHOCOLATE BUTTERCREAMS
4 large egg yolks
½ cup sugar
⅓ cup Italian or other brandy
24 tablespoons (3 sticks) unsalted butter
3 ounces semisweet chocolate + 2 tablespoons hot water
2 tablespoons instant espresso powder + 2 tablespoons hot water
2 dozen amaretti (Italian macaroons), such as Amaretti di Saronno

Confectioners' sugar for finishing

and arrange it on the stacked dome of layers, smoothly, overlapping it at the cut. Moisten with the last Marsala and spread with the remaining chocolate cream. Crush the amaretti coarsely and press them all over the outside of the cake. Chill the cake so that the filling sets. Dust lightly with the confectioners' sugar just before serving.

Makes 12 servings

CASSATA ALLA SICILIANA

SICILIAN RICOTTA-FILLED CAKE

The derivation of the name of this cake is uncertain, but everyone agrees that it is a delicate and delicious dessert. The name may come from either the Arabic *quas'at*, a large, round pan, or the late Latin *caseus*, meaning "cheese."

As with so many other Sicilian desserts, there are numerous versions of the *cassata*, as well as many different ways to finish it. The version that seems the most usual calls for lining a pan with sponge cake, or *pan di spagna*, filling it with ricotta cream, as for cannoli, and then covering the filling with more *pan di spagna*. The *cassata* can be finished with a covering of green *pasta reale*, Sicily's version of marzipan (used for many other confections besides the *cassata*), white sugar icing, or a combination. Candied fruit cut into ribbons and formed into stylized flowers is used for decoration, alone or together with elaborate rococo swirls of chocolate or sugar icing piped through a paper cone.

The first version that follows is typical of the kind found in the great pastry shops of Palermo and Catania. The second is a home-style *cassata*, less elaborate in the finishing but just as good.

Cassata di Pasticceria

Pastry Shop–Style *Cassata*

All the components of the *cassata* may be prepared 1 or 2 days in advance of assembling it, although the *cassata* needs to chill at least 12 hours before it is unmolded.

For the rum syrup, bring the sugar and water to a boil in a small saucepan, stirring occasionally. Cool and add the rum.

For the ricotta cream filling, press the ricotta through a fine sieve or strainer into a mixing bowl. Sift the confectioners' sugar over it and beat it in, either by hand, with a hand mixer set at medium speed, or in a heavy-duty mixer fitted with the whip. Continue beating the ricotta and sugar until the mixture is very light. Beat in the vanilla, cinnamon, and rum, then stir in the chocolate and candied fruit. Cover the bowl with plastic wrap and refrigerate until needed.

Butter a 9- or 10-inch springform pan, depending on the size of the *pan di spagna* layer, and line it with plastic wrap. Cut two ¼-inch horizontal layers from the *pan di spagna*, using a long, sharp, serrated knife (see the introductory material on page 148 for an explanation and illustration). Cut the remaining *pan di spagna* into ½-inch-thick vertical slices.

Place one of the horizontal layers in the bottom of the springform pan and moisten it lightly with the rum syrup, using a brush. Use the vertical slices to line the sides of the pan, and moisten them from the inside.

Pour the ricotta cream filling into the lined pan and smooth the top with a spatula. Moisten the other round layer lightly with the syrup and place it on the filling. Press gently with the palm of your hand to make the layer adhere to the filling. Cover the pan with plastic wrap. Refrigerate the *cassata* to

One 9- or 10-inch Pan di Spagna, *page 149, baked and cooled*

RUM SYRUP
½ cup sugar
½ cup water
2 tablespoons white rum

RICOTTA CREAM FILLING
2 pounds dry ricotta, commercial or homemade
2 cups confectioners' sugar, sifted after measuring
2 teaspoons vanilla extract
¼ teaspoon ground cinnamon
2 tablespoons white rum
3 ounces semisweet chocolate, finely chopped
½ cup candied citron or Zuccata, *page 15*

APRICOT GLAZE
1 cup apricot preserves
2 tablespoons water

PASTA REALE
8 ounces canned almond
    paste
1 cup confectioners' sugar
2 tablespoons light corn
    syrup
Green food coloring
Cornstarch

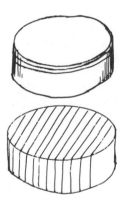

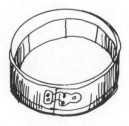

make the filling firm again. Reserve any remaining syrup for finishing the *cassata*.

While the *cassata* is chilling, prepare the apricot glaze. Combine the preserves and water in a saucepan and bring to a boil over low heat, stirring occasionally. At the boil, strain the glaze into another pan and reserve it, covered loosely, at room temperature.

For the *pasta reale*, cut the almond paste into 1-inch cubes and place in the bowl of a heavy-duty mixer fitted with the paddle or in the bowl of a food processor fitted with the metal blade. Add the sugar and corn syrup. In the mixer, mix on low speed until the *pasta reale* begins to mass around the paddle. In the food processor, pulse the mixture on and off about 10 times. The mixture will remain crumbly.

Turn the mixture out onto a clean work surface and add a drop of green food coloring to it. Knead the *pasta reale* smooth by hand. Form the *pasta reale* into a thick sausage shape, double-wrap in plastic, and reserve in a sealed plastic bag at room temperature.

To unmold the *cassata*, remove the plastic wrap from the top of the springform pan and invert a flat platter or disk of cardboard on it. Invert the pan onto the platter or cardboard and release the sides of the pan. Lift it off carefully, then lift off the pan base and peel off the plastic wrap. Moisten the outside of the *cassata* with the remaining rum syrup, using a brush.

Return the apricot glaze to a boil over low heat and brush it all over the outside of the *cassata*.

Unwrap the *pasta reale* and knead it smooth by hand, shaping it into a 5-inch disk. Dust the work surface and the *pasta reale* very lightly with the cornstarch. Roll the *pasta reale* out into a thin 14-inch disk, moving the *pasta reale* often and adding cornstarch to the work surface to prevent sticking. Slide both hands under the *pasta reale* and center it on the *cassata*, allowing the excess to drape over the sides. Press the top smooth with the palm of one hand and press the *pasta reale* against the sides of the *cassata*, easing it into place to prevent pleats and tears. Trim away the excess at the base of the *cassata* with a small, sharp knife.

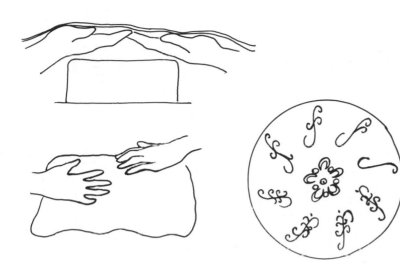

DECORATIONS
Red candied cherries
1 ounce semisweet chocolate
½ teaspoon oil
Candied citron

To decorate the *cassata*, cut the chocolate finely and place it in a small heat-proof bowl. Place the bowl over a pan of hot (but not simmering) water and stir until the chocolate is melted. Stir in the oil. Make a small cone from parchment, as in the illustration, fill with the chocolate, fold the top to seal it, and cut a small hole in the pointed end with sharp scissors. Pipe a series of designs on the top of the *cassata*, as in the illustration. Cut the citron into thin strips and make a geometric design with it and the cherries in the center of the *cassata*.

Keep the *cassata*, loosely covered with plastic wrap, in the refrigerator until time to serve it.

Makes 12 servings

ର୍ତ୍ତ ଓ

Cassata Casalinga

Home-Style *Cassata*

This is a version I have used for a long time. Although not as authentically Sicilian as the preceding one, it is a delicate and pretty dessert.

The ingredients are the same as in the previous recipe, but there is no apricot glaze or *pasta reale*. Slice the *pan di spagna* into 3 or 4 horizontal layers. Place one layer on a platter or cardboard disk and moisten it lightly with the rum syrup. Spread with some of the ricotta cream. Continue with the remaining layers and the remaining ricotta cream. Moisten the top of the *cassata* with the remaining syrup and cover with 1½ cups heavy cream whipped with 3 tablespoons sugar and 1 teaspoon vanilla extract. Press chopped, blanched pistachios against the sides of the *cassata* and decorate the top with the candied cherries and citron.

ର୍ତ୍ତ ଓ

Torta Delizia

Layer Cake with Baked Almond-Paste Topping

If there is one cake that you will see in almost every pastry shop in Italy, this is it. The interior of the *torta* is usually fairly plain, normally a sponge cake layer simply filled with jam or a bit of pastry cream. All of the cake's glory is in its exterior, completely covered with a macaroon paste piped on with a star tube. After a quick baking for the macaroon covering, the cake is glazed to make the coating shine.

The *torta delizia* has much in common with the Viennese

Punschtorte. Though the flavors and ingredients differ, each is an intensely sweet cake meant to be savored in tiny portions and is much more like a confection than a dessert.

This version is a very personal one. It is a distillation of the many interpretations of this dessert I have tasted over the course of close to twenty years. I have attempted to keep the sugariness to a minimum so that the real almond flavor emerges.

If I have some pastry cream on hand, I add 1 teaspoon grated lemon zest to it and use it with the jam for the filling, though this makes the *torta* keep less well.

Bake and cool the *torta margherita* the day before assembling the cake, if possible, to make the layer easier to slice.

For the syrup, combine the sugar and water in a small saucepan, bring to a boil over low heat, and cool. Stir in the liqueur.

For the macaroon topping, break the almond paste into 1-inch pieces and place in the bowl of a heavy-duty mixer fitted with the paddle or in a food processor fitted with the metal blade. Add one egg and mix on lowest speed or pulse in with the processor. After the first egg is almost absorbed, add the second and beat or process until smooth. Add the liqueur and work smooth again. Cover the topping until assembling the cake to prevent it from crusting.

To assemble, slice the *torta margherita* into 2 equal layers, slicing horizontally through the center of the cake. Invert the top layer onto a cardboard disk or a heat-proof platter so that what was the top of the cake as it baked is now facedown on the cardboard. Moisten with half the syrup, using a brush. Spread the layer evenly with the ¼ cup jam.

Moisten the cut surface of the remaining layer with half the remaining syrup and invert it onto the jam. The top surface of the cake is now what was the bottom as it baked. Moisten with the remaining syrup.

Spread 2 tablespoons of the macaroon topping around the sides of the cake, so that the piped macaroon mixture will adhere to it and not fall off. Place half the remaining mixture

One 9- or 10-inch Torta Margherita, *page 150, baked and cooled*

SYRUP
2 tablespoons sugar
¼ cup water
3 tablespoons Maraschino liqueur or Kirsch

MACAROON TOPPING
1 pound canned almond paste
2 large eggs
1 tablespoon Maraschino liqueur

FILLING
¼ cup sour cherry jam, homemade or commercial, or other sharp-tasting jam

GLAZE
¼ cup light corn syrup
½ teaspoon vanilla extract

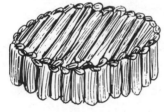

in a pastry bag fitted with a ¼-inch star tube (Ateco #1) and pipe a series of vertical lines against the sides of the *torta*. The lines should touch and cover the entire outside of the cake. Pipe the remaining macaroon mixture on the top of the *torta* in a series of horizontal lines that touch each other. Last, pipe a border at the top edge of the cake where the piping on the top and sides meet. See the illustration for help with the piping. Chill the *torta.*

Preheat the oven to 425 degrees. Place the chilled *torta* on a stack of 3 or 4 jelly roll pans or cookie sheets; using several will insulate the bottom of the cake and prevent it from heating. If using jelly roll pans, invert the stack so that the cake lies on the back of a pan for easy removal afterward. Place the *torta* in the middle level of the oven. Bake for about 10 minutes, until the macaroon topping is a deep golden color. Turn the pans or sheets frequently so that the topping colors evenly. Remove from the oven and leave on the pans or sheets.

Heat the corn syrup and vanilla to boiling and use a soft brush to glaze the still-hot surface of the topping. An atomizer also works very well for glazing the topping. Remove the *torta* from the pans or sheets and cool on a rack. Keep loosely covered with aluminum foil at room temperature or refrigerate. If you refrigerate the *torta*, bring it to room temperature before serving.

Makes 12 generous servings

༚༝ ༝༚

Baci alle Fragole
—
Meringue Kisses with Whipped Cream and Strawberries

These luscious pyramids of baked meringues interspersed with whipped cream and tiny wild strawberries normally make their appearance along with the first *fragoline* — wild strawberries — in

May. Earlier in the year the dessert is usually made with a sweet-ened chestnut puree (see the variation at the end of this recipe).

The quality of this dessert depends mostly upon the freshness and ripeness of the berries. Wild strawberries are infrequently available in the United States, but perfectly ripe local berries are a good alternative. And, although not particularly Italian, a mixture of raspberries, blueberries, and currants or gooseberries would make an admirable substitute.

For success with this recipe, choose a day that is neither overly hot nor humid for assembling, so that the cream does not melt during the time it takes to put together the *baci* at room temperature. After they are assembled, they will hold up well in the refrigerator for 3 or 4 hours; a longer wait will make the meringues soften too much.

Line 3 cookie sheets with parchment or aluminum foil. Prepare the meringue and place half of it in a pastry bag fitted with a ½-inch star tube (Ateco #4). Holding the bag perpendicular to the pan and about 1 inch above it, squeeze out large stars, about 1½ inches in diameter, spacing them at least 1 inch apart. Bake the meringues at 225 degrees (or the lowest setting on your oven) for about 1 hour. Press one to see if it is dry: if only the smallest amount in the center of the meringue remains moist (no more than the center ¼ inch), remove from the oven and cool on the pans. For advance preparation, leave the baked meringues on the parchment or foil, stack the parchment or foil, and slide into a large plastic bag. Keep in a cool, dry place for up to several weeks before assembling the dessert. If nec-essary, crisp the meringues at the lowest oven temperature and allow to cool before proceeding with assembling the dessert.

To assemble, rinse the strawberries and hull all but 6 of them (these will be used as a garnish). Halve the hulled straw-berries. Combine the cream with the sugar and vanilla and whip until firm but not separated.

Arrange 8 or 10 of the meringues in the center of a large, round platter, in the form of a circle about 8 inches in diameter. Spoon about ⅓ cup of the whipped cream on top of the me-

2 batches Meringa, *page 151*

2 pints small, ripe strawberries

2 cups heavy whipping cream

3 tablespoons sugar

2 teaspoons vanilla extract

Confectioners' sugar for finishing

ringues and scatter with some of the halved berries. Place more meringues on top of the berries, using about 6, as in the illustration. Repeat with more cream and berries, adding 1 or 2 more layers of the meringues, with fewer meringues in each layer. End with a single meringue at the top.

To decorate the dessert, place the remaining whipped cream in a pastry bag fitted with a ½-inch star tube and pipe rosettes of the cream between the meringues. Halve the remaining 6 berries, cutting right through the hulls, and arrange them here and there on the pyramid of meringues, pressing them into the whipped cream. Cover loosely with plastic wrap and refrigerate until serving time, no longer than 4 hours. Immediately before serving, dust with the confectioners' sugar.

Makes 12 ample servings

VARIATION

Baci alle Castagne
Prepare the meringues as in the preceding recipe. Substitute the chestnut puree from *Monte Bianco* (page 224) for the strawberries and assemble the dessert in the same way as for the previous recipe. After assembling, decorate with rosettes of whipped cream and chestnut puree.

ɔ୨ ୧ɕ

Torta Stregata
___

"Bewitched" Cake with Strega Liqueur

One of my earliest childhood memories centers on my fascination with the rough engraving of dancing witches on the label of a bottle of Strega. A syrupy herb liqueur, somewhat similar to Chartreuse, Strega is manufactured in Benevento, very near Grottaminarda, the birthplace of my mother and her ancestors. Consequently, Strega often appeared as an after-dinner drink on holidays and special occasions. Though I cannot recall its being used in a dessert in our home, I have often made this *torta*, which embodies many of the tastes and textures of Italian cakes. It is strictly my invention and is not part of any particular Italian dessert tradition.

For the syrup, bring the sugar and water to a boil in a small saucepan. Cool and stir in the liqueur.

For the pastry cream, bring the milk to a boil with half the sugar. Whisk the egg yolks in a bowl with the salt and whisk in the remaining sugar. Sift the flour over the yolk mixture and whisk in smoothly. When the milk boils, whisk one-third of it into the yolk mixture. Return the remaining milk to a boil and whisk in the yolk mixture, continuing to whisk until the cream thickens and comes to a boil. Boil, whisking constantly to prevent scorching, for 1 minute. Scrape the cream into a clean, nonreactive bowl and press plastic wrap against the surface. Refrigerate until cold, about 2 hours. Before assembling the cake, gently stir in the liqueur.

To assemble the cake, cut the *torta margherita* into 3 horizontal layers using a sharp, serrated knife. Place one layer on a cardboard disk or platter and moisten with one-third of the syrup. Spread with half the pastry cream. Top with another layer, another third of the syrup, and the remaining pastry cream. Place the last layer on top of the filling and moisten with the remaining syrup. Cover the *torta* loosely with the plastic wrap while preparing the meringue.

For the meringue, combine the egg whites and sugar in the bowl of an electric mixer or in a heat-proof bowl. Place the bowl over a pan of simmering water and whisk the mixture gently until the egg whites are hot and the sugar has dissolved. Test a little of the mixture on your fingertip to see if the sugar has dissolved completely. Whip by machine on medium speed until cooled and increased in volume, 4 or 5 minutes.

Spread the meringue all over the outside of the *torta*. Use a pastry bag fitted with a ½-inch star tube (Ateco #4) to pipe

One 9- or 10-inch Torta Margherita, *page 150, baked and cooled*

SYRUP
¼ cup sugar
⅓ cup water
¼ cup Strega liqueur

PASTRY CREAM
1 cup milk
¼ cup sugar
3 large egg yolks
Pinch salt
3 tablespoons all-purpose flour
1 tablespoon Strega liqueur

MERINGUE
4 large egg whites
¾ cup sugar

the remaining meringue in a series of rosettes on the top of the *torta*.

Preheat the oven to 425 degrees. Place the *torta* on a stack of 3 or 4 jelly roll pans or cookie sheets; this will insulate the bottom of the cake and prevent it from heating. If using jelly roll pans, invert the stack so that the cake lies on the back of a pan for easy removal afterward. Place the *torta* in the middle level of the oven. Bake for about 5 minutes, checking frequently that the meringue does not burn, until the meringue is a light golden color. Turn the pans or sheets frequently so that the meringue colors evenly. Remove from the oven and leave on the pans or sheets. Refrigerate the *torta* and serve on the day it is assembled.

Makes 10 servings

ಿನ ೧ಿ

Torta Bignè

Cream Puff Cake

Typical of the fancy cakes found in the elegant pastry shops of Milan and other northern Italian cities, the *torta bignè* is not particularly difficult to prepare. To make the process easier, bake the *pan di spagna* and the *bignè* the day before. Refrigerate them, tightly covered. Reheat and cool the *bignè* before assembling the cake.

One 10-inch Pan di Spagna, *page 149, baked and cooled*

SYRUP
¼ cup sugar
½ cup water
¼ cup white rum

For the syrup, bring the sugar and water to a boil. Cool the syrup and add the rum.

For the *pasta bignè*, bring the water, butter, and salt to a boil in a small saucepan. Remove from the heat and sift in the flour, all at once. Stir until smooth and return to the heat. Cook, stirring, about 30 seconds. Pour the paste into a bowl and beat in the eggs, one at a time. Pour the paste into a pastry bag fitted with a ¼-inch plain tube (Ateco #2) and pipe the paste in

⅜-inch spheres onto two parchment-lined cookie sheets. Bake the *bignè* at 375 degrees for about 15 minutes, until well puffed and deep golden. Cool the *bignè* on the sheets.

For the chocolate filling, bring the cream to a boil, remove from the heat, and add the chocolate. Allow to stand 2 minutes, then whisk until smooth. Pour into a bowl and cool. Beat the butter until soft and light. Beat in the cooled chocolate mixture, beating until light. Beat in the rum, a little at a time, being careful not to overbeat, which will make the filling separate.

To assemble the cake, cut two ¼-inch slices from the layer, using a long, serrated knife. Place one slice on a cardboard cake circle and reserve the other one, covered with plastic wrap. Cut the remainder of the cake into 3 layers, then trim one to a 9-inch-round layer, the second to an 8-inch-round layer, and the third to a 7-inch-round layer. Reserve the scraps, covered with plastic wrap. Moisten the layer on the cardboard lightly with the syrup, then spread with one-eighth of the filling. Place the 9-inch-round layer on the filling and moisten with the syrup. Spread with another eighth of the filling. Place the 8-inch-round layer on the filling, moisten with the syrup, and spread with another eighth of the filling. Place the 7-inch-round layer on and moisten. Spread with another eighth of the filling. Use the scraps to form a rough 6-inch-round layer on the filling. Moisten and spread with another eighth of the filling. Use more scraps to form a 5-inch-round layer; moisten and spread with another eighth of the filling. Use the last scraps to form a 4-inch-round layer. Moisten it and spread the entire outside of the cake with another eighth of the filling. Make a cut in the reserved layer, from the center outward to the edge, and arrange it smoothly, on the stacked dome of layers, overlapping it at the cut. Moisten with the last syrup and spread with the remaining filling. Press the *bignè* all over the outside of the cake so they adhere.

Chill briefly to let the filling set. Dust lightly with the confectioners' sugar, then with the cocoa powder. Keep the cake at a cool room temperature until served. Store leftovers in the refrigerator. Bring to room temperature before serving.

Makes about 12 servings

PASTA BIGNÈ
⅔ *cup water*
5 tablespoons unsalted butter
¼ *teaspoon salt*
⅔ *cup all-purpose flour*
3 large eggs

CHOCOLATE FILLING
1 cup heavy whipping cream
12 ounces semisweet chocolate, finely chopped
8 tablespoons (1 stick) unsalted butter, softened
3 tablespoons white rum

Confectioners' sugar and unsweetened cocoa powder for finishing

ॐ ॐ

Duchessa di Parma

Duchess of Parma Cake

Named for Maria-Luigia Bonaparte, the still-beloved duchess of Parma, this cake is a fantasy of chocolate and *zabaione*, with an unequaled richness and delicacy. This version is based on one from Ugo Falavigna's beautiful Pasticceria Torino, in Parma, where Falavigna prepares all the classic desserts and pastries of Parma's rich gastronomic history.

One 9- or 10-inch chocolate Torta Margherita, *page 151, baked and cooled*

SYRUP
¼ cup sugar
⅓ cup water
3 tablespoons white rum

CHOCOLATE FILLING
12 ounces semisweet chocolate
1 cup heavy whipping cream
2 tablespoons white rum

ZABAIONE
3 large egg yolks
⅓ cup sugar
1½ tablespoons all-purpose flour
¾ cup sweet Marsala
1 tablespoon white rum (optional)

For the syrup, bring the sugar and water to a boil in a small saucepan. Cool and stir in the rum.

For the chocolate filling, cut the chocolate finely and set aside. Bring the cream to a boil in a saucepan and remove from the heat. Stir in the chocolate and allow to stand about 2 minutes so that the chocolate melts. Whisk until smooth. Whisk in the rum, scrape into a bowl, and cool at room temperature or in the refrigerator until set and thickened.

For the *zabaione*, place the egg yolks in a medium bowl and whisk in the sugar in a stream. Sift the flour over the mixture and whisk it in smoothly. Whisk in the Marsala and optional rum.

Pour the mixture into a nonreactive saucepan, preferably enameled iron, and set the pan over medium heat. Whisk constantly until the *zabaione* thickens and comes to a boil. Allow to boil, still whisking, for 1 minute.

Scrape the *zabaione* into a clean bowl, press plastic wrap against the surface, and refrigerate it to cool.

To assemble the cake, trim the top of the *torta margherita* so it is even and slice into 4 layers. Place one layer on a cardboard disk and moisten with one-fourth of the syrup. Spread the layer with half the cooled *zabaione*. Top with another layer and moisten with another fourth of the syrup. Beat the chocolate filling, either with a hand mixer set at medium speed or in a heavy-duty mixer fitted with the paddle, for about 1 minute, until it has lightened. Spread half the filling on the layer. Top with another layer and moisten with another fourth of the syrup. Spread the layer with the remaining *zabaione*. Top with the last layer and moisten with the remaining syrup. Use half the remaining chocolate filling to cover the top and sides of the cake. Cover the entire outside of the cake with the chocolate shavings, pressing them against the cake with a metal cake spatula. Use the remaining filling to pipe a border around the top of the cake, using a pastry bag fitted with a ¼-inch star tube (Ateco #1). Chill the cake to allow the fillings to set.

Serve the cake at room temperature. Store leftovers in the refrigerator.

Makes 12 servings

Chocolate shavings for finishing

೨ ೧ ೧ ೨

Torta Nera con le Noci

"Black" Cake with Walnuts from Bologna

A specialty of Atti, Bologna's magnificent bakery and pasta store, this cake has a rich, satisfying flavor. The slight bitterness of the walnuts complements the chocolate perfectly.

Butter and line with paper a 10-inch round pan.

For the chocolate walnut cake batter, cut the chocolate finely and place in a small bowl over hot water to melt, stirring occasionally. Beat the butter with half the sugar until soft and light, either by hand, with a hand mixer set at medium speed, or in a heavy-duty mixer fitted with the paddle. Beat in the chocolate, then the egg yolks, one at a time. Combine the walnuts and flour and stir into the butter-and-chocolate mixture. In a clean, dry bowl, whip the egg whites until they hold

CHOCOLATE WALNUT CAKE BATTER
6 ounces semisweet chocolate
12 tablespoons (1½ sticks) unsalted butter, softened
⅔ cup sugar
8 large eggs, separated
1½ cups walnuts, ground
⅔ cup all-purpose flour

SYRUP
¼ cup sugar
⅓ cup water
3 tablespoons dark rum

CHOCOLATE FILLING
1½ pounds semisweet
    chocolate
1½ cups heavy whipping
    cream
⅓ cup light corn syrup
4 tablespoons butter,
    softened
4 tablespoons dark rum

Walnut halves for finishing

a very soft peak, and whip in the remaining sugar in a slow stream. Whip the whites until they hold a soft peak. Stir one-fourth of the whites into the batter, then fold in the rest with a rubber spatula. Pour the batter into the prepared pan and bake at 350 degrees for about 35 minutes. Unmold the cake onto a rack to cool.

For the syrup, bring the sugar and water to a boil in a small saucepan. Cool and stir in the rum.

For the chocolate filling, cut the chocolate finely and set aside. Bring the cream and corn syrup to a boil in a saucepan and remove from the heat. Stir in the chocolate and allow to stand about 2 minutes so that the chocolate melts. Whisk smooth, whisk in the butter and rum, and scrape into a bowl. Cool at room temperature or in the refrigerator until set and thickened.

To assemble the *torta*, trim the top of the cooled cake layer so it is even and slice into 2 layers. Place one layer on a cardboard disk and moisten with some of the syrup. Beat the chocolate filling, either with a hand mixer set at medium speed or in a heavy-duty mixer fitted with the paddle, for about 1 minute, until it is lightened. Spread one-fourth of the filling on the layer. Top with the other layer and moisten with more syrup. Use another fourth of the filling to cover the top and sides of the cake.

Use the remaining filling to decorate the *torta:* with a pastry bag fitted with a small star tube, such as Ateco #2, pipe a series of vertical lines, touching, around the sides of the *torta.* Pipe a perpendicular lattice of 5 lines in each direction on the top of the *torta.* Then pipe a series of rosettes at the top border. Fill each opening in the lattice with a walnut half.

Serve the *torta* at room temperature. Store leftovers in the refrigerator.

Makes 12 servings

∽◌ ◌∾

Torta di Amaretti

Macaroon Cake

This cake, a typical product of the sophisticated pastry shops of Milan, uses the small, crisp, commercially made amaretti both as a decoration and an ingredient in the cake batter. Though pastry shops produce many different types of macaroons, the crisp amaretti are usually purchased from a manufacturer for this type of dessert. Like pastry chefs in Italy, I use the Lazzaroni Amaretti di Saronno, which are easy to find in the United States.

Butter a 9-inch round cake pan, 2 inches deep, and line with a disk of parchment or wax paper, cut to fit.

For the cake batter, whip the egg yolks and ground amaretti, either with a hand mixer set at medium speed or in a heavy-duty mixer fitted with the whip. Continue whipping until very light, about 5 minutes. In a clean, dry bowl whip the egg whites with the salt until they are opaque and beginning to hold their shape. Increase the speed to maximum and whip in the sugar in a slow stream. Continue whipping the egg whites until they hold a soft peak. Fold the yolks into the whites, then fold in the ground almonds. Sift the flour over the batter and fold it in quickly but gently, using a rubber spatula. Pour the batter into the prepared pan. Bake the cake layer at 350 degrees for about 30 minutes, until it is well colored and a toothpick inserted in the center emerges clean. Cool 5 minutes in the pan, then invert onto a rack to finish cooling. For advance preparation, wrap the cake layer in plastic wrap and refrigerate several days or freeze up to 1 month.

For the syrup, bring the sugar and water to a boil in a small saucepan. Cool and stir in the rum.

For the amaretti filling, bring the milk to a boil with half the sugar. Whisk the egg yolks in a bowl with the salt and

CAKE BATTER
4 large eggs, separated
½ cup amaretti (Italian macaroons), ground in a food processor (about 15)
Pinch salt
½ cup sugar
¾ cup blanched almonds, ground
⅔ cup all-purpose flour

SYRUP
¼ cup sugar
⅓ cup water
¼ cup white rum

GREAT ITALIAN DESSERTS

AMARETTI FILLING

1 cup milk

¼ cup sugar

3 large egg yolks

Pinch salt

3 tablespoons all-purpose
flour

16 tablespoons (2 sticks)
unsalted butter, softened

2 teaspoons vanilla extract

½ cup amaretti (about 15),
ground in a food
processor

Crushed amaretti and
confectioners' sugar for
finishing

whisk in the remaining sugar. Sift the flour over the yolk mixture and whisk in smoothly. When the milk boils, whisk one-third of it into the yolk mixture. Return the remaining milk to a boil and whisk in the yolk mixture, continuing to whisk until the cream thickens and comes to a boil. Boil, whisking constantly to prevent scorching, for 1 minute. Whisk in the vanilla. Scrape the pastry cream into a clean nonreactive bowl and press plastic wrap against the surface. Refrigerate until cold, about 2 hours. To finish the filling, beat the butter, either with a hand mixer set at medium speed or in a heavy-duty mixer fitted with the paddle. Continue beating until the butter is very soft and light. Add the pastry cream all at once, then continue beating until smooth and light, about 5 minutes. Beat in the ground amaretti.

To assemble the *torta*, cut the cooled layer into 2 horizontal layers, using a sharp, serrated knife. Place one layer on a cardboard disk or a platter and moisten with half the syrup, using a brush. Spread the layer with one-third of the amaretti filling. Place the second layer on top of the filling and moisten with the remaining syrup. Spread the outside of the cake smoothly with another third of the filling. Press the crushed amaretti all over the outside of the cake so they adhere. Use the remaining filling to pipe a border around the top of the *torta* with a pastry bag fitted with a ¼-inch star tube (Ateco #1). Refrigerate the cake to allow the filling to set. Cover loosely with plastic wrap and refrigerate. Remove from the refrigerator about 1 hour before serving. Dust with the confectioners' sugar immediately before serving.

Makes 12 servings

ᡇ ᡇ

Torta Gianduja

Chocolate-Hazelnut Cake from the Piedmont

The combination of chocolate and hazelnuts probably originated in the Piedmont, where the *torta gianduja* is a popular dessert. Not very sweet, the *torta* derives its richness from the chocolate filling.

For the *gianduja* cake batter, preheat the oven to 350 degrees and set a rack in the middle level. Butter a cake pan that is 10 inches in diameter and 2 inches deep and line the bottom with a piece of parchment or wax paper, cut to fit. Butter the paper and dust the entire inside of the pan with flour, tapping out the excess. Place the hazelnuts on a jelly roll pan and toast them for about 10 to 15 minutes, until the skin is loose and rubs off easily. Place the hazelnuts on a towel, fold the towel over them, and rub to loosen the skins. Meanwhile, cut the chocolate finely and place in a small bowl over hot water to melt, stirring occasionally.

Combine the hazelnuts and ½ cup of the sugar in a food processor fitted with the metal blade. Pulse repeatedly to grind the sugar-and-hazelnut mixture finely. Add 2 tablespoons of the butter and continue pulsing the mixture until it is reduced to a paste, about 2 minutes. Remove the hazelnut paste from the work bowl and cool it. (Processing the mixture to a paste will heat it up somewhat.)

Beat the remaining butter with a hand-held electric mixer on medium speed until smooth and soft, about 2 minutes. Beat in the cooled hazelnut paste until smooth, then the cooled chocolate. Beat in the egg yolks one at a time, continuing to beat until the mixture is smooth and fluffy. Stir in the flour. In a clean, dry bowl, whip the egg whites, using a hand-held electric mixer on medium speed, until the egg whites are white,

GIANDUJA *CAKE BATTER*
1½ cups whole hazelnuts
7 ounces semisweet chocolate
¾ cup sugar
12 tablespoons (1½ sticks) unsalted butter
8 large eggs, separated
¾ cup all-purpose flour

CHOCOLATE FILLING
12 ounces semisweet chocolate
1 cup heavy whipping cream
4 tablespoons unsalted butter, softened

¼ cup Italian brandy or white rum

CHOCOLATE GLAZE
6 ounces semisweet chocolate
¾ cup heavy whipping cream

opaque, and beginning to hold their shape. Increase the speed to maximum and whip in the remaining ¼ cup sugar in a stream. Continue whipping the egg whites until they hold a soft peak. Stir one-fourth of the egg whites into the batter to lighten it, then fold in the remaining egg whites. Pour the batter into the prepared pan and bake at 350 degrees until firm in the center and well risen, about 35 to 40 minutes. Unmold the cake layer onto a rack to cool.

For the filling, cut the chocolate finely and set aside. Bring the cream to a boil in a saucepan and remove from the heat. Stir in the chocolate and allow to stand about 2 minutes so that the chocolate melts. Add the butter, whisk smooth, scrape into a bowl, and cool at room temperature until set and thickened, about 2 hours. Just before assembling the cake, beat the filling with a hand-held electric mixer on medium speed for about 1 minute, until the filling is light in color and texture.

To assemble the cake, trim the top of the layer so it is even and slice into 2 layers. Place one layer on a cardboard disk and moisten with some of the brandy or rum. Spread half the chocolate filling on the layer. Top with the other layer and moisten with more brandy. Use half the remaining filling to cover the top and sides of the cake, reserving the remainder to decorate the cake later on. Refrigerate the cake but leave the reserved filling at room temperature.

For the chocolate glaze, cut the chocolate finely and set aside. Bring the cream to a boil in a small saucepan and remove from the heat. Add the chocolate and allow to stand 3 minutes for the chocolate to melt. Whisk until smooth and cool to room temperature.

Place the chilled cake on a rack set over a jelly roll pan and pour the cooled glaze through a strainer onto the cake. Cover the entire cake, using a spatula to touch up the bare spots. Chill the cake for 15 minutes to allow the glaze to set.

To decorate the cake, place the reserved filling in a small pastry bag fitted with a ⅜-inch plain tube (Ateco #0). Write ''Gianduja'' on the cake. Refrigerate until 1 hour before serving.

Makes 12 servings

Zuccotto alla Ricotta

Ricotta Dome

The elegant pastry shops of Rome and Florence are filled with *zuccotti* of all flavors and appearances. Most of them are made in slightly flared, round-topped, bucket-shaped molds, although the classic *zuccotto* shape is a half-sphere. The name derives from *zucco*, or pumpkin; the dome shape recalls that of Florence's Duomo, or cathedral. The *zuccotto* is a thoroughly Florentine dessert.

I like to use a 1½-quart Pyrex bowl to mold the *zuccotto* — the shape is just right — and even though the bottom of the bowl is slightly flat, the finished dessert looks like a perfect dome.

A *zuccotto* is made in a mold lined with liqueur-soaked *pan di spagna*, filled with a creamy mousse, and covered with another disk of *pan di spagna* to make a stable base for the dessert after it is unmolded. Although a *zuccotto* is usually left fairly plain after it is unmolded, I like to cover this one with whipped cream for a more finished appearance.

Butter a 1½-quart bowl and line it with plastic wrap. Slice a horizontal disk from the *pan di spagna*; reserve for covering the filling. Cut the rest of the *pan di spagna* into 2 large wedges. Cut the wedges into thin horizontal slices and line the bowl with them. Sprinkle with the rum.

One 9- or 10-inch Pan di Spagna, *page 149, baked and cooled*
White rum

FILLING
1 pound whole-milk ricotta, commercial or homemade
1 cup confectioners' sugar

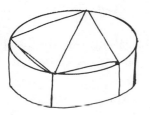  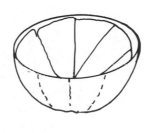

1 tablespoon anisette

3 tablespoons white rum

1 envelope unflavored gelatin

3 tablespoons unsalted
   pistachios, chopped

3 tablespoons bittersweet
   chocolate, chopped

1 cup heavy whipping cream

1 cup heavy whipping cream
   and 2 tablespoons
   unsalted pistachios,
   chopped, for finishing

Combine the ricotta and confectioners' sugar in a food processor fitted with the metal blade and process until smooth, about 1 minute. Combine the anisette and 3 tablespoons rum in a small heat-proof bowl and sprinkle the gelatin on the surface of the liquids. Allow to soak until the liquids are absorbed, then place over a small pan of simmering water to melt. Whisk the dissolved gelatin into the ricotta mixture, then stir in the pistachios and chocolate. Whip the cream until it holds its shape but is not too stiff and fold it in.

Pour the filling into the prepared bowl and cover with the reserved disk of *pan di spagna*. Cover with plastic wrap and chill until set, about 6 hours or overnight.

Invert a platter on the mold and invert the *zuccotto* onto the platter. Remove the bowl and the plastic wrap. Whip the cream and spread it on the outside of the *zuccotto*, using a metal spatula. Sprinkle with the chopped pistachios.

Refrigerate the *zuccotto*, loosely covered with plastic wrap, until serving time, no more than 6 or 8 hours later.

Makes 8 ample servings

✿✿ ✿✿

Zuccotto Toscano

Florentine Chocolate-Hazelnut Dome

This version is based on one that I tasted at the elegant Pasticceria Robiglio, in Florence, where the proprietor, Signore Pietro Robiglio, shared his vast knowledge of the traditions of Tuscan desserts and pastries.

One 9- or 10-inch Pan di
   Spagna, *page 149,*
   baked and cooled

For the fillings, place the hazelnuts on a baking pan and toast them at 350 degrees for about 15 minutes, or until the skins slip off easily. Pour the hazelnuts onto a towel, cover them with the towel, and rub to loosen the skins. Separate the hazelnuts from the skins, cool, and chop them coarsely. Chop 8 ounces of the chocolate finely. Bring 1¼ cups of the cream to a boil, remove from the heat, and add the chopped chocolate. Allow to stand 5 minutes, then whisk until smooth. Pour into a bowl and refrigerate until cold and set, several hours or overnight. Combine the remaining ¾ cup cream with the sugar and whip it until stiff peaks form. Cover and refrigerate. Chop the remaining 2 ounces of chocolate finely and set aside.

Butter a 1½-quart Pyrex bowl and line it with plastic wrap, pressing the wrap closely against the inside of the bowl. Cut a ¼-inch horizontal layer from the *pan di spagna* and reserve it, covered, to form the base of the dessert later. Cut the rest of the cake into ¼-inch vertical slices. Use the slices to line the bowl, fitting them tightly against each other, without overlapping them. Sprinkle the slices with 2 tablespoons of the rum.

Whip the chilled chocolate filling by machine until light, about 30 seconds on medium speed. Spread the chocolate filling about 1 inch thick on the slices of *pan di spagna* lining the bowl, leaving room in the center for the remaining filling. Remove the whipped cream from the refrigerator and rewhip until firm, beating in the remaining rum. Fold in the hazelnuts and reserved chopped chocolate and place the filling in the center of the other filling. Spread the top so it is even, cover with the reserved horizontal layer of *pan di spagna*, and trim the layer so that it is the same diameter as the inside of the bowl.

FILLINGS
½ cup whole hazelnuts
10 ounces semisweet chocolate
2 cups heavy whipping cream
¼ cup sugar
3 tablespoons white rum

Confectioners' sugar and unsweetened cocoa powder for finishing

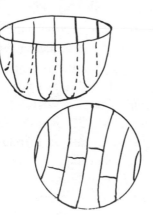

Chill the *zuccotto* in the freezer for 3 or 4 hours to allow the fillings to set. Keep in the refrigerator until serving time. To unmold, invert a platter onto the *zuccotto*, reinvert, and lift off the bowl. It should lift off easily. If not, wipe the outside of the bowl with a cloth wrung out in very hot water so that the butter between the bowl and the plastic wrap melts. Invert, lift off the bowl, and peel away the plastic wrap. If the outside of the *zuccotto* is very dry, brush with a little more rum. Dust heavily with the confectioners' sugar and lightly with the cocoa. To prepare the *zuccotto* in advance, unmold it on the platter, cover with plastic wrap, and refrigerate until serving time. Dust with the confectioners' sugar and cocoa immediately before serving.

Makes 8 to 10 servings

Polenta ed Osei

Polenta with Birds

This fanciful cake, a specialty of Bergamo, is meant to imitate a mound of polenta served with grilled game birds. The cake is molded in a half-sphere shape and covered with yellow marzipan; then some marzipan is colored and flavored with cocoa powder and molded in the shape of several tiny (cooked) birds. A spoonful of apricot glaze completes the effect, fixing the birds to the mound of "polenta" and imitating the cooking juices of the birds.

The pastry shops of Bergamo abound with this cake. Variously referred to as *polenta* or *polentina*, the cake comes in many different sizes and styles. Though many are based on a plain sponge cake like *pan di spagna*, I tasted several that used a corn flour–based cake to further the conceit of the presentation. The version that follows is a synthesis of many I tasted in Bergamo; the hazelnut filling complements the corn flavor of the cake and the richness of the marzipan perfectly.

For the syrup, bring the sugar and water to a boil in a small saucepan. Cool and stir in the rum.

For the hazelnut filling, bring the milk to a boil with half the sugar. Whisk the egg yolks in a bowl with the salt and whisk in the remaining sugar. Sift the flour over the yolk mixture and whisk smoothly. When the milk boils, whisk one-third of it into the yolk mixture. Return the remaining milk to a boil and whisk in the yolk mixture, continuing to whisk until the cream thickens and comes to a boil. Boil, whisking constantly to prevent scorching, for 1 minute. Scrape the pastry cream into a clean nonreactive bowl and press plastic wrap against the surface. Refrigerate until cold, about 2 hours. To finish the filling, beat the butter, either with a hand mixer set at medium speed or in a heavy-duty mixer fitted with the paddle. Continue beating until the batter is very soft and light. Add the pastry cream all at once, then continue beating until smooth and light, about 5 minutes. Beat in the vanilla and the ground hazelnuts.

For the marzipan, cut the almond paste into 1-inch cubes and place in the bowl of a heavy-duty mixer fitted with the paddle or in the bowl of a food processor fitted with the metal blade. Add the sugar and corn syrup. In the mixer, mix on low speed until the marzipan is beginning to mass around the paddle. In the food processor, pulse the mixture on and off about 10 times. The mixture will remain crumbly.

Turn the mixture out onto a clean work surface and add a drop of yellow food coloring. Knead the marzipan smooth by hand. Form the marzipan into a thick sausage shape. Double-wrap in plastic and reserve in a sealed plastic bag at room temperature.

To assemble the dessert, butter a 1½- to 2-quart bowl and line with plastic wrap. Cut the *polenta dolce* into thin vertical slices and line the bowl with them without overlapping the slices. Sprinkle the syrup over the cake slices in the bowl and

1 Polenta Dolce, *page 138, baked and cooled*

SYRUP
¼ cup sugar
⅓ cup water
¼ cup white rum

HAZELNUT FILLING
1 cup milk
¼ cup sugar
3 large egg yolks
Pinch salt
3 tablespoons all-purpose flour
16 tablespoons (2 sticks) unsalted butter, softened
2 teaspoons vanilla extract
1 cup hazelnuts, toasted, skinned, and finely ground

MARZIPAN
8 ounces canned almond paste
1 cup confectioners' sugar
2 tablespoons light corn syrup
Yellow food coloring

Cornstarch
*2 tablespoons unsweetened
     cocoa powder*
⅓ cup apricot preserves

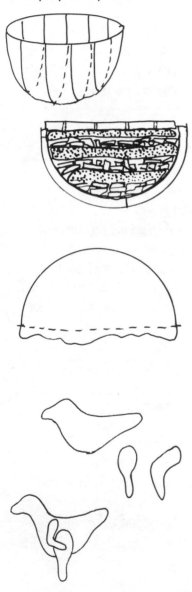

spread on a rough layer of the filling. Fill the lined bowl with alternating layers of the cake slices, cut to make even layers and moistened with syrup, and the filling. End with a layer of unmoistened cake slices, which will form the base of the dessert when it is unmolded. Reserve about ½ cup of the filling to mask the outside of the dessert so that the marzipan will adhere. Cover tightly with plastic wrap and refrigerate until firm, several hours or overnight. Wrap and refrigerate the reserved filling if you are going to store it more than a few hours.

To finish the dessert, unwrap the bowl and invert a platter on it. Invert and remove the bowl and plastic wrap. Spread the outside of the dessert with the reserved filling. (If the filling was refrigerated, let it come to room temperature.) Dust a work surface with cornstarch and place the marzipan on it. Dust the marzipan lightly with the starch and roll it out into a thin disk. Roll the marzipan up on the rolling pin and drape it over the dessert. Smooth it into place with the palms of your hands and trim away the excess at the base with a small, sharp knife. Knead the cocoa powder into the marzipan scraps and make 3 or 4 small birds, as in the illustration. Heat the apricot preserves to liquefy them; strain. Heat again until reduced and thick. Place a spoonful of the reduced preserves on the very top of the dessert and allow to cool and dry several minutes. Place the birds in the glaze, close together. Cover loosely with plastic wrap and refrigerate until serving time. Remove from the refrigerator 1 hour before serving so that the filling softens somewhat. Refrigerate leftovers tightly covered with plastic wrap.

Makes 12 ample servings

ᘯ ᘰ

Zuppa Inglese

Italian Trifle

A type of trifle, *zuppa inglese* takes its name from *inzuppare,* which means "to soak" or "moisten," since the layers of cake are soaked with syrup. Different interpretations of the *zuppa* abound, and, like a trifle, it can be varied endlessly according to what is on hand when it is prepared. This version is one that I have served and taught for about ten years, and it never fails to impress. When I have them on hand, I drizzle a few spoonfuls of sour cherry preserves on the layers of *pan di spagna* under the orange pastry cream.

This is an excellent dessert for entertaining because it can be prepared the day before and improves on standing. Cover it with the whipped cream a few hours before serving.

In Italy an unusual liqueur called Alchermes is used to flavor the syrup. Alchermes has a spicy flavor, a bright red color, and the distinction of being colored with cochineal, a natural dye derived from cochineal flies, similar to ladybugs. To achieve a similar flavor, I add a cinnamon stick and several cloves to the syrup, along with rum and vanilla. Needless to say, I dispense with the red color. If you are interested in acquiring Alchermes, it is available all over Italy — the bottle I have comes from Ai Monasteri, a store near the Piazza Navona in Rome that sells products from convents and monasteries.

One 9- or 10-inch Pan di Spagna, *page 149, baked and cooled*

For the pastry creams, bring the milk and half the sugar to a boil in a large nonaluminum saucepan. Whisk the egg yolks in a mixing bowl and beat in the remaining sugar. Sift in the flour and beat it in. Beat one-third of the boiling milk into the yolk mixture. Return the remaining milk to a boil and beat in the

PASTRY CREAMS

1 quart milk

1½ cups sugar

12 large egg yolks

⅔ cup all-purpose flour

1 tablespoon grated orange
    zest

2 teaspoons vanilla extract

6 ounces semisweet
    chocolate, coarsely
    chopped

½ teaspoon ground
    cinnamon

SYRUP

⅔ cup sugar

⅔ cup water

2-inch piece of cinnamon
    stick

3 whole cloves

½ cup dark rum

1 cup heavy whipping cream

Chocolate shavings

Candied fruit

yolk mixture, continuing to beat until the pastry cream thickens and comes to a boil. Cook, beating, about 1 minute.

Remove the cream from the heat and divide between 2 bowls, pouring half the mixture into each. Stir the orange zest and vanilla into one and the chocolate and cinnamon into the other. Press plastic wrap against the surface of each and refrigerate until cold.

For the syrup, bring the sugar and water to a boil in a small pan with the cinnamon and cloves. Cool, remove the spices, and add the rum.

To assemble the *zuppa inglese*, cut the *pan di spagna* into vertical slices about ¼ inch thick. Place a layer of the slices in the bottom of a 2½-quart glass bowl and moisten with the syrup, using a brush. Spread with half the orange pastry cream. Cover with another layer of *pan di spagna* slices, moisten with the syrup, and cover with a layer of the chocolate pastry cream. Repeat with the remaining ingredients, ending with a layer of the cake slices and moistening with the remaining syrup. Cover with plastic wrap and refrigerate up to 24 hours at this point.

To finish the *zuppa inglese*, whip the cream until it holds its shape but is not too firm, and spread it on the top. Decorate with some chocolate shavings and the candied fruit. Keep the *zuppa inglese* in the refrigerator.

Makes 12 servings

ℛℳ ℳℛ

Zuppa alle Fragole

Trifle Pudding with Ricotta and Strawberries

This pudding, layered in a bowl like *Zuppa Inglese* (see preceding recipe), was inspired by a delicious little tart filled with ricotta cream and covered with wild strawberries from the Pasticceria Spinelli, in Catania. This version, which combines syrup and *pan di spagna*, concentrates the flavors so well that the substitution of cultivated strawberries for wild ones is less noticeable.

Like all *zuppe*, this dessert has the virtue of total advance preparation. Prepare it the day before, cover it tightly with plastic wrap, and refrigerate until serving time, adding the strawberry decoration a few hours before serving.

For the syrup, combine the sugar and water in a saucepan and bring to a boil. Cool and stir in the rum and orange juice.

Place two-thirds of the sliced strawberries in a bowl and pour the syrup over them. Let them sit for several hours at room temperature to macerate. Keep the remaining berries covered in the refrigerator until ready to decorate the dessert.

For the ricotta cream filling, combine all the filling ingredients in a food processor fitted with the metal blade and process about 30 seconds. Scrape down the work bowl and process again, until smooth.

To assemble the *zuppa*, drain the strawberries and reserve the syrup. Cut the *pan di spagna* into vertical slices about ¼ inch thick and place one-fifth of the slices in the bottom of a 2- to 2½-quart glass serving bowl. Moisten with one-fifth of the syrup and spread with one-fourth of the ricotta cream filling. Strew with one-fourth of the strawberries. Continue layering the cake, syrup, filling, and berries, ending with a layer of the cake and the last of the syrup. If you are preparing the dessert the day before or more than 3 or 4 hours in advance, cover well with plastic wrap and refrigerate.

To finish the dessert, arrange the reserved sliced strawberries in a decorative pattern on the top layer of cake: start closest to the edge of the bowl and make a row of the slices, points radiating outward. Make a concentric row inside the first with the points of the berries overlapping the first row to prevent the top layer of cake from showing through. Continue until the top of the dessert is covered. Wrap loosely in plastic wrap, so as not to disturb the pattern of the berry slices, and refrigerate until serving time. Store leftovers tightly covered with plastic wrap in the refrigerator.

Makes 12 ample servings

One 9- or 10-inch Pan di Spagna, *page 149, baked and cooled*

SYRUP
⅔ *cup sugar*
⅔ *cup water*
¼ *cup white rum*
¼ *cup orange juice, strained*

3 *pints strawberries, rinsed, hulled, and sliced*

RICOTTA CREAM FILLING
2 *pounds whole-milk ricotta, commercial or homemade*
2 *cups confectioners' sugar*
2 *teaspoons vanilla extract*
1 *teaspoon grated orange zest*

ᏮᎧ ᏮᎧ

Tiramisù

Coffee and *Mascarpone* Sponge Cake Pudding

One of the traditional desserts of Treviso, not far from Venice, *tiramisù* has hundreds of variations. The dessert has achieved an incredible popularity, both all over Italy as well as in the United States. One reason it has won such a following in Italy is that, when made from *savoiardi,* Italian ladyfingers — which can be purchased easily in Italian pastry shops — most of the work is already accomplished. All that remains is to mix a few egg yolks and some sugar into the *mascarpone,* brew a pot of coffee to moisten the *savoiardi,* layer the filling and moistened *savoiardi* together, and shake a little cocoa powder over the top.

The following version is one I have been using successfully for about five years. It uses *pan di spagna* instead of *savoiardi;* espresso sweetened with sugar syrup and flavored with brandy; and a filling made from *zabaione, mascarpone,* and a little whipped cream. The top is covered with more whipped cream to give it a finished appearance.

Don't hesitate to create variations; some chefs like to add a little chopped chocolate to the filling, or even a bit of crushed *Torrone* (page 251) or *Croccante* (page 249).

One 9- or 10-inch Pan di Spagna, *page 149, baked and cooled*

ESPRESSO SYRUP
⅓ *cup sugar*
¼ *cup water*
½ *cup very strong brewed espresso*
¼ *cup Italian or other brandy*

For the syrup, combine the sugar and water in a saucepan and bring it to a boil. Cool and stir in the espresso and brandy.

For the *zabaione* filling, beat the egg yolks in the bowl of an electric mixer or another heat-proof bowl and beat in the sugar and Marsala. Whisk over a pan of simmering water until thickened. Remove and beat, either with a hand mixer set at medium speed or in a heavy-duty mixer fitted with the whip, until cold. Smash the *mascarpone* in a bowl with a rubber spatula until it is smooth. Fold in the *zabaione.* Whip the cream and fold it in.

Cut the *pan di spagna* into vertical slices about ¼ inch thick. Place a layer of the slices in the bottom of a shallow 2-quart dish, such as a gratin dish, and soak with one-third of the syrup, using a brush. Spread with half the filling. Repeat with the *pan di spagna*, another third of the syrup, and the remaining filling. Place a last layer of *pan di spagna* on the top and soak with the remaining syrup.

Whip the cream with the sugar until it holds its shape and spread it on the surface of the dessert. Decorate with the cinnamon and ground coffee or the cocoa powder. Refrigerate for several hours before serving.

Makes 12 servings

VARIATION
Substitute a layer of *Polenta Dolce* (page 138) for the *pan di spagna*. Omit the espresso from the syrup so that the corn flavor is apparent. This makes an unusually good and thoroughly nontraditional twist on the traditional *tiramisù*.

ZABAIONE *FILLING*
3 large egg yolks
⅓ cup sugar
⅓ cup sweet Marsala
½ pound mascarpone, *at
    room temperature*
*⅔ cup heavy whipping
    cream*

DECORATIONS
1 cup heavy whipping cream
2 tablespoons sugar
Ground cinnamon
Ground coffee
Unsweetened cocoa powder

❧ 8 ❧

Biscotti *and Other Cookies*

Strictly speaking, *biscotti*, as their name implies, are baked twice. The dough is formed into logs and given a first baking; then the baked logs are sliced diagonally and returned to the oven for a second baking. Nowadays the term *biscotti* is used generically for all types of cookies.

And Italians love their cookies. Pastry shops and espresso bars compete in the beauty and variety of the *biscotti* they offer. Until recently, when packaged *biscotti* began making inroads on the freshly baked variety, most pastry shops prepared immense assortments of *biscotti* for a large cookie-consuming public.

In general, many northern Italian *biscotti* are more delicate and buttery than their southern counterparts. Mantua's famous *Offelle* (page 203) offer the cookie lover a double treat — dough and batter in the same cookie, so that the delicate flavor may be experienced in two different textures. The Piedmont's *Krumiri* (page 207) and Venice's *Zaleti* (page 209), both based on corn-meal, offer a wonderful contrast of buttery sweetness and the coarse crunch of corn. Tuscany's *Biscotti di Prato* (page 187) are the model for twice-baked *biscotti*, their crispness a perfect complement to the sweet wine in which they are dunked to soften and absorb flavor.

Southern Italy and Sicily preserve many ancient traditions of cookie-making, and their *Mostaccioli* (page 210) are coarse, richly flavored honey cookies that are variations on those made in ancient Rome. Sicily, the world's leading producer of almonds, has used them in many types of *biscotti*, usually in the form of almond paste or finely ground almonds. In Sicily, too, several orders of cloistered nuns keep alive medieval traditions and bake delicate almond-paste confections in their monasteries.

Although north and south exhibit different tendencies in *biscotti* style, some types are popular throughout Italy. *Frollini* (page 200), light sugar cookies made from sweet pastry dough, are found in every region, as are *Savoiardi* (page 190), the Italian version of the ladyfinger, named for Italy's ill-fated ruling family.

Biscotti, like many other pastries, are a snack food as well as a common breakfast food. My cousin Ina Marcellino, who lives in Enna, in the center of Sicily, summed up the Italian attitude toward cookies. "Z'a Teresina [my paternal grandmother's aunt] was a very fine lady; she never ate bread for breakfast, only *biscotti*."

In this selection of *biscotti* recipes, I have attempted to cull my favorites from hundreds of varieties. Some are representative of particular regional traditions, like Aosta's *Tegole* (page 204) and Sicily's *Paste Nuove* (page 194). Others are unusual and interesting, like *Biscotti di Consuolo* (page 214), served to visitors by a bereaved family, and *Biscotti X* (page 196). Still others are recipes that Italian grandmothers prepared after emigrating to the United States, like *Cucidati* (page 198) and *Ancinetti* (page 191).

These *biscotti*, without exception, are easy to prepare. Since they keep well and many are low in fat, it is possible to keep quite an assortment on hand with relatively little effort or dietary havoc.

HINTS FOR SUCCESS WITH *BISCOTTI*

- Measure ingredients accurately. Small baked goods like *biscotti* show variations in quantities more easily than larger pastries.
- If you get a lot of bottom heat, bake the cookies on two pans stacked together to prevent the cookies from burning on the bottom. Or use insulated cookie sheets.
- Line pans with parchment or buttered wax paper for easy removal and cleanup.
- Watch cookies for signs of doneness after half the baking time has elapsed. Every oven bakes differently, and it would be a

shame to burn a batch of delicate *biscotti* by waiting until the suggested baking time in the recipe had elapsed before checking them.

- Avoid overbaking — fragile *biscotti* are often ruined by dehydrating entirely during baking. This is especially true of types that contain little or no fat, like *mostaccioli* and amaretti.

- Cool the *biscotti* as directed in the recipe. Coarser, drier varieties may cool on the pan without loss of quality. More delicate types should cool on a rack. An easy way to cool *biscotti* on a rack is to slide the paper directly from the pan to the rack, leaving the *biscotti* in place on the paper.

- Cool thoroughly before storing or the *biscotti* may become soggy from condensation generated by cooling in a closed container.

- Coarser *biscotti* may be kept in a tin or cookie jar. Store more fragile varieties between sheets of paper in a tin to prevent damage.

- Allow drier *biscotti* to age for a few days, so they may absorb a little moisture from the air and soften.

∞ ∞

Biscotti all'Anice

Anise-Flavored Biscuits

These are the classic crisp, anise-flavored biscuits so good with a cup of *caffè latte* (coffee with hot milk) or tea. They keep well stored in a tin.

I am indebted to Salvatore Maggio of the Pasticceria Maggio, in Trapani, for sharing the recipe from which this one is adapted.

3 large eggs
2 teaspoons anise extract
¾ cup sugar
Pinch salt

Combine the eggs, anise extract, sugar, and salt in a mixing bowl and whip with a hand mixer set at high speed or in a heavy-duty mixer fitted with the whip. Continue whipping until the mixture is very light and increased in volume, 6 or 7 minutes.

While the egg mixture is whipping, combine the flour, cornstarch, and baking powder and stir to mix.

Remove the whipped eggs from the mixer and sift the flour mixture over them in 3 additions, folding in after each addition with a rubber spatula. The batter will lose most of its air and become rather stiff.

Pipe the batter, using a pastry bag with ¾-inch opening but no tube, onto a jelly roll pan lined with parchment or buttered wax paper. Pipe 2 logs about 1½ inches wide and the length of the pan.

Bake the logs at 350 degrees for about 20 minutes, until they are well risen and golden. Remove the pan from the oven and slide the paper onto a cutting board to cool, about 10 minutes. Slip a knife under the logs to detach them, and, using a sharp, serrated knife, slice the logs diagonally at ½-inch intervals.

Place the *biscotti* cut side down on the pan and return them to the oven for about 10 to 15 minutes, until they color lightly on the cut surfaces.

Cool the *biscotti* on the pan and store them in a tin between layers of wax paper.

Makes 4 to 5 dozen

1½ cups all-purpose flour
¼ cup cornstarch
½ teaspoon baking powder

ॐ ॐ

Biscotti di Prato
———
Prato Biscuits

These crisp, dry almond biscuits named in honor of Prato, near Florence, are also known as *cantucci* and *cantuccini*. They are usually served with a glass of sweet Tuscan wine called *vinsanto* (holy wine), so that they may be dipped in the wine to soften. The dry texture comes from the leavener used — bicarbonate of ammonia. It works in a way similar to baking powder but has a side effect of promoting the complete desiccation of the dough during baking. Sometimes referred to as hartshorn cubes or *Hirschhornsalz*, the ammonia is available at some drugstores. Consult Sources of Equipment and Ingredients for information on ordering it. Or substitute ½ teaspoon each of baking powder and baking soda for the ½ teaspoon of bicarbonate of ammonia.

2 cups all-purpose flour
⅔ cup sugar
Pinch salt
½ teaspoon bicarbonate of
    ammonia
3 large eggs
1 teaspoon vanilla extract
¾ cup whole, unblanched
    almonds

EGG WASH
1 large egg
Pinch salt

Combine the dry ingredients and stir well to mix. If the bicarbonate of ammonia seems lumpy, crush it with the back of a spoon or a mortar and pestle before combining and sifting.

Place the dry ingredients in a mixing bowl and make a well in the center. Beat the eggs and vanilla in a bowl and pour into the well. Using either your hand or a rubber spatula, draw the dry ingredients gradually into the eggs, turning the bowl and working from the outside toward the center, to form a soft dough. When the dough is evenly mixed, let it rest for a minute so that the eggs are absorbed; then scrape the dough out of the bowl onto a lightly floured surface and flatten it into a rectangle.

Scatter the almonds over the dough and fold the dough over on itself 4 or 5 times to distribute the almonds evenly. Dust the dough and the surface very lightly with flour to prevent the dough from sticking. Divide the dough into 3 pieces and roll each into a 12-inch cylinder, using the palms of your hands. Flour your hands, not the dough or the surface, or the dough will slide rather than form a cylinder. Slide both hands under each cylinder of dough and transfer to a cookie sheet lined with parchment or dusted with flour.

For the egg wash, beat together the egg and salt until very liquid. Paint the dough evenly with the egg wash, using a flexible pastry brush. Bake at 350 degrees for about 30 minutes, until the cylinders of dough are well risen and an even, deep golden color. They should feel firm when pressed with a fingertip.

Remove the baked cylinders from the pan and place on a cutting board. Slice through them at a 45-degree angle at ½-inch intervals. Return them to the cookie sheet and stand them up with a ¼-inch space between each of the *biscotti*. (Arranging them this way for the second baking keeps them light in color; placing them cut side down for the second baking will color them deeply.) Return to the oven for another 15 minutes, until they are very dry. Cool on the pan. Store in a tin.

Makes 5 to 6 dozen

∾ ∾

Biscotti Napoletani

Honey-Almond-Cinnamon *Biscotti*

This is another easy and delicious recipe kindly given to me by Salvatore Maggio at his pastry shop in Trapani. Salvatore was so eager to share his knowledge and his recipes that he kept dictating recipes and instructions hours after his shop had closed, while one and then another member of his family would come to remind him at twenty- or thirty-minute intervals that his supper was waiting.

Be careful with the first baking of these *biscotti*. Even though they are baked a second time after being cut, the *biscotti* will have a hard, heavy core if they do not bake sufficiently the first time.

Combine all the ingredients except the honey and water in a mixing bowl and stir a minute or two to mix. Add the honey and water and stir until a firm dough forms.

Remove the dough from the bowl and divide in half. Roll each half into a log about 15 inches long. Put both logs, placed well apart, on a jelly roll pan lined with parchment or buttered wax paper. Bake at 350 degrees for about 30 minutes, until well risen, firm, and a dark gold.

Remove from the oven, cool the logs slightly, and place on a cutting board. Slice the logs diagonally at ½-inch intervals. Return the cut *biscotti* to the pan, cut side down, and bake an additional 15 minutes, until lightly colored and dry.

Cool on the pan. Stored in a tin, these keep well.

Makes about 5 dozen

2 cups all-purpose flour

¾ cup sugar

¾ cup whole, unblanched almonds, finely ground in a food processor

½ teaspoon bicarbonate of ammonia or ½ teaspoon each: baking powder and baking soda

½ teaspoon ground cinnamon

¾ cup whole, unblanched almonds

⅓ cup honey

⅓ cup water

 on oro

Savoiardi

Savoy Biscuits, or Italian Ladyfingers

These biscuits are named for the House of Savoy, Italy's ruling family during the years of the kingdom of Italy (1861 until World War II). Excellent on their own as a light and relatively low-calorie cookie, they may be used as a component in *Zuppa Inglese*, page 179, and *Tiramisù*, page 182 (though I usually prefer to use thinly sliced *pan di spagna* for those desserts). *Savoiardi* keep well in a tin and are excellent as an accompaniment to a glass of sweet wine.

4 large eggs, separated
⅔ cup sugar
1 teaspoon vanilla extract
Pinch salt
¾ cup all-purpose flour

Granulated sugar for
finishing (optional)

Line three 10 × 15-inch jelly roll pans or cookie sheets with parchment or buttered wax paper. Prepare a pastry bag fitted with a ½-inch plain tube (Ateco #6).

Whisk the egg yolks with half the sugar and the vanilla and continue whisking by hand, either with a hand mixer set at medium speed or in a heavy-duty mixer fitted with the whip, until very light and lemon-colored, about 5 minutes.

In a clean, dry bowl, whisk the egg whites with the salt and whip with a hand mixer or heavy-duty mixer fitted with the whip until they hold a soft peak. Increase the speed to maximum and whip in the remaining sugar in a slow stream. By this time the egg whites should be holding a soft, shiny peak. Remove from the mixer and fold in the yolk mixture.

Sift the flour over the egg mixture and fold in with a rubber spatula, cutting down to the bottom of the bowl to make sure the flour mixes in evenly.

Fill the pastry bag with half the batter and pipe 3½-inch fingers, 1½ inches apart, in rows on the paper-lined pans. Sprinkle the *savoiardi* with the granulated sugar, if you wish.

Bake the *savoiardi* at 375 degrees for about 15 minutes, until golden and firm to the touch. Remove them, still on the paper, from the pans and place on racks to cool. After cooling, remove the *savoiardi* from the paper and store in a tin between layers of wax paper.

Makes 2½ to 3 dozen

꙳꙳ ꙳꙳

Ancinetti

These delicate *biscotti* with their thin icing keep well in a tightly closed tin. The recipe came to me through Cathy McCauley, owner with Al Cappellini of Cooktique, one of New Jersey's most popular cooking schools and kitchenware stores. Cathy acquired the recipe several years ago from Teresa Mazzetti, her brother's mother-in-law.

For the dough, beat the butter until soft and light, either by hand, with a hand mixer set at medium speed, or in a heavy-duty mixer fitted with the paddle. Beat in the sugar, zest, and vanilla and continue beating until very light, 3 or 4 minutes. Beat in the eggs one at a time, beating until smooth after each addition. Mix the flour and baking powder together and add half of the mixture to the butter mixture, stirring it in by hand. Stir in the milk, then the remaining flour mixture, to make a sticky dough.

Form the *ancinetti* using a pastry bag fitted with a ½-inch plain tube (Ateco #6). Pipe the dough onto paper-lined pans, making ¾-inch spheres about 1 inch apart. Or use a spoon to shape them, dropping the dough in place on the pans.

Bake the *ancinetti* at 350 degrees for about 15 to 20 minutes, until they are golden and fairly firm. Cool briefly on the pans.

Immediately after removing the *ancinetti* from the oven,

DOUGH
4 tablespoons unsalted butter
½ cup sugar
1 tablespoon grated orange
   zest
2 teaspoons vanilla extract
2 large eggs
2 cups all-purpose flour
2 teaspoons baking powder
2 tablespoons milk

ICING
2 cups confectioners' sugar
1 tablespoon butter, melted
1 teaspoon vanilla extract
3 tablespoons warm water

prepare the icing. Combine all the icing ingredients in a large saucepan and stir to mix. Place over low heat and cook, stirring, until smooth and just hot to the touch, about 130 degrees. Remove from the heat and add the still-warm *ancinetti*, about 6 or 8 at a time, stirring them gently in the icing. With a slotted spoon or skimmer, remove them from the icing, draining them well, and arrange them right side up on paper-lined pans. Continue with the remaining *ancinetti*, reheating the icing if it cools and becomes too thick.

Allow the *ancinetti* to cool completely so that the icing dries, then place them in a tin between layers of wax paper.

Makes about 5 dozen

ഇൻ ഇൻ

Amaretti

Italian Macaroons

The Italian name for macaroons, *amaretti*, literally means "little bitter things," after the bitter almonds that are used in their preparation. In the United States, it is essential to use canned almond paste to achieve the taste and texture of the Italian original. The canned almond paste is flavored with oil of bitter almond, giving it the characteristic flavor. It has also been crushed very finely between granite rollers during the manufacturing process, which imparts a degree of smoothness impossible to duplicate with a food processor or blender. Although cellophane-wrapped tubes of almond paste will do for making an almond-paste covering for some of the cakes in other chapters, avoid using it for the amaretti, since it would make them rather flat both in flavor and appearance.

8 ounces canned almond paste

Break the almond paste into small pieces and combine it with the sugar in the bowl of a heavy-duty mixer. Mix on low speed with the paddle until very fine. Add the egg whites in 4 additions, mixing about 1 minute between each. Beat the paste until very smooth, about 2 to 3 minutes.

Fill a pastry bag fitted with a ½-inch plain tube (Ateco #6) with the mixture. Line 2 cookie sheets or jelly roll pans with parchment. Pipe the mixture onto the paper in 1- to 1½-inch mounds, about 1 inch apart.

Fold a clean kitchen towel into a long strip and moisten the towel with water. Squeeze lightly to eliminate excess water, leaving the towel more than damp. Slap the surface of the amaretti gently with the towel to moisten them and make the surface smooth. Sprinkle the amaretti with the granulated sugar.

Bake the amaretti at 375 degrees for about 15 to 20 minutes, until they are well risen and a deep golden color and their surface is covered with tiny cracks. Remove from the oven and place the pans on racks to cool.

To remove the amaretti from the paper, turn the paper over, with the amaretti still adhering to it, and wet the paper with hot water, using a brush. Leave for a few minutes and then pull on the paper to release the amaretti.

Makes about 3½ dozen

1 cup sugar
2 large egg whites

Granulated sugar for finishing

VARIATIONS

Amaretti ai Pignoli
After moistening the piped amaretti with the towel, strew them with 1 cup pine nuts, sprinkling them on heavily and then pressing lightly with your fingertips so that they adhere. Do not dust with sugar. Bake as for the plain amaretti.

Fior di Mandorla
This variation of amaretti is popular in southern Italy and Sicily, where green or red food coloring is sometimes added during the mixing. The rough, craggy appearance of these amaretti is a nice contrast to the smoothness of the standard ones.

Prepare as for the plain amaretti, up to and including

moistening them with the towel. Allow the piped mixture to dry at room temperature, uncovered, at least 12 hours or overnight.

After the amaretti have dried, dust them heavily with confectioners' sugar, giving them at least a ¼-inch coating. Then indent each of the piped mounds with your thumb and the first and middle fingers of one hand, positioning them an equal distance apart from each other around the circumference and pinching gently inward, about halfway into the center. Bake the *fior di mandorla* at 375 degrees for about 15 to 20 minutes. Cool and loosen the *fior di mandorla* as for the plain amaretti.

Paste Nuove

"New" Pastries

I first heard the term *paste nuove* at the Santo Spirito Monastery, in Agrigento, where it was used to describe a small spherical bun of baked almond paste filled with *zuccata*, a type of candied zucchini. (The zucchini in question is an extremely long, light green Sicilian variety. *Zuccata* resembles candied watermelon rind in concept but not flavor and is sweet and spicy, like good-quality candied citron.) I was amused at the name because I thought it meant that the pastries were an innovation, and I snickered to myself that the last time these were new was probably around five hundred years before.

It was not until I read about *paste nuove* in Giuseppe Coria's *Profumi di Sicilia* (Flavors of Sicily) that I learned that the word "new" refers to the new crop of almonds, from which these pastries are traditionally made.

Since the *zuccata* is not available in the United States, I give a recipe for it on page 15, although I have written the recipe for *paste nuove* using candied citron or a mixture of candied peel. The *paste nuove* are sweet, but they are more a confection than a pastry and are, after all, no sweeter than a macaroon.

For the dough, combine the almonds and sugar in the bowl of a food processor fitted with the metal blade and pulse repeatedly to grind the almonds very finely. Break the almond paste into 1-inch pieces and place it in the bowl of a heavy-duty mixer fitted with the paddle. Add half the sugar-and-almond mixture and beat on low speed to combine. Add the rest of the sugar-and-almond mixture, then the egg. Continue beating on low speed until the dough is smooth and masses around the paddle. Remove from the bowl and wrap in plastic until needed.

For the filling, stir the cinnamon and chocolate into the citron or *zuccata.*

Roll the dough into a cylinder about 12 inches long. Cut into 24 equal pieces. To form a pastry, roll a piece of dough into a sphere, then flatten it into a disk in the palm of your hand. Press the center of the disk into your palm with the index finger of your other hand to make the dough slightly concave. Place 1 teaspoon of the filling in the concave area and pinch the sides of the disk of dough together to enclose it. Repeat with the other pieces of dough. Arrange the pastries seam side down on pans lined with parchment or buttered wax paper. Bake at 375 degrees for about 20 minutes, until they are a light golden color. Remove the pastries, still on the paper, to racks to cool. Store between layers of wax paper in a tin.

Makes 2 dozen

DOUGH
*1 heaping cup whole,
    blanched almonds*
¾ cup sugar
*8 ounces canned almond
    paste*
1 large egg

FILLING
*½ cup candied citron, rinsed
    and finely diced, or
    Zuccata, page 15*
*½ teaspoon ground
    cinnamon*
*½ ounce semisweet
    chocolate, finely grated*

ఇం   ఛం

Palline all'Arancia

Orange and Almond Spheres

At her Pasticceria del Convento in Erice, a nearly mile-high medieval town in northwestern Sicily, Maria Grammatico makes a
version of *Paste Nuove* (preceding recipe) filled with heady, rum-
soaked candied orange peel. The flavor (and strength) of the rum
opposes the intense sweetness of the dough and filling for a very
successful liquor-imbued confection.

Dough for Paste Nuove,
   preceding recipe

FILLING
*½ cup candied orange peel,
   rinsed and finely diced
3 tablespoons dark rum*

*Granulated sugar for
   finishing*

For the filling, combine the candied peel and rum and cover
with plastic wrap. Allow to macerate at least 8 hours.

   Form and fill the *palline* as for the *Paste Nuove* (preceding
recipe). Before placing them on the pan, roll in the granulated
sugar. Bake, cool, and store as in the preceding recipe.

VARIATION
Replace the candied orange peel with raisins, dark or golden, that
have been brought to a boil in a pan of water and drained.

ఇం   ఛం

Biscotti X

Chocolate-Almond-Filled Cookies
from Sicily

I first saw these wonderful *biscotti* at Giulio and Nina Nostro's
Pasticceria Margherita, in Reggio Calabria. They make two different versions — these and a kind in which a freshly made al-

mond paste containing eggs replaces the dough, and homemade citron preserves are the filling. The Nostros are from Messina, in Sicily, where these *biscotti* are traditional.

For the dough, combine the flour, sugar, and salt in a mixing bowl. Rub in the butter finely, leaving the mixture cool and powdery. Stir in the eggs with a fork and continue stirring until the dough holds together. Knead lightly once or twice on a lightly floured surface and wrap the dough in plastic wrap. Chill the dough several hours or prepare it up to 2 days ahead.

For the filling, break the chocolate coarsely and combine with the almonds and cinnamon in the bowl of a food processor fitted with the metal blade. And the egg white and pulse the machine on and off at 1-second intervals until the filling is coarsely ground and holding together.

Preheat the oven to 350 degrees and set a rack in the middle level. Line 3 cookie sheets or jelly roll pans with parchment. To form the pastries, divide the dough into 4 parts and roll each part into a 16-inch cylinder. Flour the dough and the work surface and press to flatten the dough so it is about 3 inches wide. For the egg wash, whisk together the egg and salt. Paint the dough with the egg wash and place a line of filling down the middle of the dough. Fold both sides up to cover the filling, overlapping slightly. Cut in half crosswise and roll each half out with the palms of your hands to a 12-inch length. Cut

PASTA FROLLA
2⅓ cups all-purpose flour
⅓ cup sugar
Pinch salt
8 tablespoons (1 stick)
  unsalted butter, cold
2 large eggs, beaten

FILLING
6 ounces semisweet chocolate
1½ cups almonds, toasted
½ teaspoon ground
  cinnamon
1 large egg white

EGG WASH
1 large egg
Pinch salt

Confectioners' sugar for
  finishing

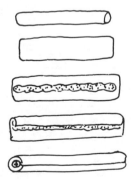

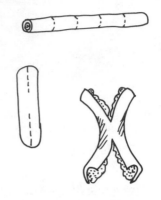

into 3-inch lengths. Repeat with the remaining dough and filling. Slash both cut edges of each *biscotto* about 1 inch deep, place 1 inch apart on all sides on paper-lined pans, and open the slashed edges to make an X. Bake about 15 minutes, until golden. Cool and dust with the confectioners' sugar.

Makes about 32 pieces

VARIATIONS

Substitute the filling for *Cucidati,* below, for the chocolate-almond filling.

For Giulio Nostro's X *Cedro Biscotti* (*Biscotti X* with Citron), use the dough and filling for *Paste Nuove,* page 194, shaping as directed for *biscotti X.*

Cucidati

Sicilian Fig-Filled Cookies

The name of these filled pastries is Sicilian dialect for *buccellati,* or "little bracelets." Popular for Christmas throughout Sicily, *cucidati* take many different forms. Some are made like ravioli: the filling is placed in mounds on one sheet of dough and another sheet of dough covers the filling before the pastries are cut out around the mounds. The following is a slightly more elaborate version, typical of some Sicilian convent pastries.

DOUGH
3⅓ cups all-purpose flour
1 cup sugar
1 teaspoon baking powder
*12 tablespoons lard or butter
    (1½ sticks), cold*
2 large eggs
2–3 tablespoons milk

For the dough, combine the flour, sugar, and baking powder in a bowl and stir to mix. Rub in the lard or butter finely, leaving the mixture powdery. Beat the eggs and 2 tablespoons of the milk to combine in a small bowl and stir into the flour mixture to form a dough. Add 1 tablespoon milk if the dough is too dry. Turn the dough out onto a lightly floured surface and knead lightly a few times. Wrap the dough in plastic and chill while preparing the filling.

For the filling, stem the figs and quarter them. Place in a bowl and cover with boiling water; steep 10 minutes. Drain and chop coarsely in a food processor fitted with the metal blade. Combine with the remaining filling ingredients. To prepare in advance, cover tightly with plastic wrap and keep at a cool room temperature or in the refrigerator up to 3 days.

Divide the dough into 12 pieces and roll each into a cylinder about 12 inches long. Flour the work surface and the dough lightly and roll it into a rectangle about 14×3 inches. Place a line of the filling down the center of each rectangle, using one-twelfth of the filling for each piece of dough. Lift up the long edges of the dough to enclose the filling and pinch to seal. Turn the filled sausage of dough over so that the seam is on the bottom and cut it into 3½- to 4-inch lengths.

Using a sharp paring knife or single-edged razor blade, make a series of diagonal slashes in the top of each little sausage. Pull and twist gently, holding the sausage at each end to open the slashes. Transfer the *cucidati* as they are formed to paper-lined cookie sheets, curving them into wide horseshoe shapes. For the egg wash, whisk the egg and salt together and paint the *cucidati*, using a soft brush.

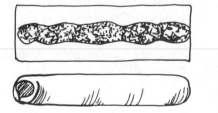 

Bake the *cucidati* in a preheated 350-degree oven for about 20 minutes, or until they are a light golden color. Cool the *cucidati* on racks.

Store in tins between layers of wax paper.

Makes about 4 dozen

FILLING
2 cups dried figs
¼ cup golden raisins
¼ cup currants or dark raisins
¼ cup candied orange peel, rinsed and diced
¼ cup almonds, toasted and sliced
¼ cup pine nuts, toasted
2 ounces semisweet chocolate, chopped
⅓ cup apricot preserves
¼ cup dark rum
1 teaspoon instant espresso powder
½ teaspoon ground cinnamon
¼ teaspoon ground cloves

EGG WASH
1 large egg
Pinch salt

Confectioners' sugar for finishing

ം‌ഇ ‌ഇം

Frollini

—

Italian Sugar Cookies

In visiting pastry shops in Italy over the course of the past twenty-odd years, I have seen hundreds of varieties of *biscotti* made from *pasta frolla*. Usually cut into rounds, ovals, and crescents after being rolled out, the *biscotti* are baked to a light golden color. Sometimes they have a little icing on top, or two of them are sandwiched around jam or chocolate. The following are several variations, all using a *pasta frolla* designed especially for cookies.

PASTA FROLLA
2 cups all-purpose flour
⅔ cup confectioners' sugar
8 tablespoons (1 stick)
   unsalted butter, cold
1 large egg
1 large egg yolk
1 teaspoon vanilla extract
2 tablespoons milk

EGG WASH
1 large egg
Pinch salt

Combine the flour and confectioners' sugar and sift into a mixing bowl. Rub the butter in by hand, making sure the mixture remains dry and powdery and does not become pasty. Beat the egg, egg yolk, vanilla, and milk together with a fork and stir into the flour mixture to form a dough. Lightly flour a work surface and turn the dough out onto it; knead lightly, folding the dough over on itself 3 or 4 times. Wrap in plastic and chill.

Roll the dough out ⅛ inch thick and pierce it at ½-inch intervals with a fork. Cut into rounds, ovals, or crescents with a fluted cutter. Transfer the cookies to a paper-lined cookie sheet. For the egg wash, whisk the egg and salt together until very liquid and brush on the cookies. Bake at 325 degrees for about 15 minutes, until pale golden. Cool on the pan.

Makes 2½ to 3 dozen

VARIATIONS
To finish the cookies, dust them with confectioners' sugar or cover them with a thin icing made from 1½ cups confectioners' sugar and 3 tablespoons milk, coffee, or liqueur, heated slightly and brushed on the cookies.

Or sandwich the cookies around 1 cup apricot preserves that have been heated, strained, and reduced until sticky, brushing the glaze on one cookie and then pressing two cookies together.

Or melt 6 ounces semisweet chocolate with 4 tablespoons butter, cool to spreading consistency, and sandwich the cookies around the chocolate filling.

⧽⧼ ⧽⧼

Biscotti Casalinghi

—

Home-Style *Biscotti*

I remember my grandmother making these homey jam-filled *biscotti* from the scraps of *pasta frolla* left over from baking all the traditional *pizze* and *torte* for Easter every year. Since this is a very casual recipe, feel free to vary it in any way you please, substituting another flavor of jam. In the next recipe (*Mosaici*), almonds, hazelnuts, candied cherries, and golden raisins are kneaded into the dough for a lovely mosaic efffect.

For the dough, combine the dry ingredients in a mixing bowl and stir well to mix. Rub in the butter, leaving the mixture cool and powdery, without allowing it to become pasty. Whisk the eggs with the orange zest and vanilla and stir into the flour mixture to form a dough. Knead lightly on a floured surface by folding the dough over on itself 3 or 4 times. Wrap in plastic and chill until firm, about 1 hour.

To form the *biscotti*, divide the dough into 3 pieces. Roll each piece into a cylinder 12 inches long. Flatten the cylinder to make a rectangle 12 × 4 inches. Spoon a line of the preserves down the middle of each rectangle, lengthwise, using less than 3 tablespoons of preserves for each piece of dough. Bring the long edges of the dough up to meet over the preserves and

PASTA FROLLA

3¼ cups all-purpose flour

⅔ cup sugar

¼ teaspoon salt

1 teaspoon baking powder

12 tablespoons (1½ sticks) unsalted butter, cold

3 large eggs

Grated zest of 1 orange

2 teaspoons vanilla extract

½ cup apricot or sour cherry preserves

pinch them together. Invert the filled logs of dough onto paper-lined cookie sheets so that the seams are on the bottom. Bake the logs at 350 degrees for about 20 minutes, until golden and firm. Cool on the pans until cool enough to handle, then cut into ½-inch diagonal slices. If the centers of the *biscotti*, where the preserves meet the dough, seem very wet, arrange the *biscotti* on cookie sheets, cut side down, and return to the oven for no more than 5 minutes. Cool, and store in a tin.

Makes 5 to 6 dozen

෩෩ ෩෩

Mosaici

"Mosaic" Biscuits

Named for the pattern of nuts and fruit visible after the *biscotti* are cut, this is an easy and infinitely variable recipe. Don't hesitate to change the combination of nuts and/or fruit to suit your personal taste — this is not a solemn recipe.

1 *batch* Pasta Frolla, *as in* Biscotti Casalinghi, *preceding recipe*
½ *cup each: whole, blanched almonds, lightly toasted; hazelnuts, roasted and skinned; candied cherries; golden raisins*

EGG WASH
1 *large egg*
Pinch salt

Prepare the *pasta frolla* and knead in the nuts and fruit, being careful not to overmix the dough. Divide the dough into 4 pieces and roll each into an even cylinder about 12 inches long. Place the cylinders on 2 jelly roll pans or cookie sheets that have been lined with parchment. For the egg wash, whisk the egg and salt together and paint the tops of the logs of dough, using a soft brush.

Bake the logs at 350 degrees for about 30 minutes, until they are well colored and firm to the touch. Remove from the pans or sheets to racks to cool. When cool, slice through the logs diagonally at ½-inch intervals, using a sharp, serrated knife. If the *biscotti* seem underdone in the center, or you wish to toast them lightly, arrange them on parchment-lined pans or cookie sheets, cut side down, and bake them at 350 degrees for

15 minutes (this is an optional step and should not be necessary).

Store the *mosaici* in a tin between layers of wax paper.

Makes about 8 dozen

ରେ ୯ଌ

Offelle Mantovane

Filled Biscuits from Mantua

A specialty of Mantua, these delicate pastries are filled with another, lighter dough, providing a subtle contrast of two delicate textures.

For the dough, beat the butter until soft and light, either by hand, with a hand mixer set at medium speed, or in a heavy-duty mixer fitted with the paddle. Beat in the sugar and continue beating until light. Beat in the egg yolks, one at a time, beating until smooth after each addition. Stir in the flour by hand. Scrape the dough onto a piece of plastic wrap, then wrap and chill the dough until firm.

While the dough is chilling, prepare the filling: combine the flour and confectioners' sugar and sift once to avoid lumps. Beat the egg with the vanilla and butter and fold into the flour-and-sugar mixture.

To form the *offelle*, roll half the dough out ⅛ inch thick on a floured surface and cut into 3-inch disks with a fluted cutter. Arrange the disks on a paper-lined cookie sheet and paint with the egg white. Place 1 teaspoon of the filling in the center of each disk and fold each side of the disk over the filling to make an oblong shape, as in the illustration. Repeat with the remain-

DOUGH
12 tablespoons (1½ sticks)
    unsalted butter, softened
½ cup sugar
2 large egg yolks
2 cups all-purpose flour

FILLING
¼ cup all-purpose flour
¼ cup confectioners' sugar
1 large egg
1 teaspoon vanilla extract
1 tablespoon butter, melted

1 large egg white for sealing

Confectioners' sugar for
    finishing

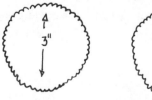

ing dough and filling. Finally, press the scraps together gently and reroll, or chill until firm and then reroll, to make the last *offelle*. Discard any remaining scraps, since the dough will toughen too much if rolled a third time.

Bake the *offelle* at 325 degrees for about 20 minutes, until light golden. Cool on racks and dust with the confectioners' sugar.

Store in a tin between layers of wax paper.

Makes 24 to 30

ഛൗ ൕൟ

Tegole d'Aosta

Aosta "Tiles"

These thin, crisp almond-and-hazelnut wafers are a specialty of Aosta, capital city of the Val d'Aosta region, Italy's French-speaking enclave. Aosta has everything — breathtaking mountain views, Roman ruins, and excellent food. The wonderful Pasticceria Boch, right in the center of the city on Piazza Chanoux, is a typical Old World pastry shop. There is an elegant salesroom, a bustling stand-up bar, and indoor and outdoor café tables where residents and tourists alike savor coffee or other drinks and, of course, the heavenly pastries.

Tegole have been part of the Pasticceria Boch's assortment of cookies since early in the century, when the establishment was founded by the grandfather of the present owner, Augusto Boch. Signore Boch explained that the *tegole* were so popular that his father, Edmondo, capitalized on this and named them *tegole d'Aosta*. Now every pastry shop and restaurant in the city has them, in varying versions.

Signore Boch was happy to share the recipe, which translated into American measurements very easily. In his pastry shop, where they make hundreds of *tegole* at a time, they use a metal stencil as large as the pan on which the cookies are baked, with many 3-inch circular openings in it. Then they simply spread the batter over the stencil, lift it, and an entire pan of *tegole* is ready to be baked. You can simulate the stencil (with one modest opening) using a piece of flexible plastic, like the lid of a ricotta container or a piece of stiff, thin cardboard, with a 2½-inch circle cut out of the center, according to the illustrations.

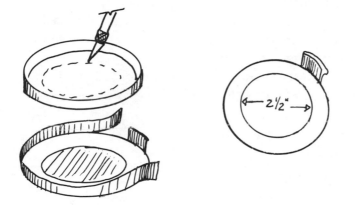

If you use unblanched almonds and hazelnuts, the finished *tegole* will be attractively speckled. If the nuts are already blanched, the cookies will be lighter in color.

Combine the almonds, hazelnuts, and sugar in the bowl of a food processor fitted with the metal blade and pulse repeatedly to grind to a fine powder. Pour into a medium bowl and stir in the flour. In a clean, dry bowl, whip the egg whites with the salt and continue whipping until they hold a soft peak. Stir the egg whites into the nut mixture. They will fall, but it does not matter, since the *tegole* will leaven slightly while they are baking.

Butter 4 or 5 jelly roll pans or cookie sheets thickly. For this purpose it is better to use very soft (but not melted) butter, applying it with a brush. Place twelve ½-teaspoon mounds of the batter on the pan, in 4 rows of 3 mounds, then use the back of a spoon to widen and flatten the mounds into 2½- to 3-inch disks. Or, to shape the *tegole* with your plastic stencil, position

¼ cup whole almonds
¼ cup whole hazelnuts
½ cup sugar
*3 tablespoons all-purpose
     flour*
2 large egg whites
Pinch salt

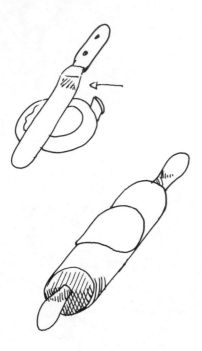

the stencil on the prepared pan. Place ½ teaspoon of batter in the stencil and then spread back and forth once or twice with an offset spatula. Repeat with all the batter. Bake the *tegole* at 375 degrees for about 10 minutes, until they are an even, deep golden color. Remember to bake only one pan at a time, so that the shaping is not too hurried.

Immediately upon removing the pan from the oven, pry the *tegole* off the pan with a flat, sharp-edged spatula and drape them over a rolling pin or a roll of aluminum foil so that they curve and become crisp. Repeat with the remaining batter. Remove the *tegole* from the rolling pin or roll of foil after they have cooled enough to hold their shape, and finish cooling on a rack.

Store the *tegole* airtight or they will absorb humidity and become soggy.

Makes 4 to 5 dozen

ঔত ৎ৫

Esse di Raveo

"S" Cookies from Raveo

These crisp, buttery cookies are a specialty of the Carnia region, a subdivision of the Friuli that includes the provinces of Udine, Gorizia, and Pordenone.

Esse di Raveo (*essis di Ravièi* in the local dialect) are quickly made and keep well in a tin. Commercialized versions of the *esse* are found in Udine and other parts of the Carnia, but these are a purely homemade type.

8 tablespoons (1 stick)
    unsalted butter, softened
½ cup sugar
1 large egg

Combine the butter and sugar in a mixing bowl and beat for 3 or 4 minutes, until soft and light, either by hand, with a hand mixer set at medium speed, or in a heavy-duty mixer fitted with the paddle.

Add the egg and continue beating until the mixture is smooth. Mix the flour with the baking powder and soda. Sift the flour mixture over the butter mixture and stir it in gently with a rubber spatula.

Line 2 or 3 cookie sheets with parchment and pipe the batter onto the paper, using a pastry bag fitted with a ¼-inch plain tube (Ateco #2) in the form of S's, about 3 inches long. Keep the *esse* at least 1 inch apart on all sides, so that they do not touch when they spread.

Bake the *esse* at 325 degrees for about 12 minutes, until they spread and turn a deep golden color. Carefully remove them from the cookie sheets with a thin spatula or pancake turner and cool them on racks. Store the *esse* in a tin between layers of wax paper.

Makes about 3 dozen

1 cup all-purpose flour
¼ teaspoon baking powder
¼ teaspoon baking soda

ᘉ ᘏ

Krumiri

——

Cornmeal Cookies from the Piedmont

I first encountered *krumiri* on one of my first visits to Italy, in the early seventies. I have to confess that I was mainly attracted to the brightly lithographed red tin they came in and wanted to add it to my growing collection. Later, on the train back to Zurich, I opened the tin and was pleasantly surprised to find a bonus of delicious *biscotti*.

Krumiri are delicately buttery with a strong, sweet corn flavor. If you do not have the patience to pipe them, use the dough for *Schiacciatine di Granturco*, which follows.

Beat the butter with the sugar, either by hand, with a hand mixer set at medium speed, or in a heavy-duty mixer fitted with the paddle. Continue beating until the mixture lightens

16 tablespoons (2 sticks)
*   unsalted butter, softened*
⅔ cup sugar

1 teaspoon vanilla extract
3 large egg yolks
1½ cups all-purpose flour
1 cup yellow cornmeal

both in texture and color, about 4 or 5 minutes. Beat in the vanilla, then the egg yolks, one at a time, beating smooth after each addition. Stir the flour and cornmeal together to mix and stir into the butter mixture by hand.

Line 2 or 3 cookie sheets with parchment and pipe the *krumiri* in horseshoe or stick shapes, according to the illustration, using a pastry bag fitted with a ½-inch star tube (Ateco #4).

Bake the *krumiri* at 325 degrees for about 15 minutes. Remove from the pans and cool on a rack.

Makes 4 or 5 dozen

VARIATION

Schiacciatine di Granturco
These wonderful *biscotti* are always on the bar at Tonino and Claudia Verro's charming inn, La Contea, at Neive, near Alba, in the Piedmont. The surrounding area, known as the Langhe for its location in the Langa Hills, has some of Italy's most breathtaking natural scenery, as well as excellent wine and *grappa*.

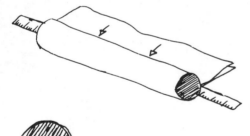

Follow the recipe for *krumiri* but do not pipe the dough. Divide it in half and place each half at the midpoint of a piece of parchment or wax paper, parallel to the shorter side. Shape each piece into a rough log about 1 inch in diameter × 6 inches long. Lift the far edge of the parchment or wax paper up over the log of dough and place it directly on top of the near edge of the paper, forming a loop around the dough. Take a ruler or the side of a jelly roll pan and place it on top of the paper, just at the edge of the log of dough, as in the illustration. Push the ruler or pan down toward the dough to make it perfectly cylindrical. Roll the dough up in the paper. Repeat with the other piece of dough. Chill the cylinders of dough about 1 hour, until firm. Remove one piece at a time from the refrigerator and slice the cylinder into disks ¼ inch thick. Arrange the disks of dough on paper-lined cookie sheets, 1 inch apart on all sides. Continue with the other cylinder of dough. Bake as for the *krumiri*.

Sometimes Claudia adds a handful of coarsely chopped

hazelnuts to the dough, which she says adds the "perfume of the Langhe" to the cookies.

Makes about 4 dozen

ᴈᴑ ᴄᴐ

Zaleti

Venetian Cornmeal Diamonds

Another wonderful cornmeal biscuit, this time from Venice. *Zaleti* are to be found in all the Venetian pastry shops and are popular in one form or another in all of northeastern Italy.

Although there are some large *zaleti*, they are a little rich, and I prefer to make small ones. The Venetians pronounce the name "sah-HET-ee."

Mix the dry ingredients in a large bowl. Rub in the butter finely, leaving the mixture cool and powdery. Stir in the currants or raisins.

Or pulse the dry ingredients in the work bowl of a food processor fitted with the metal blade. Add the butter, cut into 8 pieces, and pulse again 6 or 8 times until finely mixed. Pour into a bowl and stir in the currants or raisins.

Beat the eggs with the lemon zest and vanilla. Stir into the flour mixture with a fork.

Flour the dough lightly and divide it into 4 pieces. Roll them into cylinders about 1 inch in diameter. Flatten the cylinders slightly and cut them diagonally at 1½-inch intervals, making diamond shapes.

1½ cups yellow cornmeal
1½ cups all-purpose flour
½ cup sugar
¼ teaspoon salt
1 teaspoon baking powder
12 tablespoons (1½ sticks)
    unsalted butter, cold
¾ cup currants or dark
    raisins
2 large eggs
Grated zest of 1 small lemon
2 teaspoons vanilla extract

Confectioners' sugar for
    finishing

Arrange the *zaleti* on paper-lined cookie sheets and bake them at 350 degrees for about 15 minutes, until they are light golden in color. Cool on racks and dust with the confectioners' sugar.

Makes 2½ to 3 dozen

VARIATION

When I am pressed for time, I bake the dough in 3 logs, then slice the logs diagonally after they are baked. These *biscotti* do not need a second baking. A handful of very green pistachios is spectacular added to the dough; this little variation of mine is not one seen in Italy.

MOSTACCIOLI

Though the name of these southern Italian and Sicilian Christmas cookies would seem to derive from *mosto*, or "must," the unfermented juice of grapes that is made into wine, it actually comes from the late Latin *mustaceum*, a type of cake baked in leaves that was served at weddings and fertility rites. Mentioned by Cato in his *De agri cultura*, the cake is described as a mixture of rye flour, anise, cumin, cheese, and eggs, wrapped in leaves of *mustace*, a type of laurel.

Modern versions are usually made from a mixture of flour, honey, ground almonds, and spices, resulting in hard biscuits that are aged to soften them. In the Basilicata, there is a chocolate version flavored with cocoa powder, and Neapolitan *mustacciuoli* are covered with a chocolate icing.

The following recipes are for *mostaccioli* from Naples and the Basilicata.

❧ ❧

Mustacciuoli Napoletani

————

Neapolitan *Mostaccioli*

These iced *biscotti* are flavored with mixed spices. The chocolate icing is simple to prepare, and since it is used to cover all the exposed surfaces of the *mustacciuoli*, it helps to keep them from becoming excessively dry.

For the dough, combine the flour and sugar in a mixing bowl. Pour the water into a small bowl and stir in the remaining dough ingredients. Stir the water mixture into the flour and sugar and continue mixing until the dough begins to hold together. Turn the dough out onto a lightly floured surface and knead lightly until smooth. Do not knead too much or the dough will be difficult to roll and the resulting *mustacciuoli* will be tough. Wrap the dough in plastic and allow it to rest at room temperature for about 30 minutes.

    Place the dough on a lightly floured surface, flour it lightly, and roll it out ¼ inch thick, to a 12 × 9-inch rectangle. With a floured knife or cutting wheel, cut the dough into 6 strips, each 2 × 9 inches. Cut each strip diagonally at 2-inch intervals to make 6 diamond shapes, about 36 in all. Do not mass the scraps back together but bake them as they are. Transfer the *mustac-*

DOUGH
2 cups all-purpose flour
1 cup sugar
⅓ cup water
¼ teaspoon ground cinnamon
¼ teaspoon ground nutmeg
¼ teaspoon ground cloves
¼ teaspoon ground pepper
Grated zest of 1 orange
½ teaspoon bicarbonate of ammonia or ½ teaspoon each: baking powder and baking soda

CHOCOLATE ICING
6 ounces semisweet chocolate
¼ cup water
¼ cup light corn syrup
¾ cup sugar

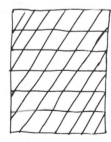

ciuoli to paper-lined cookie sheets and bake them in the middle level of a 325-degree oven for about 20 minutes, until they are very lightly colored. Slide the papers off the pans and cool the *mustacciuoli* on racks.

For the icing, chop the chocolate finely and set aside. Combine the water, corn syrup, and sugar in a small saucepan. Bring to a boil, stirring often. Remove the pan from the heat and add the chopped chocolate, swirling the mixture around in the pan to make sure the chocolate is immersed in the syrup. Allow to stand 3 minutes. Then whisk the icing smooth and paint it on the underside of each *mustacciuolo*, using a brush. Allow the *mustacciuoli* to dry for 5 minutes, turn them over, and brush the tops with the icing. If the icing becomes firm, add 1 tablespoon water and reheat it gently over low heat, stirring constantly.

Allow the *mustacciuoli* to dry at room temperature for 1 hour, then pack them in a tin between layers of wax paper. They keep well.

Makes about 36

⮞⮜ ⮞⮜

Mustazzuole Lucane

Mostaccioli from the Basilicata

The addition of cocoa powder to these *biscotti* makes them richer and denser. They keep well, and a week's rest will help them to absorb a little moisture before you serve them. Be careful not to overbake them. Their dark color makes it difficult to determine when they are done, so watch for the first sign of the dough's becoming dull-finished; this signifies that the liquid that made it shiny during the beginning of the baking has evaporated.

For the dough, sift the cocoa powder through a fine strainer to eliminate any lumps. Combine in a mixing bowl with all the remaining dough ingredients except the honey and water.

Make a well in the center of the dry ingredients and add the honey and water. Stir until a smooth, sticky dough forms. Allow to stand for 1 minute to absorb the liquid.

Turn the dough out onto a generously floured surface and pat into a 6 × 12-inch rectangle about ¼ inch thick. Flour the dough lightly and roll over it once or twice with a rolling pin to even it out.

Cut the dough into 1½-inch strips, then cut the strips diagonally to make diamond shapes and transfer to a parchment-lined pan. Bake at 325 degrees for about 15 minutes. Remove from the pan to cool.

For the icing, mix the confectioners' sugar and water in a small saucepan. Bring to a boil, stirring occasionally. Brush over the cooled *mustazzuole*. The icing will crystallize as it dries.

Makes about 24

DOUGH
½ cup unsweetened cocoa
   powder
⅔ cup all-purpose flour
¼ cup sugar
1 cup whole almonds, finely
   ground in a food
   processor
½ teaspoon ground
   cinnamon
½ teaspoon ground cloves
1 teaspoon baking soda
½ cup honey
¼ cup water

ICING
1 cup confectioners' sugar
¼ cup water

പന്ധ ഡ

Pizzelle alle Nocciole ed alla Cioccolata

Chocolate-Hazelnut *Pizzelle*

Although you need a special type of waffle iron to make these (Pizzelle Chef — see Sources of Equipment and Ingredients), it is well worth the trouble and expense to find one. Either leave the *pizzelle* in disks, divide them into fourths with a sharp knife after they are baked, or mold them around a cylinder, like a thick wooden spoon handle or cone, for easy cannoli shells or ice cream cones. Work quickly; the *pizzelle* become crisp as they cool. This is loosely based on a recipe by my friend Anna Teresa Callen.

4 *large eggs*
1 *cup sugar*
¼ *teaspoon salt*
8 *tablespoons (1 stick)*
   unsalted butter
2 *cups all-purpose flour*
¼ *cup unsweetened cocoa*
   powder
½ *teaspoon ground*
   cinnamon
1 *tablespoon baking powder*
¾ *cup hazelnuts, ground*

Whisk the eggs with the sugar and salt until light. Melt the butter and stir in. Sift together all the remaining ingredients except the hazelnuts and fold in. Stir in the hazelnuts last.

Heat the *pizzelle* iron and place 1 teaspoon of batter on each imprint. Close the iron and bake for 30 seconds. Cool on racks.

Makes about 32 pizzelle

പന്ധ ഡ

Biscotti di Consuolo

Consolation Biscuits

Although these biscuits have an unhappy association, they are tender and tasty. The name refers to the time during which a bereaved family receives callers and serves them these *biscotti* with a glass of wine. In Campania and the Basilicata, these customs survive in out-of-the-way mountain villages that still cling to ancient traditions.

Combine the flour, salt, and baking powder in a mixing bowl. Combine the egg, honey, and olive oil or butter in a bowl, beat to mix, and pour into the flour mixture. Stir well to form a firm dough.

Remove the dough from the bowl to a floured surface and knead well, about 2 or 3 minutes. Flour the dough lightly, wrap in plastic, and allow to rest at room temperature about 1 hour.

Unwrap the dough, cut it into 12 pieces, and roll each piece into a rope about ¼ inch in diameter × 12 inches long. Divide each rope into 3 pieces. Join the ends and form each piece into a figure eight, making sure that the seam lies at the midpoint of the figure eight and underneath it. Transfer the *biscotti* to parchment-lined cookie sheets and bake them in a preheated 350-degree oven for about 10 minutes, until puffed and light golden. Cool the *biscotti* on a rack and store in a tin between sheets of wax paper.

Makes 3 dozen

2 cups all-purpose flour
¼ teaspoon salt
1½ teaspoons baking powder
1 large egg
½ cup honey
¼ cup mild olive oil or
*   melted butter*

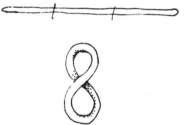

❧ 9 ❧

"Spoon" Desserts

Dolci al cucchiaio is one of my favorite Italian gastronomic terms: literally translated as "spoon sweets," it signifies soft foods, like creams and custards, eaten with a spoon. I have also included several fruit desserts that are favorites of mine, as well as the triumph of Sicilian grain cookery, the famous pistachio couscous from the Santo Spirito Monastery, in Agrigento.

❧ ❧

Arance Caramellizzate

Caramelized Oranges

This most typical Italian restaurant dessert has the advantage of being both easy to prepare and low in calories. Use good, firm eating oranges, such as Valencias, for this recipe.

Aurum is a wonderful Italian orange liqueur not widely available in the United States. Cointreau is an excellent substitute.

8 seedless oranges
2 cups sugar
⅔ cup water
¼ cup orange liqueur

Strip the zest from the oranges with a vegetable peeler, avoiding the white pith underneath. Then stack 3 or 4 pieces of the zest at a time on a cutting board and cut into ⅛-inch shreds with a large, sharp knife. Place the zest in a saucepan, cover with water, bring to a boil, drain, and rinse.

Combine the sugar and water in a small saucepan, bring to a boil, and cook the syrup until it thickens slightly, about 3 minutes.

While the syrup is cooking, cut away the white pith that remains on the oranges with a sharp knife to expose the flesh of the oranges: slice off each end and stand the orange on one of the ends. Then, following the contour of the orange, remove the pith from top to bottom. The oranges may exude a little juice during the peeling. If this happens, add the juice to the syrup.

Lower the heat so that the syrup is barely simmering around the edges of the pan. Place the oranges, one or two at a time, in the syrup and cook for about 2 minutes. Be careful that the oranges do not become too soft. Continue until all the oranges are cooked, making sure that the syrup does not become too thick. If it does, add 2 or 3 tablespoons of water at a time to thin it.

Remove the oranges from the syrup with a slotted spoon, allowing the syrup to drain back into the pan, and place them in a serving bowl or deep platter.

Add the blanched, shredded zest to the syrup and cook the zest for 1 or 2 minutes. Remove the zest from the syrup and strew it over the oranges.

Chill the oranges and sprinkle with the orange liqueur just before serving.

Makes 8 servings

☙ ❧

Pesche alla Piemontese

Baked Peaches from the Piedmont

A quick, easy dessert for the height of peach season, after the novelty of the first ripe ones has passed. Very ripe pears are also excellent this way.

Baked Peaches

6 ripe peaches
1/3 cup sugar
8 amaretti (Italian
    macaroons), such as
    Amaretti di Saronno,
    crushed
1 large egg yolk
4 tablespoons unsalted butter
Heavy whipping cream
    (optional)

Rinse, halve, and stone the peaches.

Puree 2 of the peach halves in a food processor fitted with the metal blade. Place the puree in a bowl and add the sugar, crushed macaroons, and egg yolk.

Cover each peach half with this filling and place the peach halves in a baking dish greased with about 1 tablespoon of the butter. Sprinkle the remaining butter over the peaches and bake at 350 degrees for about 45 minutes. Serve hot or cold, with or without heavy cream.

Makes 12 servings

ꙮꙮ ꙮꙮ

Zabaione Marsala

Warm Marsala Cream

Although many old texts use the spelling *zabaglione,* the currently accepted form is without the *g* and the *l. Zabaione,* variously attributed to different regions of Italy, was usually served as a dessert in itself. Nowadays, however, it is often used as a component in a more elaborate dessert, though normally not served with fruit, as is the custom in the United States.

The traditional *zabaione* is made with sweet Marsala, a fortified Sicilian wine made in a manner similar to that in which sherry is made. By all means, try substituting other wines for the Marsala; a combination of strong coffee and brandy also makes a flavorful, though not traditional, *zabaione.*

4 large egg yolks
1/3 cup sugar

Bring a quart of water to a simmer in a medium saucepan. Place the egg yolks in a heat-proof bowl and whisk by hand until liquid. Whisk in the sugar in a stream, then the Marsala. Regulate the heat under the pan so that the water simmers gently and place the bowl over the pan, with the bottom of the bowl above the surface of the water. Whisk vigorously; the *zabaione* will begin to absorb air fairly quickly. Continue whisking for a total of 4 minutes, until the *zabaione* is very aerated and thickened. Pour into stemmed glasses, dust with a dash of cinnamon, and serve immediately.

½ cup sweet Sicilian Marsala, such as Florio or Pellegrino

Ground cinnamon for finishing

To serve the *zabaione* cool (an untraditional method): after whisking until thickened, continue whisking, either by hand, with a hand mixer set at medium speed, or in a heavy-duty mixer fitted with the whip, until the *zabaione* is cool.

Makes 4 servings

❧ ☙

Crema Pasticciera

Italian Pastry Cream

Use this custard cream as a filling for pastries or cakes. Flavor it according to the directions following the recipe.

Bring the milk to a boil with half the sugar in a 2-quart non-reactive saucepan over medium heat.

Whisk the egg yolks in a bowl with the salt and whisk in the remaining sugar in a stream. Sift the flour over the yolk mixture and whisk in.

When the milk boils, remove it from the heat and whisk one-third of it into the yolk mixture. Return the remaining milk to a boil and, beginning to whisk the milk first, pour in the yolk mixture. Continue whisking constantly until the cream thickens and comes to a boil. Allow to boil, whisking constantly, for 30 seconds.

Remove from the heat, whisk in the vanilla, and pour into a clean nonreactive bowl. Press plastic wrap against the surface and refrigerate until cold. Use the cream within 24 hours.

2 cups milk
½ cup sugar
Pinch salt
6 large egg yolks
¼ cup all-purpose flour
2 teaspoons vanilla extract

VARIATIONS

Crema Pasticciera all'Arancia — Orange Pastry Cream
Add the grated zest of 1 orange to the cold milk and sugar.

Crema Pasticciera al Limone — Lemon Pastry Cream
Add the grated zest of 1 lemon to the cold milk and sugar.

Crema Pasticciera alla Cioccolata — Chocolate Pastry Cream
Add 4 ounces chopped semisweet or bittersweet chocolate and
½ teaspoon ground cinnamon to the hot pastry cream as it
comes off the heat. Stir in and allow to stand 2 minutes; then
whisk smooth and store as described previously.

Crema Pasticciera al Caffè — Coffee Pastry Cream
Add 2 tablespoons instant espresso powder to the cold milk and
sugar.

Crema Pasticciera al Rum — Rum Pastry Cream
Add 2 tablespoons rum or liqueur to the hot pastry cream as it
comes off the heat. Whisk in well and store as described previously.

Gattò di Ricotta

Sicilian Ricotta Cheesecake

Typically Sicilian, this ricotta cake is similar in style to an American cheesecake but much lighter. Italian ricotta is much more firm
and less watery than the typical American ricotta. If you live near
a store that sells freshly made ricotta in perforated containers, use
it and the result will be more creamy.

Note that the instructions call for stirring rather than beating
the ingredients together: beating the batter will incorporate air,
which will cause the *gattò* to rise too much during baking and sink
dismally as it cools.

Preheat the oven to 300 degrees. Set a rack in the middle level. Butter and flour a 9½-inch springform pan and tap out the excess flour.

Place the ricotta in a large mixing bowl and stir it as smooth as possible with a rubber spatula.

Stir the sugar and flour together and stir them thoroughly into the ricotta. Stir in the eggs one at a time, then the remaining ingredients.

Pour the mixture into the prepared pan and bake the *gatto* from about 1¼ to 1½ hours, until it is a light golden color, fairly firm in the center, and the point of a sharp knife inserted 1 inch from the center emerges without any batter clinging to it. Cool the *gatto* on a rack in a draft-free place; it will sink slightly as it cools. Cover the *gatto* with plastic wrap and chill until serving time. Before serving, release the sides of the springform pan but leave the *gatto* on the pan base.

Makes 10 to 12 servings

2 pounds whole-milk ricotta,
    commercial or
    homemade
⅔ cup sugar
⅓ cup all-purpose flour
6 large eggs
¼ teaspoon ground
    cinnamon
2 teaspoons grated orange
    zest
2 teaspoons vanilla extract
Pinch salt

Bonet al Caffè

Coffee Custard from the Piedmont

One of the most typical and traditional desserts of the Piedmont, this version is from La Contea, Tonino and Claudia Verro's lovely restaurant and inn. Rich and satisfying, the *bonet* is a perfect dessert after a light meal.

While it is baking, a crust forms on the *bonet*, so that there is a thin, firm layer on the bottom when the dessert is unmolded. Be careful not to bake the *bonet* too long or it will be coarse-textured instead of delicate and creamy.

CARAMEL
½ cup sugar
½ teaspoon lemon juice
2 tablespoons hot water

BONET
¾ cup water
½ cup ground espresso
2 cups heavy whipping
    cream
1 cup milk
⅓ cup sugar
8 large eggs
2 tablespoons white rum

For the caramel, combine the sugar and lemon juice in a small saucepan. Mix well with a metal spoon (a wooden spoon might carry traces of grease, which could make the sugar crystallize as it melts) and place over low heat. At the first sign of smoke, stir occasionally until the caramel is deep golden in color. Add the water, allow to return to a boil, and cool the caramel for about 1 minute.

Pour the caramel into a 1½-quart Pyrex loaf pan and tip the pan in all directions to coat it well. Pour out the excess caramel and allow the loaf pan to cool while preparing the *bonet*.

For the *bonet*, preheat the oven to 300 degrees and set a rack in the middle level. Bring the water to a boil in a small saucepan and remove from the heat. Stir in the coffee, cover the pan, and allow to steep for 5 minutes. Strain through a fine strainer into a measuring cup, then line the strainer with a paper towel or coffee filter and strain again. Measure ½ cup of the coffee.

Combine the cream, milk, and sugar in a saucepan. Bring the mixture to a boil over medium heat, stirring occasionally. In a large bowl, whisk the eggs to break them up and whisk in the rum and coffee. Whisk in the boiled cream mixture in a stream.

Pour the mixture into the caramelized loaf pan and set in a pan that contains 1 inch of warm water. Bake the *bonet* for about 1 hour, until it is firm to the touch and well colored on top. Be careful that the water in the pan does not simmer; add cold water to prevent it from becoming too hot, if necessary.

Cool the *bonet* at room temperature for half an hour, then cover with plastic wrap and refrigerate.

To unmold the *bonet*, insert the point of a paring knife about ½ inch deep between the *bonet* and the loaf pan and, scraping against the pan, loosen it at the top. Invert a platter onto the pan, then invert the pan and the platter. The pan should lift off easily. If it does not, shake gently from side to side so that some air gets in between the *bonet* and the pan; the pan should then lift off. If not serving immediately, cover loosely with plastic wrap and refrigerate. Serve the *bonet* in 1-inch slices.

Makes 10 to 12 servings

ক্তেও ড়ে

Panna Cotta

"Cooked" Cream

Despite this dessert's name, the cream is not cooked at all beyond being heated. It is really a cream jelly poured into a caramelized mold and results in a lighter and more flavorful version of a baked custard.

To dress up the *panna cotta,* prepare it in a ring mold and fill the center with mixed berries or with mixed cut fruit sprinkled with a tablespoon or two of white rum.

For the caramel, combine the sugar and lemon juice in a small saucepan. Mix well with a metal spoon (a wooden spoon might carry traces of grease, which could make the sugar crystallize as it melts) and place over low heat. At the first sign of smoke, stir occasionally until the caramel is deep golden in color. Add the water, allow to return to a boil, and cool the caramel for about 1 minute. Pour the caramel into a 1½-quart ring mold or eight 6-ounce ramekins. Swirl the caramel around inside the mold or ramekins and pour out the excess. Allow the caramel to set while preparing the cream.

For the cream, pour the milk into a bowl and sprinkle the gelatin on the surface. Allow to stand 5 minutes, until the gelatin absorbs the milk and softens.

Combine the cream, sugar, lemon zest, and cinnamon in a saucepan and bring to a simmer. Remove from the heat, cover, and allow to stand 5 minutes so that the cream absorbs the flavor from the lemon and cinnamon. Stir in the softened-

CARAMEL
½ cup sugar
½ teaspoon lemon juice
2 tablespoons hot water

CREAM
2 cups milk
2 envelopes unflavored
    gelatin
4 cups heavy whipping
    cream
1 cup sugar
Zest of 1 lemon, stripped
    with a vegetable peeler
3-inch piece of cinnamon
    stick

gelatin-and-milk mixture and return to a boil, stirring to dissolve the gelatin. Strain the mixture into the mold or ramekins, then refrigerate until set, at least 6 hours. Overnight is best.

To unmold, dip the mold or ramekins briefly in hot water. Loosen the top of the dessert by inserting the point of a sharp paring knife between the cream and the mold or ramekins, about ¼ inch below the top of the cream, scraping it against the mold all around. For the ring mold, place a platter on the dessert and invert. Tap the mold at the top and lift it off. For the ramekins, unmold each onto a dessert plate. Refrigerate until serving.

Makes 8 servings

ა

Monte Bianco

Mont Blanc

Named after one of the highest peaks in the Alps at the border between France and Italy, this dessert is claimed by both countries. Although it is not unusual for the *Monte Bianco* to be served on its own, as it is here, with whipped cream, the chestnut cream is often used as an accompaniment to meringues (see *Baci alle Castagne*, page 162). Americans associate chestnuts with late fall and early winter, but in Italy chestnut desserts are in the pastry shops for most of the year.

Make the chestnut cream up to 3 or 4 days in advance, if you wish, and assemble the dessert a few hours before serving.

CHESTNUT CREAM
1½ pounds fresh chestnuts
3 quarts water
1 teaspoon salt

Pierce each chestnut on its rounded end with the point of a small knife. Bring the water to a boil in a large pan and add the salt. Add the chestnuts and return to a boil over medium heat. Lower the heat and cook the chestnuts for about 20 minutes, until they are tender. Test one of the chestnuts after 20 minutes. If it peels easily under warm running water, remove the pan from the heat, drain the chestnuts in a colander, and peel. Keep them warm while peeling; if they cool too much, it will become difficult to remove the shell and the brown interior skin.

Place the peeled chestnuts in a heavy pan with the milk, sugar, and butter and simmer over low heat until very tender, stirring often to prevent scorching, about 20 minutes.

Cool the cooked chestnuts and puree the mixture in a food processor fitted with the metal blade, adding the brandy or Cognac and the vanilla. Force the cooled chestnut cream onto a platter through a food mill, potato ricer, or colander so that it falls in fine shreds. As much as possible, shape the shreds of chestnut cream into a cone-shaped mound.

Whip the cream until firm but not grainy and spread it on the top third of the chestnut cream, pulling it to a point with a thin metal spatula. Or pipe the whipped cream onto the chestnut cream with a pastry bag fitted with a ½-inch star tube (Ateco #4), piping long, pointed streaks, beginning one-third of the way down the mound of chestnut cream and joining the streaks in a point at the top.

Sprinkle with the chocolate shavings and dust very lightly with the confectioners' sugar.

Keep the *Monte Bianco* in the refrigerator up to 4 hours before serving. Cover any leftovers tightly with plastic wrap and store in the refrigerator.

Makes 8 to 10 servings

2 cups milk
⅔ cup sugar
3 tablespoons unsalted butter
2 tablespoons Italian brandy or Cognac
2 teaspoons vanilla extract
1 cup heavy whipping cream

Chocolate shavings and confectioners' sugar for finishing

෨෪ ෬෮

Gelo di Melone

—

Sicilian Watermelon Pudding

Popular during midsummer in Palermo, where it is called *gelu 'i muluni*, this dessert carries the humble watermelon to new heights of sophistication. Though the Sicilians like to make the mixture dense enough to unmold, I prefer to go easy on the cornstarch and serve the ice-cold watermelon pudding from a bowl. Some like to add a drop or two of jasmine flavor to the mixture, but it is not obligatory.

Make sure to choose a very ripe watermelon for this dessert or you will wind up with a pink cucumber pudding.

¼ ripe watermelon, about 3
    pounds
⅔ cup sugar
½ cup cornstarch
1 teaspoon vanilla extract
2 tablespoons blanched
    pistachios, chopped
½ ounce semisweet
    chocolate, coarsely grated
3 tablespoons candied citron
    or Zuccata (page 15),
    rinsed and chopped

Ground cinnamon for
    finishing

Spoon the flesh away from the rind of the melon and place in a large bowl. Remove the seeds and liquefy in a blender or a food processor fitted with the metal blade.

Combine the sugar and cornstarch in a 3-quart nonreactive saucepan and add the watermelon juice gradually, whisking it in. Place over low heat and bring to a boil, stirring constantly with a flat-edged wooden spatula. At the boil, continue cooking about 5 minutes, stirring constantly, over lowest heat.

Remove from the heat, stir in the vanilla, and pour into a mixing bowl. Cool to room temperature, stirring occasionally to prevent a skin from forming on the surface.

After the *gelo* has cooled, stir in the remaining ingredients, except the cinnamon. Pour into an attractive glass serving bowl and chill.

To serve the *gelo*, spoon into dessert bowls and sprinkle with cinnamon at the table.

Makes 4 to 6 servings

ବ୍‍ଠ ଓ

Cuscusu di Pistacchi,
Monastero di Santo Spirito d'Agrigento

———

Pistachio Couscous
from the Santo Spirito Monastery, Agrigento

I first heard of the famous pistachio couscous of Agrigento from Paula Wolfert, shortly before leaving on a trip through Italy with my friend Sandy Leonard in May 1988 to look for unusual recipes. Soon after Sandy and I arrived in Sicily, Paula's friend Pasqualino Giudice put me in touch with the dean of Agrigento's chefs, Professore Salvatore Schifano of the Favara Hotel School. Professore Schifano immediately offered to take us to the Santo Spirito Monastery to meet the abbess and prioress and to taste the pastries they make.

The abbess, Madre Ildegarde Pirrone, and the prioress, Madre Mafalda Pascucci, received us in a simply furnished parlor separated from the cloister by a thin, waist-high partition. The corridor of the cloister — off-limits to all — was clearly visible behind them, and I longed for a glimpse of their pastry shop. They described their great specialty, the *cuscusu di pistacchi,* made from a secret monastery recipe. An early noble abbess supposedly had an Arab servant who first cooked the couscous in the monastery, and it has remained a delicacy there since the end of the thirteenth century.

Unfortunately, none of the couscous had been prepared recently, and there were no leftovers for us to taste. Since the minimum order was twenty kilos and the nuns needed a week's advance notice, we decided to forgo a special order, though we were able to taste all the *biscotti* and confections made in the convent. You will find the recipe for their pistachio confection, *Bocconcini di Dama,* on page 252, as well as their *Paste Nuove,* page 194.

We chatted about antique Sicilian pastries, and at a certain point I asked Madre Mafalda to what religious order they belonged. She explained that they were Cistercians (also called Trappists), and I asked if she had ever heard of Thomas Merton, the famous American Cistercian monk whose devotional works were popular when I was growing up. This was the link needed to bridge the enormous cultural gap that lay between us, and after that both nuns gave us liberal descriptions of their pastries and the couscous, but no recipes, since they are maintained in the strictest secrecy.

I vowed to return to taste the couscous, and I did so a year later with my friends Miriam and Lester Brickman. This time I phoned ahead to Professore Schifano before leaving New York and asked him to order the twenty-kilo batch of couscous. Our friend Anna Teresa Callen would be bringing a tour group to Agrigento the day we were to pick up the longed-for dessert, and her group would be able to help us consume the enormous quantity.

On the appointed day, Professore Schifano again accompanied us to the monastery, and we were ushered into the same parlor. This time the couscous was ready, on little plates. The first taste was indescribably delightful. Deep green in color, with each grain of the couscous totally intact and separate, the dessert had a rich flavor combining pistachio and bitter almond, with a sweetness that was intense but not cloying. The platter of couscous was garnished with candied cherries and tangerines, and sprinkled all over with grated chocolate and confectioners' sugar. Suora Benedetta, the actual maker of the couscous, made an appearance and graciously answered my scores of questions, cautioning me to listen only to her, since she and not the others actually prepared it. She added with a smile that a bit of intelligence was only needed to reproduce it.

The version that follows is partly based on Paula Wolfert's method of cooking couscous in her magnificent book *Couscous and Other Good Food from Morocco* and on specific information about Sicilian couscous from Giuseppe Coria's *Profumi di Sicilia* (Flavors of Sicily). To cook the couscous you will need a *couscousière*, a perforated pan that sits in another larger pan, usually available at stores that carry imported cookware. Or you can improvise with a colander or steamer basket. For best results, buy couscous loose in a health food store and follow the instructions in the recipe exactly.

SEALING DOUGH
1 cup all-purpose flour
½ cup water

COUSCOUS
1 cup couscous (NOT instant)
3 cups water

First prepare the pan for steaming the couscous. For the sealing dough, mix the flour and water together in a bowl and scrape out onto a floured work surface. Knead briefly to form a rough, sticky dough, adding 1 or 2 tablespoons of flour if necessary. Roll into a rope as long as the circumference of the bottom pan and apply the dough to the rim of the pan. Add water to the pan to a point below the bottom of the *couscousière* or colander and press the *couscousière* or colander into place. Bring the water to a boil on high heat, until steam is escaping freely through the perforations, then lower to a simmer in which the steam escapes very gently.

While the water is coming to a boil, prepare the couscous to be cooked: place the grain in a bowl and add the water. Swish the water through the grain with the fingers of one hand splayed apart, raking through it. Tilt the bowl and drain away any excess water. Set aside for 5 minutes.

Line the *couscousière* or colander with a dampened napkin or piece of cheesecloth and add the grain. Cover and steam for 15 minutes.

While the grain is cooking, prepare the flavoring. Half fill a saucepan with water and add the pistachios. Bring to a boil and drain in a strainer. Pour the pistachios onto a towel, fold the towel over them, and rub to loosen the skins. Separate the pistachios from the skins, going over them carefully.

Combine the freshly blanched pistachios, almond extract, and cinnamon in the bowl of a food processor fitted with the metal blade and process for 2 or 3 minutes, until very finely ground and beginning to become pasty. Add the oil 1 table-spoon at a time and continue processing the mixture until it forms a smooth paste, stopping the machine and scraping the inside of the work bowl 3 or 4 times. Reserve the pistachio paste.

After the couscous has steamed for 15 minutes, remove it from the *couscousière* or colander in the cheesecloth and place it in a large nonreactive roasting pan. Spread it out with a fork and allow it to cool. Combine the water and salt and work into the cooled couscous, raking through with one hand. Add the pistachio paste in 3 or 4 additions, rubbing it and the couscous together with your fingertips.

Return the water in the bottom pan to a simmer and line the *couscousière* or colander with the dampened cheesecloth. Add the seasoned couscous to the *couscousière* or colander, cover, and steam for 15 minutes. Remove the couscous to the roasting pan, spread out with a fork, without compressing the mixture, and leave uncovered until cool.

Bring the sugar and water to a boil, stirring to dissolve all

FLAVORING FOR SECOND
    STEAMING
1½ cups unsalted, shelled,
    very green pistachios
1 teaspoon almond extract
1 teaspoon ground cinnamon
¼ cup almond oil or mild
    vegetable oil
1 tablespoon water
½ teaspoon salt

½ cup sugar
2 tablespoons water

1 ounce semisweet chocolate,
    finely grated; ¼ cup
    confectioners' sugar; and
    candied cherries, or other
    candied fruit, for
    finishing

dough seal

bottom

the sugar granules, and cool the syrup. Work the cooled couscous between the palms of your hands to separate the grains, and add the syrup in 5 or 6 additions, fluffing the couscous with a fork. Allow the couscous to dry uncovered for several hours in a cool place, fluffing it with a fork occasionally until all the grains are separate. For advance preparation, cover tightly with plastic wrap and refrigerate up to several days.

To finish, fluff up the couscous with a fork so that the grains separate well, and mound on a platter. Sprinkle the couscous evenly with the grated chocolate, then the confectioners' sugar, and decorate with no more than 5 or 6 pieces of the candied fruit.

Makes 8 to 12 servings

❧ 10 ❧

Ices and Frozen Desserts

Early in the twentieth century even the celebrated French chef Escoffier, in his now-classic compendium of French cooking, *Le guide culinaire*, prefaced his remarks on and recipes for ices by saying that the Italians were the acknowledged masters of this field. Ices and frozen desserts, in their many variations, are still celebration foods in Italy, where the acquisition of a half-gallon of ice cream is still an undreamed-of luxury. This is mainly because large-scale industrial production of ice cream specialties is still devoted primarily to popsicles and other packaged items that can be picked up at the corner store and to fancy frozen desserts meant to be served in medium- to lesser-quality restaurants.

In Italy, ice cream, as Americans know it, and high-quality frozen desserts come from pastry shops and from *gelaterie*, establishments dedicated to the preparation of freshly made ices. Ices are mainly consumed in cones, carried away from the *gelateria*, and in the form of *coppe*, or coupes, fancy sundaes that combine one or several ices with fruit or other garnishes; these are served at tables and eaten on the premises.

Because of the long history of preparation of ices in Italy, many variations have developed over the course of centuries, and just as many confused explanations of these forms have been the result. The following is a list of Italian frozen specialties with definitions and examples.

Gelato alla crema — literally, "ice cream," made with a cooked custard cream like the French *crème anglaise.* I have encountered this rich, classic ice cream only in high-quality restaurants. Sometimes also called *gelato all'uovo* ("egg ice").

Gelato al latte — literally, "milk ice." This is the type served in *gelaterie* and pastry shops all over Italy. Unfortunately, many of these *gelati al latte* are made from prepared mixes, though some establishments make them from fresh ingredients. *Gelato al latte* is what we know simply as *gelato* — a combination of milk, cream, nonfat milk powder, and flavoring. *Gelato al latte* comes in all flavors, from the chocolate, vanilla, coffee, and nut flavors we normally associate with ice cream, to fruit and berry flavors we normally associate with sherbets or water-based ices. Recently, especially in large cities, there has been a trend toward bizarre flavors, like the turquoise-streaked *dentifricio,* or "toothpaste," hopefully a passing fad.

The typical *gelato* has a light, airy texture due to its low fat content and the fact that it is held at a fairly high dipping temperature to emphasize its rather slushy texture and to prevent the formation of large ice crystals, which its leanness would cause to form at a lower temperature.

Gelato all'acqua — literally, "water ice." Though recipe books contain many references to and recipes for this type of ice, I have never encountered it in Italy. Like the French *sorbet,* made from sugar, water, and fruit pulp, water ices seem to be gaining popularity in cookbooks, but not in the *gelaterie.*

Granita — literally, "grained" or "grainy," a water ice with a low sugar content and a grainy texture. Large ice crystals form due to the high water content of the mix, which may either be turned in an ice cream freezer, stirred occasionally while it is freezing in a pan, or frozen solid and then chopped by hand to a flexible consistency. Sometimes *granite* are prepared by pouring a strongly flavored syrup over shaved ice. Coffee, lemon, and assorted berry flavors are the most popular variations.

Granite and *gelati* are frozen in an ice cream maker — an iced container with a mechanism to scrape away the mixture that freezes to the inside walls of the container and, while turning, also incorporates air into the mixture. Known as a *gelateria* in Italy, this kind of machine comes in many different models, both commercial and domestic. Many home models have become available in the United States during the past few years.

Semifreddi — "half-frozen" mixtures that are not frozen in an ice cream maker but in a mold in the freezer. *Semifreddi* have air incorporated into them by means of whipped egg preparations, or meringue and whipped cream. Very much like a mousse, they are easy to prepare without an ice cream maker.

Spumone — a very light *semifreddo* mixture made from equal parts of meringue and whipped cream, with flavoring added.

HINTS FOR SUCCESS
WITH *GELATI* AND *SEMIFREDDI*

- Measure ingredients accurately. Whether a *gelato* or *semifreddo* freezes successfully depends on a delicate balance of the ingredients, especially sugar and alcohol, which control the formation of ice crystals and the degree of firmness at freezer temperature.
- Follow manufacturer's directions for the ice cream maker carefully. If using a machine that requires the addition of ice and salt, use shaved ice and rock salt.
- Place containers for finished ices or molds for *semifreddi* in the freezer for at least 30 minutes before packing ice or a mixture into them. If the molds are at room temperature, the ice cream may begin to melt and acquire an icy texture where it has melted against the warm mold. With *semifreddi*, if the mixture does not begin freezing quickly after being placed in the freezer, the mixture may separate.
- Make sure all egg mixtures or meringues for *semifreddi* are cool before adding the whipped cream. If the mixture is still warm when the whipped cream is added, the cream will separate and ruin the mixture.

Gelati

Italian Ices

MILK-BASED ICES

The following recipes fall into the category of milk-based ices frequently found in ice cream and pastry shops in Italy today. Fairly light in texture, these ices combine standard ice cream flavors, as well as fruit flavors, with a fairly lean mixture of milk and cream that contains no eggs. Often a little granulated gelatin is added to the mixture, to allow diverse elements to freeze together evenly, rather than to thicken it.

Information about and recipes for *gelati* are loosely based on *Il gelato artigianale italiano* (Artisanal Italian Ices), by G. Preti — the best source of information about Italian ices.

ক্৳ ৻৵

Basic Mixture for Milk-Based Ices

Use this formula as the basis of the recipes for milk-based ices in the following section, adding flavoring to the mixture before freezing.

2 cups whole milk

¾ cup heavy whipping cream

3 tablespoons light corn syrup

⅓ cup nonfat dry milk powder

⅔ cup sugar

½ teaspoon granulated gelatin

Combine the milk, cream, and corn syrup in a saucepan. Combine the dry milk, sugar, and gelatin in a bowl and stir to mix. Add the dry ingredients to the milk mixture, whisking to prevent lumps. Place the saucepan over low heat and bring the mixture to a simmer, whisking occasionally.

Makes about 1½ pints

ᖆᔕ ᘓᖆ

Gelato al Caffè

Coffee Ice Cream

This coffee ice cream has the deep, rich flavor of a cup of espresso. Try serving it with a dab of unsweetened whipped cream and a dusting of cinnamon.

Prepare the basic mixture up to the point where the mixture comes to a simmer. Whisk in the coffee, remove from the heat, and cover. Allow to steep for 10 minutes. Strain the mixture, then pour through a coffee filter to remove any remaining grounds. Cool the mixture and freeze in an ice cream maker.

Pack the *gelato* in a cold container, press plastic wrap against the surface, and cover the container with a lid. Store in the freezer. Serve the *gelato* on the day it is prepared for best texture.

Makes about 1½ pints

1 batch Basic Mixture for Milk-Based Ices, preceding recipe
½ cup ground espresso

ᖆᔕ ᘓᖆ

Gelato alla Cannella

Cinnamon Ice Cream

Use the freshest cinnamon possible for maximum flavor in this *gelato*. After the *gelato* has frozen, stir in a handful of coarsely chopped, skinned, toasted hazelnuts for an interesting variation.

1 batch Basic Mixture for
    Milk-Based Ices, page
    234
1 tablespoon ground
    cinnamon

Mix the cinnamon with the dry ingredients in the basic mixture. Follow the directions for the basic mixture, bringing the mixture to a simmer and whisking occasionally. Cool the mixture and freeze in an ice cream maker.

Pack the *gelato* in a cold container, press plastic wrap against the surface, and cover the container with a lid. Store in the freezer. Serve the *gelato* on the day it is prepared for best texture.

Makes about 1½ pints

 exy   cxe

Gelato alla Gianduja

Chocolate-Hazelnut Ice Cream

Although this type of *gelato* is usually prepared using praline paste, an industrially made paste of sugar and hazelnuts, I find the flavor of the freshly toasted hazelnuts in this version fresh and vivid. Use the best-quality chocolate possible for this recipe.

1 batch Basic Mixture for
    Milk-Based Ices, page
    234
5 ounces semisweet
    chocolate, finely chopped
1 cup whole hazelnuts,
    toasted, skinned, and
    finely ground in a food
    processor

Prepare the basic mixture up to the point where the mixture comes to a simmer. Whisk in the chocolate and hazelnuts, remove from the heat, and cover. Allow to steep for 10 minutes. Pour the mixture through a fine mesh strainer. Cool the strained mixture and freeze in an ice cream maker.

Pack the *gelato* in a cold container, press plastic wrap against the surface, and cover the container with a lid. Store in the freezer. Serve the *gelato* on the day it is prepared for best texture.

Makes about 1½ pints

VARIATION

Gelato di Nocciole — Hazelnut Ice Cream
Omit the chocolate and add 2 teaspoons vanilla to the mixture before freezing.

ɞɔ ɕɞ

Gelato al Pistacchio

___

Pistachio Ice Cream

The pale green color of this ice cream is as delicate as the natural pistachio flavor. Try to find the greenest pistachios available for the recipe.

Half fill a saucepan with water and add the pistachios. Bring to a boil over medium heat. Immediately drain the pistachios and pour them onto a towel. Gather up the edges of the towel to enclose the pistachios and rub hard to loosen the skins. Go over the pistachios to separate them from the skins. Measure ½ cup of the pistachios, place them on a jelly roll pan, and bake in a preheated 300-degree oven for 10 minutes. Cool the pistachios on the pan, chop them coarsely, and reserve them. Grind the remaining pistachios very finely in a food processor fitted with the metal blade.

Prepare the basic mixture up to the point where the mixture comes to a simmer. Whisk in the ground pistachios, remove from the heat, and cover the pan. Allow to steep for 10 minutes. Pour the mixture through a fine mesh strainer. Cool the strained mixture, add the almond extract, and freeze in an ice cream maker. Add the chopped pistachios immediately before removing the *gelato* from the ice cream maker so that they are evenly distributed throughout the *gelato*.

Pack the *gelato* in a cold container, press plastic wrap against the surface, and cover the container with a lid. Store in the freezer. Serve the *gelato* on the day it is prepared for best texture.

Makes about 2 pints

1 batch Basic Mixture for Milk-Based Ices, page 234
1½ cups unsalted, shelled pistachios
½ teaspoon almond extract

꿍ꜝ ꜭ꿍

Gelato al Croccante

Caramel-Almond Ice Cream

The recipe for *Croccante,* on page 249, provides more than you need for this *gelato.* If you grind up only the amount needed for the *gelato,* the rest will keep for use as a confection. Or grind the whole batch and sprinkle extra on the *gelato* when you serve it.

1 batch Basic Mixture for Milk-Based Ices, page 234
1 cup Croccante, page 249, finely ground
1 tablespoon dark rum

Prepare the basic mixture. Cool the mixture, add the ground *croccante* and rum, and freeze in an ice cream maker.

Pack the *gelato* in a cold container, press plastic wrap against the surface, and cover the container with a lid. Store in the freezer. Serve the *gelato* on the day it is prepared for best texture.

Makes about 2 pints

FRUIT ICES

Although the recipes that follow are also milk-based ices, the proportions of the basic mixture differ to allow for the water content of the fruit.

꿍ꜝ ꜭ꿍

Basic Mixture for Fruit Ices

1½ cups whole milk
½ cup heavy whipping cream

Combine the milk, cream, and corn syrup in a saucepan. Combine the dry milk, sugar, and gelatin in a bowl and stir to mix. Add the dry ingredients to the milk mixture, whisking to prevent lumps. Place the saucepan over low heat and bring the mixture to a simmer, whisking occasionally.

Makes about 1 pint mix, to be combined with fruit

3 tablespoons light corn syrup
⅓ cup nonfat dry milk powder
⅔ cup sugar
½ teaspoon granulated gelatin

❧ ☙

Gelato alle Fragole

Strawberry Ice Cream

If possible, use fresh, very ripe strawberries in season for this recipe. Failing that, individually quick-frozen strawberries will have more flavor than the underripe, out-of-season fruit.

Prepare the basic mixture and cool to room temperature. While the mixture is cooling, rinse, hull, and puree the strawberries in a blender. Measure 1½ cups puree. Stir the puree and the mixture together and freeze in an ice cream maker.

1 batch Basic Mixture for Fruit Ices, preceding recipe
1 pint fresh strawberries

Pack the *gelato* in a cold container, press plastic wrap against the surface, and cover the container with a lid. Store in the freezer. Serve the *gelato* on the day it is prepared for best texture.

Makes about 2 pints

❧ ☙

Gelato al Mandarino

Tangerine Ice Cream

Use the sweetest tangerines possible for this ice. The tiny clementines that appear around the end of the year in American markets are ideal for this recipe.

1 batch Basic Mixture for
    Fruit Ices, page 238
1½ cups strained tangerine
    juice

Prepare the basic mixture and cool to room temperature. Stir in the tangerine juice and freeze in an ice cream maker.

Pack the *gelato* in a cold container, press plastic wrap against the surface, and cover the container with a lid. Store in the freezer. Serve the *gelato* on the day it is prepared for best texture.

Makes about 2 pints

 howdy ⁘

Gelato alle Amarene

Sour Cherry Ice Cream

Though sour cherries are not particularly easy to obtain, this is best made with fresh ones in season. Frozen cherries make a good substitute, but canned ones tend to be watery-tasting.

1 batch Basic Mixture for
    Fruit Ices, page 238
1 pound fresh sour cherries
    or one 12-ounce bag
    individually quick-frozen
    sour cherries
⅓ cup sugar

Prepare the basic mixture and cool to room temperature. While the mixture is cooling, rinse and pit the cherries and combine with the sugar in a nonreactive saucepan. Bring to a simmer, stirring occasionally, and allow to reduce to about 1½ cups, stirring often. Puree in a blender or a food processor fitted with the metal blade and let cool. Stir into the basic mixture and freeze in an ice cream maker.

Pack the *gelato* in a cold container, press plastic wrap against the surface, and cover the container with a lid. Store in the freezer. Serve the *gelato* on the day it is prepared for best texture.

Makes about 2 pints

Granite

As refreshing in flavor as they are easy to make, *granite* are popular throughout Italy. These mixtures of syrup and flavoring (usually fruit juice or coffee) are grainy in texture, as their name indicates, and are frozen in a pan in the freezer. They develop the characteristically large ice crystals as the mixture is stirred occasionally during the freezing. Feel free to experiment with your own *granite* — lime or grapefruit would work equally well in the *Granita al Limone* (page 242), as would the strained juice of berries other than strawberries in the recipe for *Granita alle Fragole* (page 243).

Granita al Caffè

Coffee *Granita*

Only a good, strong, dark-roasted espresso will make a flavorful *granita*. I have frequently used the Medaglia d'Oro brand with good results.

Bring the water to a boil in a nonreactive saucepan with a tight-fitting lid. Remove from the heat, whisk in the espresso, cover and allow to steep for 10 minutes. Strain once to eliminate most of the grounds, then strain through a coffee filter or dampened napkin or paper towel to eliminate all the remaining grounds. Measure the coffee: there should be 3 cups. If not, add water to make 3 cups. Stir in the sugar until it is dissolved and cool to room temperature.

1 quart water
1 cup ground espresso
1 cup sugar

Pour the mixture into a nonreactive gratin dish or roasting pan and place in the freezer. When the mixture starts to freeze, stir it every 10 minutes, scraping the *granita* off the bottom and sides of the pan so that it freezes evenly. When the *granita* no longer has any unfrozen liquid in it, stir well and pack in a chilled container. Press plastic wrap against the surface, cover the container with a lid, and store in the freezer. The *granita* is best on the day it is made. Serve the *granita* in chilled stemmed glasses with a spoonful of unsweetened whipped cream.

Makes 6 to 8 servings

Note: If the *granita* freezes to a solid block, pop it out of the container, cut into thick slices with a stainless steel knife, and chop the slices finely. Replace in the container and freeze until serving time.

 confucius ornament

Granita al Limone

Lemon *Granita*

Nothing is easier to prepare — or more refreshing on a hot day — than lemon *granita*. Taste the mixture before freezing. If it seems too tart, add more sugar to taste.

2 cups water
1 cup sugar
2 cups freshly squeezed
    lemon juice

Combine the water and sugar in a small nonreactive saucepan. Bring to a boil, stirring occasionally to dissolve the sugar. Cool the syrup. Strain the lemon juice into the syrup through a very fine strainer, to eliminate pulp and tiny seeds. Stir well to combine.

Pour the mixture into a nonreactive gratin dish or roasting pan and place in the freezer. When the mixture starts to freeze, stir it every 10 minutes, scraping the *granita* off the bottom and sides of the pan so that it freezes evenly. When the *granita* no longer has any unfrozen liquid in it, stir well and pack in a chilled container. Press plastic wrap against the surface, cover the container with a lid, and store in the freezer. The *granita* is best on the day it is made. Serve the *granita* in chilled stemmed glasses.

Makes 6 to 8 servings

Note: If the *granita* freezes to a solid block, pop it out of the container, cut into thick slices with a stainless steel knife, and chop the slices finely. Replace in the container and freeze until serving time.

❧ ☙

Granita alle Fragole

Strawberry *Granita*

Again, try to use the ripest strawberries for this. Substitute unsweetened frozen strawberries rather than underripe ones.

Combine the water and sugar in a small nonreactive saucepan. Bring to a boil, stirring occasionally to dissolve the sugar. Cool the syrup. Rinse the berries. Wrap and refrigerate a few attractive ones to garnish the *granita*. Hull and puree the remaining strawberries in a blender. Measure 2½ cups strawberry puree and add to the cooled syrup. Stir well to combine.

1½ cups water
¾ cup sugar
2 pints strawberries

Pour the mixture into a nonreactive gratin dish or roasting pan and place in the freezer. When the mixture starts to freeze, stir it every 10 minutes, scraping the *granita* off the bottom and sides of the pan so that it freezes evenly. When the *granita* no longer has any unfrozen liquid in it, stir well and pack in a chilled container. Press plastic wrap against the surface, cover the container with a lid, and store in the freezer. The *granita* is best on the day it is made. Serve the *granita* in chilled stemmed glasses topped with a spoonful of unsweetened whipped cream. Garnish each portion with a whole berry.

Makes 6 to 8 servings

Note: If the *granita* freezes to a solid block, pop it out of the container, cut into thick slices with a stainless steel knife, and chop the slices finely. Replace in the container and freeze until serving time.

Semifreddi

Frozen Desserts

The term *semifreddi* can sometimes be ambiguous. Although it certainly refers to certain types of frozen mousse preparations, it is sometimes also used to describe desserts like *Zuccotto alla Ricotta* (page 173) or *Tiramisù* (page 182), which are really chilled rather than frozen.

The following *semifreddi* use either an aerated, cooked egg base or an Italian meringue for lightness, along with whipped cream for richness and more aeration. They may be frozen in molds and unmolded, but they are equally well suited to being molded in an attractive bowl and spooned out for serving.

∾ ∽

Semifreddo all' Amaretto

Amaretto Frozen Dessert

The combination of amaretto liqueur and the crisp amaretti makes for a frozen dessert with a suave flavor tempered by a bit of crunch.

1½ cups heavy whipping cream
¼ cup amaretto liqueur
2 large eggs
4 large egg yolks
½ cup sugar

Combine the cream and the amaretto and whip until the mixture begins to hold its shape but is still soft and smooth. Set aside in the refrigerator.

Bring a small pan of water to a boil and reduce to a simmer. Whisk the eggs, egg yolks, and sugar in a heat-proof bowl or in the bowl of a heavy-duty mixer and place over the pan of simmering water so that the bottom of the bowl is above, not in, the water. Whisk as for *Zabaione Marsala* (page 218), continuing to whisk until the eggs are hot, increased in volume, and thickened. Remove the egg mixture from the pan of water and whip the mixture to cool it, either with a hand mixer set at medium speed or in a heavy-duty mixer fitted with the whip. Fold in the amaretto-flavored whipped cream and the crushed amaretti.

Pour the mixture into a chilled 2-quart mold or soufflé dish, cover with plastic wrap, and freeze overnight.

To unmold the *semifreddo*, dip it briefly into a pan of warm water, then loosen it from the mold with a thin, sharp knife, running the knife between the *semifreddo* and the mold. Invert a chilled platter onto the *semifreddo*, invert again, and remove the mold. Touch up the outside with a cake spatula if necessary, sprinkle with the crushed amaretti, and cover loosely with plastic wrap. Return to the freezer until serving time.

Makes 10 servings

VARIATIONS

Semifreddo al Aurum — Frozen Dessert
 with Italian Orange Liqueur

Aurum is not easy to find; Cointreau will yield good results but a slightly different flavor.

Follow the directions for *Semifreddo all'Amaretto*, preceding recipe, substituting Aurum or Cointreau for the amaretto. Add the finely grated zest of 1 large orange to the egg mixture before heating it and omit the amaretti crumbs.

Semifreddo all'Anice — Anise-Flavored Frozen Dessert

Follow the recipe for *Semifreddo all'Amaretto*, substituting anisette for the amaretto. Add 1 teaspoon finely grated lemon zest to the egg mixture before heating it and omit the amaretti crumbs. Garnish the dessert with 1 teaspoon of ground coffee.

½ cup amaretti (Italian macaroons), such as Amaretti di Saronno, crushed

¼ cup amaretti, crushed, for finishing

❧ ❧

Semifreddo alla Cioccolata

Frozen Chocolate Dessert

This is the most suave and velvety of all chocolate desserts, in my opinion. Use a fine-quality chocolate for best results.

1¾ cups heavy whipping
 cream
2 tablespoons white rum
8 ounces semisweet chocolate
4 tablespoons unsalted butter
1⅓ cups sugar
⅓ cup water
1 tablespoon light corn syrup
5 large egg whites
Pinch salt

Chocolate shavings for
 finishing

Combine the cream and rum and whip until it begins to hold its shape but is still soft and smooth. Set aside in the refrigerator.

Bring a small pan of water to a boil and turn off the heat. Combine the chocolate and butter in a heat-proof bowl and place over the pan of water. Stir occasionally to melt the chocolate and butter. After the mixture is melted and smooth, remove the bowl from the pan and cool the mixture.

Combine the sugar, water, and corn syrup in a saucepan, preferably one with a pouring lip. Stir well and place over low heat, stirring often and washing the inside of the saucepan with a clean brush dipped in cold water to prevent stray sugar crystals from accumulating there. When the syrup boils, insert a candy thermometer, increase the heat to medium, and continue cooking the syrup until it reaches the soft-ball stage, 240 degrees.

As soon as the syrup begins to boil, combine the egg whites and salt in a clean, dry mixing bowl and whip the whites, either with a hand mixer set at medium speed or in a heavy-duty mixer fitted with the whip. If the egg whites seem to be becoming stiff or grainy before the syrup has reached 240 degrees, add 2 tablespoons sugar and decrease the speed of whipping to the lowest setting. When the syrup reaches the desired temperature, pour it over the egg whites while they are whipping on medium speed and continue whipping until the meringue has cooled. (If using a hand mixer, move the mixer all around inside the bowl while adding the syrup to distribute it quickly.)

After the meringue has cooled, fold in the chocolate mixture, then the whipped cream. Pour the *semifreddo* into a 2½-quart mold or soufflé dish or two 1½-quart loaf pans. Cover with plastic wrap and freeze. Unmold as for *Semifreddo all'Amaretto*, page 244. Decorate with the chocolate shavings.

Makes 8 servings

VARIATION

Semifreddo alla Gianduja — Chocolate-Hazelnut
        Frozen Dessert
Toast 1 cup hazelnuts, rub off the skins, and reduce to a paste with 2 tablespoons butter in a food processor fitted with the metal blade. Add to the chocolate mixture before combining with the meringue.

❧ 11 ❧

Confections

The following recipes for simple confections are mostly of the type that would be prepared in the home. Italians are great lovers of all kinds of candies and little sweets, though nowadays the simple homemade and artisanal varieties are being replaced rapidly by industrially prepared candies. Most of these sweets date from the time when white sugar was still considered a rare and precious commodity, and they may seem primitive to those of us accustomed to fancy French chocolates. The most outstanding characteristic of these confections is their emphasis on flavor and texture over sweetness. Though they are not low in sugar, the sugar is secondary to the intrinsic flavor that it accompanies.

HINTS FOR SUCCESS WITH CONFECTIONS

- Always choose a dry day for making any confections that call for cooked sugar. Excessive humidity in the air will be absorbed by the sugar after it is cooked, causing it to become soft and sticky.
- For safety, always have a bowl of ice water (mostly ice) at hand when cooking sugar. In case of burns, a quick immersion in the cold water will stop the effects of the hot sugar, which has a tendency to stick to the skin.
- When a pan of cooked sugar comes off the heat, rest it for a moment in the same bowl of ice water. This will prevent the heat retained by the pan from continuing to cook the sugar beyond the degree necessary for the recipe.

- Washing the inside of the pan with a clean brush dipped in cold water is the most important part of cooking a sugar syrup. Doing so keeps stray sugar crystals from sticking to the pan and crystallizing the entire batch of syrup during cooking.
- If a batch of syrup does crystallize, add 2 tablespoons water and lower the heat to the minimum, stirring occasionally until the syrup returns to a boil. Wash the inside of the pan with a clean brush dipped in cold water before and after the syrup returns to a boil.

∽ ∾

Croccante

Almond Brittle

Popular throughout Italy, especially in the south and Sicily, *croccante* (literally, crunchy) is a mixture of caramelized sugar and almonds left to harden. It is then broken into pieces for use as a confection or ground up for use as a flavoring. *Croccante* is fairly simple to prepare, but it must be handled quickly and deftly to avoid having the sugar overcook and become bitter, as well as to avoid burns.

Combine the sugar and corn syrup in a wide, shallow pan, like a straight-sided sauté pan. Stir continuously with a metal spoon (a wooden spoon might carry traces of grease, which could make the sugar crystallize as it is melting) until the mixture looks like wet sand. Set over low heat and allow to melt and caramelize, stirring occasionally.

1 cup sugar
1 tablespoon light corn syrup
1½ cups whole or slivered blanched almonds, lightly toasted

While the sugar is melting, butter or oil a jelly roll pan and set it on several towels to protect the surface under the pan.

When the sugar is a clear amber color, remove the pan from the heat and quickly stir in the almonds. Pour the molten *croccante* out on the pan and spread it out with the spoon. Allow the *croccante* to cool and harden.

After the *croccante* has cooled, break it into coarse pieces for use as a confection. To use the *croccante* as a flavoring, chop it finely with an old knife or put it through a meat grinder fitted with the fine blade. Use a food processor only as a last resort, since it reduces the *croccante* to too fine a powder.

Store the *croccante* in a tin in a cool, dry place.

Makes about 1 pound

ꙮ ꙮ

Cubbaita di Giugiulena

Sicilian Sesame Brittle

The name and origin of this Sicilian sweet are both Arab. Though many versions of it exist, I have chosen one from Tommaso d'Alba's *Cucina siciliana di derivazione araba* (Sicilian Cooking of Arab Origin), which chronicles all Sicilian dishes with Arab ancestry. D'Alba suggests that *cubbaita*, alone among sweets, has retained the purity of its Arab origins, since it has never been subjected to the refinements of fancy cooking or cooks.

1½ cups sesame seeds
⅓ cup sugar
1 cup honey
Finely grated zest of 1 lemon
¼ teaspoon ground cinnamon

Combine all the ingredients in a wide, deep pan and stir with a metal spoon to mix evenly. Place over low heat and bring to a boil, stirring occasionally. Be careful that the mixture does not boil over, since the honey foams a great deal as it is cooking. Insert a candy thermometer in the mixture and cook, stirring occasionally, until the mixture reaches 325 degrees, a light caramel.

While the *cubbaita* is cooking, butter or oil a jelly roll pan and set it on several towels to protect the surface under the pan.

When the temperature reaches 325 degrees, remove the pan from the heat and quickly pour the molten *cubbaita* out onto the pan and spread it out with the spoon. Allow the *cubbaita* to cool slightly. Slide a spatula under the *cubbaita* and loosen it from the pan. While it is still flexible — before it cools to the point where it becomes brittle — butter or oil an old knife and cut the *cubbaita* into strips 1 inch wide. Then cut the strips diagonally into diamond shapes. If the *cubbaita* cools so much that you can't cut it, slide the pieces onto a buttered or oiled cookie sheet and reheat them briefly in a 250-degree oven to soften.

Store the *cubbaita* in a tin between layers of wax paper in a cool, dry place.

Makes about 1 pound

ல் ல

Torrone

Italian Honey and Egg White Nougat

Making *torrone* at home is quite a production, though it is not difficult. The indispensable ingredient is edible wafer paper, available through mail order (see Sources of Equipment and Ingredients). The type that I use is German and comes in 4 × 6-inch rectangles in packages of 10 sheets. Called *ostia* (host) in Italian, it is the same material that altar breads are made from. Besides the wafer paper, you need a candy thermometer and a heavy-duty mixer.

Combine the sugar and corn syrup in a deep pan and stir with a metal spoon until the mixture looks like wet sand. Place over low heat and allow to caramelize, stirring occasionally. In another pan, heat the honey until bubbles form around the edges and set aside. When the sugar has caramelized, pour the honey into the caramel and remove the pan from the heat (avert your face, because the sugar may splatter). Insert a candy thermometer, return the pan to the heat, and cook until the syrup reaches the soft-ball stage, 240 degrees.

1 cup sugar

1 tablespoon light corn syrup

¾ cup honey

2 egg whites

1 tablespoon vanilla extract

1½ cups whole, blanched almonds, lightly toasted

1½ cups whole hazelnuts, toasted and skinned

4 sheets edible wafer paper

While the sugar is cooking, begin whipping the egg whites on medium speed, in a heavy-duty mixer fitted with the whip, until they hold a firm peak. If the egg whites are beginning to become firm before the syrup is ready, add 1 tablespoon sugar and lower the speed to the minimum. When the syrup is ready, pour it over the egg whites while they are whipping on medium speed. Whip 5 minutes to cool slightly.

Bring 2 inches of water to a boil in a pan large enough to hold the mixer bowl. Lower the water to a simmer. Remove the bowl with the *torrone* from the mixer, stir in the vanilla, and place the bowl in the water. Stir the *torrone* mixture constantly for about 20 minutes, or until a small spoonful cooled to room temperature becomes very firm.

Remove the *torrone* from the water bath and stir in the almonds and hazelnuts. Line the bottom of a jelly roll pan with 2 sheets of the edible wafer paper and spread the *torrone* about ½ inch thick on the paper. Top with 2 more sheets of the paper and press lightly with another pan to make the paper adhere and to even out the *torrone.* Allow to cool until just tepid, then cut into 1½-inch bars with a sharp, heavy knife. When the *torrone* is cool, double-wrap it in plastic and store in a cool, dry place.

Makes about 1½ pounds

ন্ত্ৰ   ত্ৰে

Bocconcini di Dama

Ladies' Delights

These delicious pistachio confections are a specialty of the Santo Spirito Monastery, in Agrigento, where I have enjoyed them several times. Agrigento and pistachios go hand in hand, since it is in Favara, right outside the town, that the pistachios grow. Seeing these confections for the first time made me understand why some pistachios are dyed red. For the *bocconcini*, the skins (natural and undyed) are left on the pistachios, and they tint the sugar coating a delicate pink as their color bleeds into it. The mammoth, deep green, flavorful pistachios of Favara are unfortunately not available to us for duplicating the recipe. I usually purchase pistachios in a Middle Eastern store, where they are guaranteed to be deep green and fresh.

Pick over the pistachios to remove any bits of shell and set aside.

Combine the remaining ingredients in a saucepan and bring to a boil over low heat, making sure to wash down the insides of the pan occasionally with a clean brush dipped in cold water. At the boil, insert a candy thermometer and raise the heat to medium. Cook the syrup until it reaches the soft-ball stage, 240 degrees. Remove the pan from the heat and pour the syrup into another saucepan to cool until the bottom of the pan may be held comfortably on the palm of your hand. Beat the cooled syrup with a small spoon until it hardens and crystallizes, then add 1 teaspoon water and place the pan on the lowest possible heat until the sugar is smooth, melted, and creamy. Remove the pan from the heat, stir in the pistachios, then remove 1-teaspoon clusters of the mixture to a pan lined with parchment, to cool and set. If the sugar recrystallizes after the pistachios have been added, add ½ teaspoon water and reheat until the sugar liquefies again.

Makes about 20 bocconcini

*1 cup unsalted pistachios,
    skins left on*
1 cup sugar
1 tablespoon light corn syrup
¼ cup water

Sources of Equipment and Ingredients

Though few unusual pieces of equipment are called for in the recipes, you may wish to purchase pans, molds, or tools for particular preparations. Local restaurant-supply stores carry heavy-duty equipment that may be more expensive, but is more durable, than lighter-weight domestic cookware and baking pans. Failing that, a great many excellent pans, molds, and tools are available in department and hardware stores.

For imported Italian food products, grocery stores in Italian neighborhoods usually carry a full line of ingredients necessary for the recipes.

The following list of mail order sources for particular equipment and foods will be helpful if you have difficulty with local sources.

EQUIPMENT

Bridge Kitchenware
214 East Fifty-second Street
New York, NY 10022
Telephone (212) 688–4220
No catalogue
   Couscousières, cannoli tubes, and assorted pastry equipment and cookware.

Maid of Scandinavia
3244 Raleigh Avenue
Minneapolis, MN 55416
Telephone (800) 328–6722
Illustrated catalogue
   Cannoli tubes, decorating supplies.

ITALIAN FOOD PRODUCTS

Balducci's
424 Sixth Avenue
New York, NY 10011
Telephone (212) 673–2600
Illustrated catalogue
    Good-quality candied fruit, arborio rice, Italian food products
of all kinds.

Mozzarella Company
2944 Elm Street
Dallas, TX 75226
Telephone (214) 741–4072
    Ricotta, mozzarella, and ricotta *pecorina* in season.

Paprikas Weiss
1546 Second Avenue
New York, NY 10028
Telephone (212) 288–6117
Catalogue
    Edible wafer starch paper (*ostia* or *Oblaten*) for *panforte* and
torrone, bicarbonate of ammonia, excellent candied fruit, and baking equipment.

Raymond Hadley Corporation
P.O. Box 492A
Spencer, NY 14883
Telephone (607) 589–4415
No catalogue
    Semolina, cornmeal, corn flour, wheat berries.

Todaro Brothers Mail Order
557 Second Avenue
New York, NY 10016
Telephone (212) 679–7766
Catalogue
    Semolina, corn flour, wheat kernels.

Bibliography

Anon. *L'antica cuciniera genovese.* Genoa: Nuova Editrice Genovese, 1983.

Adami, Pietro. *La cucina carnica.* Padua: Franco Muzzio & C. Editore, 1985.

Adimari, Fiamma Niccolini, e Manuela Wezel Grosso. *Il libro della cioccolata.* Milan: Gruppo Editoriale Fabbri, Bompiani Sonzogno, Etas S.p.A., 1984.

Alberici, AnnaLisa. *Biscotti & biscottini.* Milan: Idealibri S.p.A., 1989.

Antonini, Giuseppina Perusini. *Mangiare e ber friuluno.* Milan: Franco Angeli Editore, 1984.

Bartelletti, N. Sapio. *La cucina siciliana nobile e popolare.* Milan: Franco Angeli Editore, 1985.

Bonetti, Silvia Tocco. *Antichi dolci di casa.* Milan: Idealibri S.R.L. Milano, 1984.

Boni, Ada. *Il talismano della felicità.* Rome: Editore Colombo, 1972.

Bonino, MariaLuisa. *Le autentiche ricette della cucina ligure.* Genoa: Edizioni Realizzazioni Grafiche Artigiano, 1982.

Borzini, Luigi. *Memorie di pasticceria.* Milan: Rizzoli Libri S.p.A., 1986.

Braccili, Luigi. *Abruzzo in cucina.* Pescara: Costantini Editori, 1988.

Capnist, Giovanni. *I dolci del Veneto.* Padua: Franco Muzzio & C. Editore, 1983.

————. *La cucina veronese.* Padua: Franco Muzzio & C. Editore, 1987.

Capuozzo, Toni, e Michele Neri. *Feste e sagre dei paesi italiani.* Milan: Arnoldo Mondadori Editore S.p.A., 1985.

Casati, Maria, ed. *135 ricette delle scuole di cucina italiana.* Milan: Gruppo Editoriale Fabbri, Bompiani Sonzogno, Etas S.p.A., 1987.

Cavalcanti, Ottavio. *Il libro d'oro della cucina e dei vini di Calabria e Basilicata.* Milan: U. Mursia Editore S.p.A., 1979.

Ciocca, G. *Il pasticciere e confettiere moderno.* Milan: Ulrico Hoepli Editore, 1921.

Codacci, Leo. *Le chicche.* Florence: Edizioni del Palazzo, 1987.

Coltro, Dino. *La cucina tradizionale veneta.* Rome: Newton Compton Editori S.R.L., 1983.

Coria, Giuseppe. *Profumi di Sicilia.* Palermo: Vito Cavallotto Editore, 1981.

Correnti, Pino. *Il libro d'oro della cucina e dei vini di Sicilia.* Milan: U. Mursia Editore S.p.A., 1976.

Corsi, Guglielma. *Un secolo di cucina umbra.* Assisi: Edizioni Porziuncola, 1976.

Cùnsolo, Felice. *La cucina lombarda.* Milan: Novedit Milano, 1963.

D'Alba, Tommaso. *La cucina siciliana di derivazione araba.* Palermo: Casa Editrice Vittorietti, n.d.

della Salda, Anna Gosetti. *Le ricette regionali italiane.* Milan: Casa Editrice Solares, 1967.

Dellea, E. *Il pasticciere.* Bergamo: Editrice San Marco, n.d.

Delledonne, Gino, e Rino Quagliotti. *Ricette parmigiane vecchie e nuove.* Parma: Luigi Battei, 1986.

Del Soldo, Marco. *Il manuale del pasticciere moderno.* Milan: Giovanni de Vecchi Editore S.p.A., 1973.

De Zuliani, Mariù Salvatori. *A tola coi nostri veci—La cucina veneziana.* Milan: Franco Angeli Editore, 1987.

Falavigna, Ugo. *L'arte della pasticceria a Parma.* Parma: Luigi Battei, 1987.

Francesconi, Jeanne Carola. *La cucina napoletana.* Naples: Edizioni del Delfino, 1977.

Gavotti, Giuseppe. *La cucina tradizionale dell'Ennese.* Caltanissetta: Papiro Editrice Enna, 1977.

Gleiseses, Vittorio. *A Napoli si mangia così.* Naples: Edizioni del Giglio, 1987.

Goria, Giovanni, e Claudia Verro. *In cucina a quattro mani.* Chieri (Turin): Daniela Piazza Editore, 1985.

Imbriani, Luciano. *Dolci.* Novara: Istituto Geografico de Agostini S.p.A., 1987.

Kompatscher, Anneliese. *La cucina nelle Dolomiti.* Bolzano: Casa Editrice Athesia, 1985.

Lodomel, Vera Rossi. *Il nuovo cucchiaio d'argento.* Milan: Editoriale Domus, 1965.

Lucrezi, Nice Cortelli. *Le ricette della nonna.* L'Aquila: Japadre Editore, 1974.

Luraghi, Anna Mavri e Paola. *Enciclopedia dei dolci.* Genoa: Casa Editrice Anthropos S.R.L., 1986.

Maffioli, Giuseppe. *La cucina trevigiana*. Padua: Franco Muzzio Editore, 1983.

————. *La cucina veneziana*. Padua: Franco Muzzio & C. Editore, 1982.

Montorfano, Emilio. *Storia e tradizioni nella cucina lariana*. Milan: Casa Editrice Xenia, 1987.

Oberosler, G. *Il tesoretto della pasticceria e della dispensa*. Milan: Ulrico Hoepli Editore S.p.A., 1983.

Ortana, Giorgio. *A scuola di pasticceria da Elio Casati*. Bologna: Edizioni Calderini, 1987.

Padovan, Rachele. *La cucina ampezzana*. Padua: Franco Muzzio Editore, 1981.

Paleari, Laura e Nia. *Tutto dolci*. Editoriale Albero Zoate di Tribiano, 1986.

Panza, Giovanni. *La checine de nononne*. Schena Editore/Grafischena S.p.A., 1984.

Papa, Sebastiana. *La cucina dei monasteri*. Edizioni il Formichiere S.R.L., 1981.

Parenti, Giovanni Righi. *La grande cucina toscana*. (2 vols.) Milan: Sugarco Edizioni, 1986.

Pomar, Anna. *La cucina tradizionale siciliana*. Giuseppe Brancato Editore, 1986.

Portinari, Folco. *Voglia di gelato*. Milan: Idealibri S.p.A., 1987.

Preti, G. *Il gelato artigianale italiano*. Milan: Ulrico Hoepli Editore, 1985.

Ragusa, Vittorio. *La vera cucina casareccia a Roma e nel Lazio*. Rome: Iniziative Editoriali Esercizi Pubblici, 1985.

Russo, Anna. *La pasticceria napoletana*. Guidonia: Casa Editrice Anthropos S.R.L., 1988.

Savoldi, Giovanna. *La cucina emiliana e romagnola*. Florence: Edizioni del Riccio, 1987.

Serra, Piero. *Pasticceria meridionale*. Naples: Adriano Gallina Editore, 1986.

Spagnol, Elena. *I gelati fatti in casa*. Milan: Rizzoli Libri S.p.A., 1977.

Toto, Lorenzo. *La cucina delle valli piemontesi e lombarde*. Milan: Rusconi Libri S.p.A., 1978.

Trombetta, Silvia. *Dolci tradizionali siciliani*. Catania: Giuseppe Brancato Editore, n.d.

Usuelli, Catullo. *I segreti del pasticciere*. Milan: Giovanni de Vecchi Editore S.p.A., 1986.

Zucchi, Linda. *La cucina friulana*. Florence: Edizioni del Riccio, n.d.

Selected Recipe Index

LOW-FAT/LOW-CHOLESTEROL DESSERTS

DESSERTS TO BE STORED TIGHTLY COVERED AT ROOM TEMPERATURE

DESSERTS THAT CAN BE STORED FROZEN FOR SEVERAL WEEKS

DESSERTS THAT CAN BE STORED REFRIGERATED FOR SEVERAL DAYS

DESSERTS THAT CAN BE STORED REFRIGERATED FOR 1–2 DAYS AND FINISHED BEFORE SERVING

200

33
34
17
128
129
145
146
185
186
187
188
189
218
220
221